September 11 in History

American Encounters/Global Interactions
A series edited by Gilbert M. Joseph
and Emily S. Rosenberg

This series aims to stimulate critical perspectives
and fresh interpretive frameworks for scholarship
on the history of the imposing global presence of
the United States. Its primary concerns include the
deployment and contestation of power, the construction and deconstruction of cultural and political borders, the fluid meanings of intercultural encounters, and the complex interplay between the
global and the local. American Encounters seeks
to strengthen dialogue and collaboration between
historians of U.S. international relations and area
studies specialists.

The series encourages scholarship based on multi-
archival historical research. At the same time, it supports a recognition of the representational character
of all stories about the past and promotes critical inquiry into issues of subjectivity and narrative. In the
process, American Encounters strives to understand
the context in which meanings related to nations,
cultures, and political economy are continually produced, challenged, and reshaped.

September 11 in History

A Watershed Moment?

Edited by Mary L. Dudziak

Duke University Press

Durham and London 2003

© 2003 Duke University Press

All rights reserved

Printed in the United States

of America on acid-free paper ♾

Designed by Mary Mendell

Typeset in Melior by Tseng

Information Systems, Inc.

Library of Congress Cataloging-

in-Publication Data appear

on the last printed page of

this book.

To our students

Contents

September 11 in History

Introduction

MARY L. DUDZIAK

The first plane could have been an accident. It was the second plane, flying into the south tower of the World Trade Center in New York City that led many to think that the world had changed on September 11, 2001. United Airlines flight 175 had sixty-five people on board, including five hijackers, when it exploded in flames as it crashed. Many died instantly. In the World Trade Center, people were trapped on the floors above the impact zone, unable to escape through damaged stairwells. Some scrambled toward the roof, hoping for rescue from above, only to find the way blocked. Some returned to their desks. They called home. They said good-bye before the floors collapsed beneath them as first the south tower and then the north tower fell, turning thousands, in a moment, into dust.[1]

While New Yorkers looked in horror at the smoke arising from lower Manhattan, news broke of a third plane crashing into the Pentagon. The geographic scope of this developing nightmare expanded with news that a fourth plane had been hijacked that same morning. The hijacking of United flight 93 was the final act of terrorism in the series of events that were soon referred to simply by their common date: September 11. The full impact of these events on security, politics, culture, economics, and international relations was just beginning to unfold. Perhaps it was passengers on flight 93 who were the first to act on the basis of an understanding that the events of that morning had changed their world. From in-flight telephone calls to loved ones, they learned that other hijacked planes had been used as missiles, with devastating consequences. With hijackers in control of the aircraft, passengers stormed the cockpit.

Rather than reaching its target, the plane crashed in a Pennsylvania field, killing all on board, but no one on the ground.[2]

Across the United States, across the world, many turned quickly to an effort to make sense of a series of events that seemed incomprehensible. Among the sea of American flags, among the memorial displays around the world, amid the developing international crisis, many felt that the United States, and perhaps the world, had entered a new age of terror. "Nothing Will Ever Be the Same" read a full-page headline in a September 11 special edition of the *Philadelphia City Paper*. The idea that September 11 had "changed everything" was ubiquitous, the date a dividing line between a "before" and an "after." So pervasive was this idea that in the new "terror slang" that quickly emerged among U.S. teenagers, the new put-down was "That's *so* September 10."[3]

But how transformative was September 11? Would it become an iconic historical event, marking a transition in the history of the United States and of the world? Or was it instead best understood as an aspect of pre-existing historical trajectories? Did it change law, politics, religion, and culture, or did it instead simply provide a new site for political and cultural conflicts that were already in play?

Moments of crisis in the history of the United States and the world have been a traditional focus of scholarly study. Some social scientists and historians argue that moments of crisis can be moments of social change. Economic dislocations, natural disasters, and war are the context for changes in politics and culture, as the crisis creates an environment that seems to require new responses that before may not have been imaginable.[4] For social change scholars, the question is whether September 11 is this sort of moment. Has it shifted popular conceptions of the good in a way that will affect politics, ideas about justice, or perhaps our toleration of conditions of inequality?

For historians, moments of historical change give the story of the past a narrative structure. They provide the breaks than enable periodization into one age or another, into what came before and what came after. Some historical moments emerge as cultural symbols, as icons for a broader set of ideas, values, and politics. Hiroshima is one such moment. The atomic bomb dropped on that Japanese city is remembered not only for its role in the military history of World War II, or for its destruction. The event ushered in a "nuclear age." Nuclear weapons and fear of nuclear holocaust eventually would have entered popular consciousness without Hiroshima, but, as the first major nuclear event, Hiroshima became the iconic moment, the point in time between a "before" and an "after." The contested construction of that moment—as a heroic Allied victory over a treacherous foe, or as a horrific humanitarian disaster wreaked on civilians—had consequences for the way the new "nuclear age" would be understood.[5]

The idea of change affects the way an event enters historical memory. It also constructs present-day politics. If circumstances are new, then arguably the policies needed to address them should be new as well. According to President George W. Bush, the terrorist attacks were the beginning of "a new kind of war." This new war is thought to require new tactics. The idea of newness was invoked by prior American presidents. World War I and World War II were thought to be new forms of warfare as well, and the new circumstances of "total war" were seen to justify a softening of constitutional restraints on the executive.[6] Has a new age of terror dawned that makes constitutional restraints and the restraints of international law, crafted by earlier generations, anachronistic? Does a new approach to warfare require unfettered executive power? Does it justify the unilateralism of the United States as a global police power? These are defining questions for American politics and international politics.

This volume takes up the question of whether the assumption that September 11 "changed everything" holds up under closer scrutiny. The essays—by leading scholars and by newer voices in history, literature, Islamic studies, and law—approach the issue from different disciplinary perspectives. Out of this cross-disciplinary exchange comes a complex sense of the evocative power of iconic moments in history, yet also the enduring nature of political power, in the United States, within Islam, and around the world.

The idea that the world was transformed on September 11 was pervasive in popular culture, but can this idea be sustained? According to diplomatic historian Marilyn Young, one aspect of global politics that did not change was the basic orientation of American foreign policy. She sees parallels in the Korean War where, as in post–September 11, "the enemy . . . was a vast, amoebic 'ism' that could take up residence in any number of surprising places." During the Cold War, "the United States did not fight Koreans . . . but Communists," just as in the military campaign after September 11, the United States fought not Afghans but terrorists. Rather than transformation, Young sees long-term continuity in American foreign policy before and after September 11. September 11 became a site for reinforcement of a preexisting U.S. unilateralism. Different administrations, she argues, "have attempted to order the world so as to sustain the dominant power of the United States," supporting absolute sovereignty for the United States and limited sovereignty for others. In this regard, "September 11 did not change the world," she argues, "but it has enabled the Bush administration to pursue, with less opposition and greater violence, policies that might otherwise have appeared too aggressive."

U.S. social and cultural historian Elaine Tyler May turns to domestic culture and politics. She examines the way that the past serves as a frame of reference, drawn on to make sense of a new crisis. In this sense, the presence of change itself called forth an embrace of the familiar. New experiences were understood by grounding them in memories of the past. In the aftermath of September 11, leaders invoked Pearl Harbor as their reference point. Yet it is the Cold War, May argues, not World War II, that is the reference point most fitting here. The September 11 terrorists "seemed to personify the characteristics of the Communist threat: foreigners who infiltrated the nation, studied our technology, and used our own power against us." Like the Cold War focus on civil defense, the new Department of Homeland Security creates domestic security systems, such as airport screenings, that are "performances of security," offering "the illusion of safety against an unpredictable enemy." Cultural reactions to September 11 have included a new focus on the home, marriage, and relationships, and also the marketing of American patriotism, from flags to patriotic trading cards. Yet there was no call to sacrifice, as there had been during other moments of crisis such as World War II. Americans instead were told after September 11 that buying consumer goods and participating in leisure activities would help safeguard the American way of life.

Amy Kaplan, a literature and American studies scholar, takes up the language of September 11, exploring the meaning of particular words and spaces: ground zero, homeland, and Guantánamo Base. Did these words signify continuity or change? The first use of "ground zero" was in the aftermath of the use of nuclear weapons during World War II, and one definition of the term, evoking widespread devastation, is the site of a nuclear explosion. Another use of the term is the idea of starting from the very beginning, the point of origin. This thinking, Kaplan argues, "might be called a narrative of historical exceptionalism, almost an antinarrative that claims that the event was so unique and unprecedented as to transcend time and defy comparison or historical analysis." In contrast, the idea of homeland evokes connections to the past.

Kaplan's examination of the particular language of September 11 sets the subject in a global context. In the face of the great sense of insecurity in the aftermath of September 11, did the idea of a homeland contribute to "the cultural work of securing national borders?" To speak of the United States as a homeland, Kaplan suggests, implicitly evokes the foreign and a boundary between domestic and foreign. The international dimension appears again in Kaplan's third space: Guantánamo Base. She sees Guantánamo as a lawless site, neither quite foreign nor domestic, and the repository of a repressed imperial history.

A central interpretive question after September 11 has been the way Islam is understood. Many have viewed September 11 as impacting the relationship between Islam and the West. For some, September 11 was the apex of what Samuel Huntington has called the "clash of civilizations." Even though President Bush suggested that "Islam is a religion of peace," Muslims and those who appeared to Americans to be Muslims were harassed in American cities, with several deaths attributed to anti-Muslim hate violence.[7] Two contributors to this collection raise, however, a different set of interpretive questions. Their essays go beyond the dichotomy between Islam and the West and ask instead what the debate has been *within* Islamic communities. Has September 11 had an impact on Islamic self-identity? And is the East/West construction even an accurate way to depict Muslims who live in nations around the world?

Islamic law scholar Khaled Abou El Fadl argues that culture and religion matter, but his interest is not in a "clash of civilizations" between Islam and the West; instead, he is concerned with the effect of September 11 on the understanding of Islam within Islam. The idea of a "clash of civilizations" is present not only among Western scholars like Huntington but also among Muslim fundamentalists. In the dichotomy between Islam and the West, critics of fundamentalism are seen within the Islamic community as Western apologists. Yet Abou El Fadl argues that this dichotomous thinking is due to the fact that Islamic thought has been affected by "the shadow of colonialism and postcolonialism." The Islamic experience "has struggled to come to terms with modernity, with its own marginality and loss of autonomy, and with the concentration of power in the hands of the non-Muslim 'other.' "

The September 11 attacks affect how Islam is understood, for "meaning in Islam is acquired through the formation of communities of interpretation. In effect, Osama bin Laden, through his actions, has offered an interpretive community that is at odds with the main interpretive communities of classical Islam." According to Abou El Fadl, the only way to respond effectively to bin Laden "is to offer alternative communities of meaning that are more convincing to Muslims and that would act to challenge and negate the worldview of the bin Ladens of the world." Abou El Fadl sets contemporary fundamentalism within the context of the historical development of Islamic thought, arguing that classical Islam "does not bear a message of violence." Instead, he argues, Muslims should strive for "a collective enterprise of goodness." By embracing such an alternative vision, Muslims might move beyond bin Laden, "the quintessential example of a Muslim who was created, shaped, and motivated by postcolonialism."

However, have arguments over the nature of Islam proceeded from false assumptions about the essence of Islam? Near Eastern studies scholar Sherman A. Jackson argues that in the aftermath of September 11, critics of Islamic fundamentalism have themselves essentialized Islam and have attempted to substitute one false universal for another. Setting his critique in the context of postcolonialism, Jackson argues that the truth sought by fundamentalists is not the truth of Muhammad, but rather, quoting Franz Fanon, a truth that "hurries on the break-up of the [post-]colonialist regime. In this . . . context there is no truthful behavior: and good is quite simply that which is evil for 'them.'"[8] Yet in responding to fundamentalism, Western Muslims embrace and privilege another false universal, essentializing Islam in a different way. Jackson argues instead for a deconstruction of Islam, based on a recognition of the diversity among Muslims. While it has been appealing and politically expedient for Western Muslim reformers to argue that Muslim fundamentalism is wrong, for American Islam to be truly pluralistic, Jackson argues, "it will have to be bold and vigilant in its refusal to ignore or jettison" any of the histories of Islam.

Abou El Fadl and Jackson are concerned with identity and meaning within Islam, while Leti Volpp, a critical race theory and immigration law scholar, focuses on identity within the United States. The construction of citizenship has been tremendously important since September 11, as the government has justified new policies by arguing that they only apply to noncitizens who are outside the ambit of full constitutional protection. Volpp argues that "September 11 facilitated the consolidation of a new identity category" of those "who appear to be 'Middle Eastern, Arab, or Muslim.'" She finds this construction a "redeployment of old Orientalist tropes." Meanwhile post–September 11, the category of "loyal American," encompassing an understanding of citizenship as inclusion and solidarity, was constructed in opposition to the foreign other. The solidarity of citizenship came at a cost to those who appeared to be Middle Eastern, Arab, or Muslim, who were "formally citizens of the United States" but were "thrust outside the protective ambit" of this new solidarity.

The consequences of the response to terrorism for the law are particularly stark in the area of citizenship, as described by Volpp, yet the consequences for law within the United States and internationally are much broader. After September 11, courts began to face the question of whether a "new kind of war" justified a new legal regime. Constitutional theorists Christopher Eisgruber and Lawrence Sager raise the question of whether September 11 has led to an erosion of the usual border between the domestic sphere governed by law and the area traditionally thought of by American courts as the forbidden region outside the nation, "the domain of realpolitik rather than reason." According to Eisgruber and Sager, in crafting antiterrorism measures, "the president and Congress have invoked their discretion over foreign affairs in order to escape restrictions that courts have imposed on domestic police activities." They focus in particular on the use of military tribunals to prosecute terrorists. While Eisgruber and Sager do not argue that military tribunals under all circumstances should be unlawful, they argue for judicial involvement in a way that would "enable courts to negotiate the blurred boundary between domestic policy and foreign affairs, preventing the government's traditional discretion with regard to the latter domain from destroying rights carefully cultivated in the former one."

As an international crisis, has September 11 had an impact on international law? According to international law scholar Laurence Helfer, the post–September 11 notion of unlimited U.S. sovereignty has had consequences for the U.S. role in international law. U.S. unilateralism, he argues, is in tension with international efforts to develop effective mechanisms for responding to crimes that transcend borders, such as the International Criminal Court. In spite of this, Helfer argues that September 11 should not be thought of as a transformative moment in international law. The idea of transformation is appealing, he suggests, bringing "coherence to a world that existing paradigms no longer adequately explain." He argues, however, that the response to September 11 should occur within the existing framework of international law. He analyzes responses to the terrorist attacks within three current paradigms: terrorism as crime, terrorism as armed conflict, and terrorism as atrocity. While he urges that international law should not change, he suggests that "what has changed since September 11 . . . is the readiness of the United States to pick and choose among these three categories and to claim for itself the right to respond to terrorism unilaterally."

What are the consequences of the U.S. unilateralism so often criticized by world leaders before and after September 11? What are the consequences of continued repression of what Amy Kaplan calls a "repressed imperial history"? In an age of international terrorism, perhaps security derives from power; perhaps autonomy enables the U.S. to respond effectively to new threats. Yet democratic legitimacy is threatened, legal and political theorist Ruti G. Teitel argues, when responses to emergency occur outside of law.

Teitel's focus is on the relationship between law and politics, particularly the question of "how the sense of the transformative significance of these political events is constructed by the law." Teitel describes the debate over the proper response to September 11 as a debate over the competing juridical-political models of justice and war. Yet rather than employing the legal regime associated with justice (criminal law) or with war (international law), September 11 has been characterized as exceptional, justifying a departure from both. The legal model employed by the United States, she argues, is the model of the sovereign police, justifying U.S. intervention and enforcement, but excepting the nation from external limitations. The logic, she argues, "is that the United States constitutes the world sovereign," so it follows that the United States can never be the subject of police action. It is inconsistent with the U.S. position for the United States to be the object of enforcement. Teitel argues that democratic legitimacy requires that states of exception must be limited in duration and that there must be checks on executive authority so that responses to states of emergency are not outside law.

Teitel's examination of the impact of September 11 on democracy sharpens the question of the political consequences of the construction of September 11 as a moment of change. Since September 11, the idea of change has been deployed to justify departure from past practices, from a new secrecy in detention and deportation of noncitizens to the preemptive use of American military power. This use of the idea of change to justify new policies requires that we examine critically whether this justification rests on a firm foundation, whether the idea of transformation holds up under closer scrutiny, and whether any changes are of the sort that would justify these new government policies. It may well be that this generation lacks the distance to fully measure the question of how transformative an event September 11 has been. However, as we seem perched on the entryway to a new age of terror, there are immediate consequences of the idea of transformation. We do not have the luxury to wait for this moment to settle more firmly into historical memory. Understanding September 11 and its impact is a need, and a responsibility, of our own.

Notes

1. Jim Dwyer, et al., "102 Minutes: Last Words at the Trade Center," *New York Times,* May 26, 2002, late edition, sec. 1, p. 1. First person accounts of the events on September 11 are available at the *September 11 Digital Archive,* http://911digitalarchive.org.

2. *September 11 Timeline,* http://www.september11news.com/AttackImages.htm; Jere Longman, *Among the Heroes: United Flight 93 and the Passengers and Crew Who Fought Back* (New York: HarperCollins, 2002).

3. Frank Lewis, ed., "Nothing Will Ever Be the Same," *Philadelphia City Paper,* September 11, 2001, extra edition, http://www.september11news.com/USAPapers3.htm; Julian Borger, "War in Afghanistan — Weapons Grade Slang Updates Putdowns," *Guardian* (London), March 20, 2002, 4.

4. On wartime and social change, see Philip A. Klinkner, with Rogers M. Smith, *The Unsteady March: The Rise and Decline of Racial Equality in America* (Chicago: University of Chicago Press, 1999); Mary L. Dudziak, *Cold War Civil Rights: Race and the Image of American Democracy* (Princeton: Princeton University Press, 2000).

5. See Paul Boyer, *By the Bomb's Early Light: American Thought and Culture at the Dawn of the Atomic Age* (New York: Pantheon, 1985); Michael J. Hogan, ed., *Hiroshima in History and Memory* (Cambridge: Cambridge University Press, 1996); John Whittier Treat, *Writing Ground Zero: Japanese Literature and the Atomic Bomb* (Chicago: University of Chicago Press, 1995). See also "History and September 11 — A Special Issue," *Journal of American History* 89, no. 2 (September 2002); "The Road to and from September 11th: A Roundtable," *Diplomatic History* 26, no. 4 (fall 2002).

6. See Edward Corwin, *Total War and the Constitution* (New York: Knopf, 1947).

7. Samuel P. Huntington, *The Clash of Civilizations and the Remaking of World Order* (New York: Simon and Schuster, 1996); President George W. Bush, "Remarks at the Islamic Center of Washington, September 17, 2001," *Weekly Compilation of Presidential Documents* 37, no. 38 (September 24, 2001): 1327–28; President George W. Bush, "Address before a Joint Session of Congress on the United States Response to the Terrorist Attacks of September 11, September 20, 2001," *Weekly Compilation of Presidential Documents* 37, no. 38 (September 24, 2001): 1347–51.

8. Quoting Franz Fanon, *The Wretched of the Earth* (New York: Grove Press, 1963), 50.

Ground Zero: Enduring War

MARILYN B. YOUNG

I dread our own power and our own ambition; I dread our being too much dreaded.
—Edmund Burke

Good afternoon. Today I ordered our armed forces to strike at terrorist-related facilities in Afghanistan and Sudan because of the imminent threat they presented to our national security. Our target was terror. . . . [Osama bin Laden and the groups associated with him] have made the United States their adversary precisely because of what we stand for and what we stand against. . . . [The U.S. strikes] were not aimed against Islam. . . . [The struggle against terrorism] will require strength, courage and endurance. . . . This will be a long, ongoing struggle between freedom and fanaticism, between the rule of law and terrorism. . . . America is and will remain a target of terrorists precisely because we are leaders; because we act to advance peace, democracy and basic human values; . . . because, as we have shown yet again, we take an uncompromising stand against terrorism.—President William Jefferson Clinton, August 20, 1998.

Over the past twenty years or so, American presidents have periodically declared war against terrorism.[1] William Jefferson Clinton's war against terrorism included efforts to assassinate Osama bin Laden, a doubling of the budget for counterterrorism and direct, if ineffective, acts of war: the bombing of a Sudanese pharmaceutical plant and the blasting of a bin Laden camp in Afghanistan, well known to the United States because it had originally been set up to train the same people to fight against the Soviet Union. Clinton also placed a $5 million price on bin Laden's head and pressured the government of Sudan to expel him. The one counter-terrorist strategy Clinton did not consider was a major change in U.S. policy in the Middle East.[2] Meanwhile, on and off throughout his presidency, sometimes with great intensity and almost always unnoticed by the American public, Clinton bombed Iraq and bombed it again. In mid-December 1998, just before hearings on his impeachment were about to begin, Clinton launched a particularly heavy series of raids, explaining that bombing was the only way to deal with Saddam Hussein's noncompliance with UN inspections: "If Saddam defies the world and we fail to respond, we will face a far greater threat in the future. Saddam will strike again at his neighbors; he will make war on his own people. And mark my words, he will develop weapons of mass destruction. He will deploy them, and he will use them. Because we are acting today, it is less likely that we will face these dangers in the future."[3] The future then arrived.

The initial response of most commentators to September 11 was that we had witnessed a historical watershed, one of those topographic metaphors historians favor. Jonathan Schell captured the feeling best in his first "Letter from Ground Zero," written for the *Nation:* "In an instant and without warning on a fine fall morning, the known world had been jerked aside like a mere slide in a projector, and a new world had been rammed into its place. . . . Has the eye of the world ever shifted more abruptly or completely than it did on September 11?"[4]

What made it a new world? Editorials, politicians, sermons, and on-line opinion sites mourned America's loss of innocence.[5] But pundits and politicians have regretted the end of American innocence before, as recently as the failed intervention in Somalia or, for those with greater historical reach, Vietnam. Terrorism did not create a new world, for, as a tactic, terrorist incidents were already familiar to Americans at home and abroad, as, on a more regular basis, they had become familiar to the Israelis, British, Irish, Italians, and French. The only new aspect of this act of terror was its happening in the United States, whose citizens had imagined themselves invulnerable. Many commentators, both here and abroad, expressed a kind of pleasure: now Americans would know how it felt to be unsafe, to be a target, to experience war, and this would have an effect on how they understood other countries with a longer history of devastation. Some, in this country, believed the attack would wake a hedonistic public to a renewed sense of self-sacrifice, civic responsibility, and ethical commitment.[6]

Neither compassion nor spiritual renewal occurred. Instead, as is sometimes the case with individuals facing crises, the country became even more itself, almost to the point of caricature. Unlike other nationals, Americans often fly flags outside their homes on national holidays. After September 11, there were flags everywhere, all the time, even in New

York. A headline in the humor newspaper the *Onion* reflected what has become a national problem: "Local Man Uncertain When to Take Down Flag." Unlike the French, who know the answer and don't care, or the British, who would never ask, Americans often wonder whether other people love them. After September 11, newspapers and television anchor people asked, plaintively or angrily or both: why do people hate the United States? The most frequent answer was reassuring: Americans were hated because they were envied, for their wealth, their freedom, their liberty.

The world that had seemed to crumble with the Berlin Wall in 1989 reappeared, a little dusty. Good and Evil, Us and Them, Enemies Everywhere. The view was bipartisan. Senator Joseph Lieberman, who could have been vice president on September 11, described the war on terrorism as a struggle between "the medieval zealotry and religious fanaticism of a holy war against the universalistic, humanitarian, democratic and tolerant ideals of America." The country's fundamental principles were "as much on the line in this war against terrorism as they were in our battles with Nazism and communism."[7]

Along with the Manichean language came a revivification of a number of Cold War tactics, such as psychological warfare, embodied in the short-lived Office of Strategic Influence, whose open purpose was to spread disinformation abroad. Washington and Hollywood fell into each other's arms. In late October, forty Hollywood executives met with Chris Henick, deputy assistant to the president, and Adam Goldman, associate director of the administration's Office of Public Liaison. Leslie Moonves, president of CBS, explained their mission: "I think you have a bunch of people here who were just saying, 'Tell us what to do. We don't fly jet planes, but there are skill sets that can be put to use here.' " There was a clear need, both "domestically and internationally to tell the story that is our story."[8]

The government acted quickly to blunt any questioning of administration policy, passing the "Uniting and Strengthening America by Providing Appropriate Tools Required to Intercept and Obstruct Terrorism Act." Known as the USA Patriot Act for short, it provides for an unprecedented peacetime abrogation of civil liberties in a piece of legislation whose name itself discourages dissent.[9] Nine months after its passage, in a move that makes the FBI Cold War informant network look benign, the administration launched Operation TIPS, whose acronym must also have preceded its full naming. Through a pilot project in ten cities, the Terrorism Information and Prevention System will enable one million letter carriers, train conductors, utility employees, and ship captains to report "suspicious activity" by calling a toll-free number which will connect them "directly to a hotline routing calls to the proper law enforcement agency."[10] The U.S. Postal Service declined to participate, and protests in Congress make it likely that Operation TIPS will follow the Office of Strategic Security into the rubbish bin. But Operation TIPS was the formalization of a system already in place, the Neighborhood Watch Program, whose original anticrime mandate was now expanded: "With the help of the National Sheriffs' Association, the Neighborhood Watch Program will be taking on a new significance. Community residents will be provided with information which will enable them to recognize signs of potential terrorist activity, and to know how to report that activity, making these residents a critical element in the detection, prevention and disruption of terrorism."[11] One alert citizen in Williamsburg, Virginia, John Chwaszczewski, shot at a helicopter as it landed in his neighborhood to pick up a local businessman. "Maybe I overreacted," Mr. Chwaszczewski said.[12] A Federal Express driver working in a Middle Eastern neighborhood in Brooklyn told a reporter: "Whenever I would go to a place where there was a lot of them [Arab Americans], I would tell the landlord, hey, you got nine people living up there or whatever, and they would call the F.B.I. and get them checked out."[13] Raymond Arnold, a field-service representative for a local gas company, made the Cold War connection explicit, recalling his earlier effort on behalf of patriotic observation: "A long time ago, I saw a Communist flag [sic] in someone's basement."[14]

A presidential executive order made it legal to try alien terrorists in military tribunals, and the Geneva Conventions on prisoners of war was abrogated with respect to Taliban and Al Qaeda prisoners, who would be held indefinitely, irrespective of any evidence, at the Guantánamo Bay military base in Cuba. Nongovernmental witch-hunters set up organizations to monitor thought. Among the first was Lynne Cheney, the wife of the vice president. Mrs. Cheney, a veteran defender of Western Civilization, had successfully opposed the National History Standards for being insufficiently patriotic. Now, as head of the American Council of Trustees and Alumni (ACTA), she published the names of over 100 academics guilty of criticizing U.S. foreign policy. In March 2002, William Bennett founded a new disciplinary organization, Americans for Victory over Terrorism (AVOT), whose mandate was to "take to task those groups and individuals who fundamentally misunderstand the nature of the war we are facing." Like ACTA, AVOT has a list of "internal threats" to America that includes Congresswoman Maxine Waters, President Jimmy Carter, Congressman Dennis Kucinich, and the editors of several magazines. In Maine, a student teacher lost his internship in a local high school for offering a course on Islam when parents complained that he was trying to convert their children.[15] Meanwhile, in the first few weeks after September 11, some 1,200 immigrants, especially those from Middle Eastern countries, were rounded up and held in secret detention, while on the streets they were assaulted and, on occasion, killed. An unknown number continue to be held; the rest have been deported on various immigration charges.[16]

Fifty years ago, the country had been informed it must gird itself for a long, indefinite struggle against godless Communism; now, the appeal was for fortitude in a struggle of indefinite duration against terrorism. Tactic was thus transformed into an ideology. A universal explanation transcended local sites of conflict: wherever acts of terror, as defined by the United States, occurred, there was Al Qaeda, if not literally, then metaphorically. Resistance movements that endangered governments judged legitimate by the United States were a danger to American security as well. Homeland security alerts recalled the mobilization for civil defense of the 1950s: the public was alerted to dangers that neither they nor the government could do much to avert.

Since 1945, American presidents have routinely drawn on the tropes of World War II to justify their own wars. President George W. Bush compared September 11 to Pearl Harbor, and one can see the similarities: surprise; planes; many dead.[17] The differences are more telling: Pearl Harbor was a military target; the attack came as the culmination of long-standing tension between the United States and another nation-state; there was a formal declaration of war. A more apt historical analogy might have been June 25, 1950, the beginning of the Korean War. Harry Truman responded to the North Korean invasion, which he cast as aggression across an international border, by securing support for U.S. military moves from a compliant UN, putting American troops in the field, and calling for a worldwide mobilization against Communism. The stated goal was to drive the North Koreans out of the South in what was at first an unnamed military effort (later, a police action) but never a declared war. Having driven the North Koreans back, Truman went on to make war against North Korea, as Bush, who set out to capture bin Laden dead or alive, went on to make war on the Taliban. Along the way, the Truman administration was able to pass legislation contemplated earlier but deemed unlikely to succeed — in particular, the tripling of the defense budget. The enemy then, as now, was an amoebic "ism" that could take up residence in any number of surprising places, instantly deterritorializing them. The United States did not fight Koreans on that devastated peninsula, but Communists. The only Koreans (or, later, Vietnamese) around were America's allies, as, if the Bush administration has its way, the only Iraqis around will be those so designated by the United States, with the rest of the country subsumed under the single figure of Saddam Hussein, a personified weapon of mass destruction.

After the Chinese joined the North Koreans, Truman denounced them as "the inheritors of Genghis Khan and Tamerlane, who were the greatest murderers in world history." At an informal lunch with reporters, Truman explained that Western jurisprudence had "originated with Hammurabi in the Mesopotamian Valley, [was] propounded by Moses and 'elaborated on by Jesus Christ, whose Sermon on the Mount is the best ethical program by which to live.'" Led by the United States, others could join the battle: "I have been trying to mobilize the moral force of the world—Catholics, Protestants, Jews, the eastern church, the Grand Lama of Tibet, the Indian Sanskrit code—I have been trying to organize all these people to the understanding that their welfare and the existence of decency and honor in the world depends on our working together, and not trying to cut each other's throats."[18] The idiom, and the grammar, have a contemporary ring.

The comparison between the current war against terrorism and the early days of the Cold War has been made by members of the Bush administration itself. In an interview with Nicholas Lemann, the National Security Adviser Condoleezza Rice said she thought "this period is analogous to 1945–1947 . . . in that the events so clearly demonstrated that there is a big global threat."[19] As in those early postwar years, the United States is the sole superpower, now so much the superior of any possible rival it is relieved of even the appearance of multilateralism. "It's good to have the Europeans supporting us to the degree they do," Richard Perle told the Foreign Policy Research Institute, but "the price you end up paying for an alliance is collective judgment, collective decision-making."[20] The administration feels the price is too high. Zalmay Khalilzad, a former aide to Secretary of Defense Dick Cheney and currently the U.S. envoy to Afghanistan, put it even more bluntly in his 1995 book, *From Containment to Global Leadership?* The United States is and must remain the only world power. It should "preclude the rise of another global rival for the indefinite future." To prevent "multipolarity," the United States "must be willing to use force if necessary."[21]

Khalilzad did not so much describe an arc of policy running from containment to global leadership, as define what containment has always been about: the establishment and sustenance of the United States as the dominant power in the world. So long as the Soviet Union existed, there was a rough sort of balance, skewed in favor of the United States, requiring negotiation, alliances, a degree of caution. The disappearance of the Soviet Union, immediately reflected in U.S. military thinking, made all this unnecessary. The 1992 Defense Planning Guidance, prepared by Paul Wolfowitz, then serving the first President Bush as undersecretary of defense for policy, stated the lineaments of American empire. It argued that the United States "must continue to dominate the international system and thus to 'discourage' the 'advanced industrial nations from challenging our leadership or . . . even aspiring to a larger regional or global role.'" In the unguarded language of the document, the United States "must provide its allies with . . . 'adult supervision,'" establishing a "military protectorate over Europe's and East Asia's worldwide interests, so that they need not develop military forces capable of 'global power projection.'"[22]

If one keeps this ambition in mind, many puzzling aspects of U.S. policy become clearer. Why, for instance, discourage Korean unification? Because, Benjamin Schwarz and Christopher Layne write, citing here not Wolfowitz but Zbigniew Brzezinski, peace in Korea would remove the justification for stationing troops; this "could lead to a U.S. pullback from East Asia which could, in turn, lead to Japan's becoming 'militarily more self-sufficient,' which would lead to political, military, and economic rivalry among the region's states." And what of the Middle East? They refer not to any of the current right-wing militarists in the Bush administration but rather to Walter Russell Mead, a member of the Council on Foreign Relations: "One of the reasons that we are sort of assuming this role of policeman of the Middle East, more or less, has to do with making Japan and some other countries feel that their oil flow is assured . . . so that they don't then feel more need to create a great power, armed forces, and security doctrine, and you don't start getting a lot of great powers with conflicting interests sending their militaries all over the world."[23]

Yet to note the preferences of Brzezinski and Mead for preponderant American power and the will to use it is not to argue that nothing has changed. The tactics through which various post-1945 administrations have attempted to order the world so as to sustain the dominant power of the United States have been shaped by the individual predilections of the president and his men, domestic opposition, the state of the economy, and the actions of other nations. And tactics have consequences, certainly to those on the receiving end. There is a difference between the interim bombing of Iraq, however brutal and futile, and an all-out war against the country; between a war against drugs that may mask counterinsurgency, but is sensitive to charges of human rights abuses, and one that ignores all constraint; between the veiled, cautious, unilateralism of the Clinton administration and the naked, crusading version with which we live today.[24] Clinton's Plan Colombia, for example, drew a line, barely visible though it might have been, between military support for the campaign against narcotics and counterinsurgency. That line is now erased: the insurgents have been conveniently labeled terrorists, and Bush has asked for an increase in military aid to fund counterinsurgency directly. In Bolivia as well, the fragile protection against human rights abuses that accompanied the drug war under Clinton has been eliminated, and, in its place, Bolivian peasants now face a U.S. embassy–controlled paramilitary force engaged in the usual brutalities.[25]

More than tactics are involved. The way in which the Bush administration articulates its vision of the world brings latent tendencies to full potency and, in so doing, changes the policy, altering and in some cases overwhelming its balance. The Clinton administration, for example, also worried about a "Saddam Hussein with nukes," and in 1993, under Secretary of Defense Les Aspin, prepared a Counter-Proliferation Initiative (CPI) to deal with "radical regimes that appear on the verge of acquiring WMD [weapons of mass destruction]." The initiative was heavy on weapons development but stressed that "diplomacy, treaty restrictions, security assurances, export controls, non-military sanctions, and economic cooperation" were the primary means by which the United States planned to prevent the proliferation of such weapons. Then, covering all bases, Aspin declared that the CPI would improve the capacity of the United States to deal with "dangerous and hostile radical regimes" either in a "reactive or a preemptive mode, primarily the former, but also the latter when no other option provides a better means of defense."[26] The Bush administration, by contrast, explicitly rejects the reactive mode and plans "unilateral world domination through absolute military superiority," as Anatol Lieven put it.[27]

Nowhere is this clearer than in the new National Security Strategy, a thirty-three-page *in memoriam* to September 11, 2001, released by the White House on September 17, 2002. It opens with a bold assertion. The twentieth century ended in "a decisive victory for the forces of freedom and a single sustainable model for national success: freedom, democracy, and free enterprise."[28] Potential alternatives—"militant visions of class, nation, and race"—have been defeated; in their place, the United States will use its economic power abroad to encourage "pro-growth legal and regulatory policies," "lower marginal tax rates," "sound business policies to support business activity," and free trade, defined as a "moral principle."[29]

The National Security Strategy joins the American domestic order, American prescriptions for the world, and American military supremacy.

For along with the age of militant class struggle and nationalism, the age of deterrence has also passed. "Given the goals of rogue states and terrorists, the United States can no longer rely on a reactive posture as we have in the past." Against such enemies, preemptive war is the only possible policy. To be sure, the United States "will not use force in all cases to preempt emerging threats, nor should nations use preemption as a pretext for aggression."[30] There is no definition of when preemption is appropriate or when it is a pretext for aggression; these definitions are in American hands. American forces will be such as to "dissuade potential adversaries from pursuing a military build-up in hopes of surpassing, or equaling, the power of the United States." However, they will be used "to promote a balance of power that favors freedom." This turns out to be the Bush administration's understanding of internationalism: "The U.S. national security strategy will be based on a distinctly American internationalism that reflects the union of our values and our national interests. The aim of this strategy is to help make the world not just safer but better."[31] Or, as Condoleezza Rice put it in a television interview, no power will ever again be allowed "to reach military parity with the United States in the way that the Soviet Union did." Why? Because "when that happens, there will not be a balance of power that favors freedom; there will be a balance of power that keeps part of the world in tyranny the way that the Soviet Union did."[32]

There has been a shift from the recognition of the fact of American preponderance of power to an insistence on maintaining exclusive power; from a multilateral vocabulary, however honored mostly in the breach, to an unabashed unilateralist posture; from an understanding of physics in which a balance requires a fulcrum to one in which exclusive American power constitutes a balanced world. September 11 did not change the world; but it has enabled the Bush administration to pursue, with less opposition and greater violence, policies that might otherwise have appeared too aggressive.

Consider, for example, that September 11 instantly affected the availability to the public of government documents under the Freedom of Information Act. On October 12, 2001, Attorney General John Ashcroft circulated a memorandum to all government agencies suggesting the withholding of information under the Freedom of Information Act in any case where a "sound legal basis" to do so could be asserted. The standard ground for refusal, that the release of a particular document would endanger national security, though often abused as an excuse, was no longer necessary. One month later, Bush issued an executive order that severely limited public access to presidential records. Any former president can assert executive privilege with respect to the records of his administration, and, in the absence of "compelling circumstances," the incumbent president is compelled to protect those records.[33]

Under cover of the war against terrorism, the Bush administration stilled opposition to the missile defense system, expanded programs to secure U.S. dominance of space,[34] declared the unilateral right to conduct preemptive war using nuclear weapons against nonnuclear powers ("offensive deterrence"),[35] and, covering all bases, proposed a new policy of limited sovereignty with respect to all other countries save the United States.[36] One could argue that the United States has often behaved as though the sovereignty of other countries was not of compelling interest. The views of the Bush administration are only a more explicit statement of Reagan administration policies in Central America in the mid-1980s, when the sovereignty of Nicaragua was regularly violated. In 1986, the International Court at The Hague officially condemned the United States "for unlawful use of force," ordered an end to support for the contras, and required the United States to pay reparations. The court's ruling was ignored.

However, Richard Haass, director of the State Department's Policy Planning Staff, has suggested that the current policy of "limited sovereignty" represents "the emergence of a new principle or body of ideas— I'm not sure it constitutes a doctrine." According to Haass, "Sovereignty entails obligations," principally "not to massacre your own people" and "not to support terrorism in any way." Failure to meet these obligations means forfeiting "the normal advantages of sovereignty, including the right to be left alone inside your own territory." Massacring your own population would give other governments the "right to intervene." But supporting terrorism could "lead to a right of preventive, or peremptory, self-defense. You essentially can act in anticipation if you have grounds to think it's a question of when, and not if, you're going to be attacked."[37]

The right to preventive self-defense appears to be exclusively American. Otherwise, under Haass's rules, Haiti, for example, should have the right of preemptive war against the United States, which has for years ignored requests for the extradition of convicted terrorist Emmanuel Constant; Cuba could retaliate for the pardoning, by the first President Bush, of another convicted terrorist, Orlando Bosch, responsible for the bombing of a domestic Cuban airline, and so on.[38] One of Bosch's most enthusiastic supporters is Otto Reich, the recipient of a "recess appointment" (and thus spared Congressional hearings) as assistant secretary of state for Western Hemisphere affairs.[39] Reich's goals for the Western Hemisphere have not changed since the Reagan administration. He was in touch with Pedro Carmona Estanga on the day the military installed Carmona as president of Venezuela in place of Hugo Chavez. We know this because the administration announced the call as a demonstration of its commitment to democracy in Latin America. Reich urged Carmona not to dissolve the National Assembly, an administration official informed the press, because it would be " 'a stupid thing to do' and provoke an outcry." Not unconstitutional, not undemocratic, just plain stupid, as indeed it proved to be. But the call led to speculation that "Mr. Reich or other officials were stage-managing the takeover by Mr. Carmona."[40] The entire Iran-Contra gang is back, including the twice-convicted Elliott Abrams, now head of the Office of Democracy and Human Rights in the State Department, the felon John Poindexter,[41] who will head the Pentagon's Information Awareness Office, Rogelio Pardo-Maurer, the former chief of staff to the representative of the contras in Washington, now deputy assistant secretary of defense for Western Hemisphere affairs and John Negroponte, U.S. ambassador to the UN.

The Negroponte appointment is especially interesting. As Reagan's ambassador to Honduras, Negroponte supervised the transformation of Honduras from a relatively peaceful, if poor, country into a base for military operations in El Salvador and Nicaragua.[42] This entailed, as well, repression of the Honduran left, and the United States worked closely with the head of the Honduran security police, General Gustavo Alvarez Martinez, whose approach to the problem of domestic subversion, the journalist Stephen Kinzer observed, was "the simple expedient of murder." The most feared unit of Alvarez's forces was Battalion 3-16, many of whose members were trained in the United States or by U.S.-funded Argentine "counterinsurgency experts." During Negroponte's tenure in Honduras, Kinzer wrote, "[h]ardly a day passed without a newspaper article about a kidnapping, assassination, or 'disappearance'; by one count, over three hundred such articles appeared in 1982 alone."[43] Despite its knowledge of numerous crimes committed by Battalion 3-16, the embassy not only continued to work with its leaders but rewarded them. In 1983, Alvarez received the Legion of Merit for "encouraging the success of democratic processes in Honduras," and the State Department report on human rights in Honduras declared the country free of political prisoners.[44] When Alvarez's own officers arrested him, Washington offered him a job as a "consultant on unconventional warfare." In 1989 Negroponte was appointed ambassador to Mexico; in 1993 President Clinton appointed him ambassador to the Philippines. On September 14, 2001, Negroponte was approved as ambassador to the UN with little discussion.[45]

The clearest expression of the principle of limited sovereignty for the rest of the world and absolute sovereignty for the United States is reflected in the number of international conventions the United States has refused to sign on grounds of infringement of U.S. sovereignty: treaties on global warming, arms control, land mines, chemical and biological warfare, child labor, small arms trade, and the International Criminal Court. Negotiations on the Biological Weapons Convention were "deliberately scuttled" in December 2001, leading an angry European delegate to observe: "In decades of multilateral negotiations, we've never experienced this kind of insulting behavior."[46] But that was before the United States insisted that American soldiers engaged in UN peacekeeping missions must be granted immunity from the International Criminal Court and threatened to use its veto power against renewal of such missions unless it had its way.[47]

When it does not withdraw from international bodies, the Bush administration seeks to control them. There has been an ongoing effort to remove from office UN officials whose policies in any way challenge those of the United States. According to the reporter George Monbiot, the director-general of the Organization for the Prohibition of Chemical Weapons was forced from office on the grounds that he was "biased" and had undertaken various "ill-considered initiatives." Jose Bustani's offense was that he pressed the United States to adhere to international standards of inspection. Worse, Bustani had sought to persuade Iraq to reopen itself to international inspection.[48] Paul Wolfowitz instructed the CIA to investigate Hans Blix, chair of the UN Monitoring, Verification and Inspection Commission, in hopes of discrediting him and preventing negotiations to renew weapons inspections in Iraq. According to the *Washington Post,* Wolfowitz and his allies were worried that Saddam Hussein might agree, which would "delay and possibly fatally undermine their overall goal to start a military campaign against Iraq." When the CIA reported that it could find nothing untoward in Blix's record, Wolfowitz is reported to have " 'hit the ceiling.' "[49] Finally, environmental groups charge that Robert Watson, head of the UN Intergovernmental Panel on Climate Change, whose insistence on the dangers of global warming had annoyed ExxonMobil, was forced out of office in favor of a hopefully more compliant scientist.[50]

The United States has returned to the Alice's wonderland of the Vietnam War years, when words meant whatever Humpty Dumpty said they meant. When the United States supported Afghan mujahideen, they were freedom fighters, and Ronald Reagan declared a national day in their honor.[51] When civilian Afghans were killed by a missile, the Pentagon declared them an "appropriate target," albeit "we do not know yet exactly who it was."[52] More recently, the military coup in Venezuela was deemed a "victory for democracy" and Ariel Sharon, a "man of peace." The power of definition is at the heart of all power.

The ripple effect of this power has been felt worldwide. Everywhere, local conflicts involving local insurgents have been redefined as wars against terrorism, to the benefit of the governments of Russia, Pakistan, China, Israel, several former Soviet republics, Yemen, Malaysia, Indonesia, the Philippines, and Colombia.[53] Relieved of the onus of humanitarian intervention, which the Republicans have always opposed (except, as in Somalia, when undertaken by a Republican), the rapid, widespread deployment of American troops is now declared to be in the national interest. The battlefront is global. Whereas, after the fact, victory in the Cold War was defined as the collapse of the Soviet Union, victory in this war has a far more ambitious goal. As defined by Secretary of State Colin Powell, this goal means "reaching a state where people are no longer afraid of terrorist activities, where they can go about their lives not concerned about the kinds of things that happened on the 11th of September or the kinds of car bombings that take place in Jerusalem or the kinds of terrorism that [are] meted out by the [left-wing] guerrillas in Colombia."[54] Nothing links these three examples except the tactic of terrorism. The vast differences among Al Qaeda, the Palestinian Authority, and the FARC are erased, as is the possibility of political, rather than military, solutions. As Senator Robert Byrd warned, "If we expect to kill every terrorist in the world, that's going to keep us going beyond Doomsday."[55]

What September 11 permitted the Bush administration to do has reshaped the domestic order. The new defense budget will constrict spending on education, health, and social welfare, already curtailed by massive tax cuts, even more severely. Over the next five years, the United States will spend $2 trillion, twice the military spending of all the countries in the European Union combined and 40 percent of the military expenditure of the entire world.[56] Rather than being prepared to fight a modest number of regional wars simultaneously, the United States will now work toward the capacity to defeat "two aggressors at the same time, while preserving the option for one massive counter-offensive to occupy an aggressor's capital and replace the regime."[57] Reporting on American bases in the Caucasus and Central Asia, *Jane's Foreign Report* explained them in terms of the Pentagon's doctrine of "full-spectrum dominance."[58] With the new defense budget, the military-industrial complex is well on its way to establishing full-spectrum dominance domestically as well.

In addition to the expansion of military bases (those since September 11, many of them in areas previously closed to the United States, include Afghanistan, Pakistan, Kyrgyzstan, Uzbekistan, and Tajikistan), the Bush administration has used September 11 to advance an approach to nuclear weapons long held dear by the president's military advisers. This may be the most dangerous use of the attack. For almost twenty-five years, one of the mechanisms working to control the proliferation of nuclear weapons has been the pledge not to use them against non-nuclear powers. These negative security assurances reflect a "fundamental bargain: the non-nuclear-weapon states agree to submit to international verification that they will never acquire nuclear weapons in exchange for a pledge from the nuclear-weapon states to work toward eliminating these weapons entirely."[59] The terms of such assurances have not been absolute. As defined by the Carter administration, the United States would not use nuclear weapons against countries that had signed the Nuclear Non-Proliferation Treaty "except in the case of an attack on the United States, its territories or armed forces, or its allies, by a state allied to a nuclear-weapon state, or associated with a nuclear-weapon state in carrying out or sustaining the attack." In 1995 the Clinton administration reiterated this pledge, and, for good measure, the UN Security Council, including its four nuclear members, passed a resolution to that effect. A year later, however, Clinton's secretary of defense, William Perry, introduced another modification: a country attacking with biological or chemical weapons would "have to fear the consequences of a response from any weapon in our inventory. . . . We could make a devastating response without the use of nuclear weapons, but we would not forswear the possibility."[60] The country in everyone's mind was Iraq. During the Iraq-Iran war—itself encouraged and prolonged by the United States—the United States, Britain, Germany, Saudi Arabia, and South Africa were the sources of Iraq's weapons of mass destruction: the "feeder stocks" for germ warfare came from a U.S. laboratory; the development technology from Britain; the chemical equipment from Germany; the nuclear technology from Saudi Arabia and South Africa. Meanwhile Israel, acting as a conduit for the United States, armed Iran.[61]

John Bolton, Bush's undersecretary of state for arms control and international security, indicated a further shift in nuclear policy in February 2002. The pledge not to use nuclear weapons against nonnuclear countries, he told reporters, represented "an unrealistic view of the international situation." September 11, Bolton went on, demonstrated that "fine theories of deterrence . . . implicit in the negative security assurances ha[ve] . . . been disproven."[62] Then, in March, copies of the Bush administration's Nuclear Posture Review were leaked to the press, and the full extent of the departure from the balmy days of the Carter administration became clear. The review lists a range of situations in which nuclear weapons might be used: if Iraq attacked Israel; if China attacked Taiwan; if North Korea attacked South Korea. Other countries, all signatories to the Non-Proliferation Treaty, were also named as possible targets: " 'Iran, Syria and Libya are among the countries that could be involved in immediate, potential or unexpected contingencies' that would require 'nuclear strike capabilities.' "[63] The review looked forward as well to the development of new nuclear weapons, such as the Robust Nuclear Earth Penetrator or RNEP, not a Toys "R" Us special but a weapon to be used against buried targets impervious to conventional weapons.[64] Jonathan Schell summarized the effect of the Nuclear Posture Review, along with the abrogation of the ABM treaty and the development of a missile defense shield: "The United States, safe behind its missile shield, will, at its sole discretion and unconstrained by treaties or even consultation with allies . . . protect its territory and impose its will in the world by using its unmatched military power to coerce or destroy, if possible by preemptive attack, every challenger."[65]

The potential boon to the U.S. oil industry should be added to the list of post–September 11 profit-taking. In 1998 the vice president of Unocal, an energy giant with close ties to the Bush family, described his vision of a "new Silk road" to the House Committee on International Relations: a 1,040-mile long oil pipeline beginning in northern Turkmenistan and running through Afghanistan to a terminal on the Pakistan coast, which would "once again make Central Asia the crossroads between Europe and Asia." He called on Congress to "support international and regional efforts to achieve balanced and lasting political settlements within Russia, other newly independent states and in Afghanistan" and to encourage "economic reforms and the development of appropriate investment climates in the region."[66] War has made all Unocal's wishes accessible. "Having pushed, cajoled and bribed its way into [central Asia]," Simon Tisdall reported, "the U.S. clearly has no intention of leaving any time soon. . . . [T]he potential benefits for the U.S. are enormous: growing military hegemony in one of the few parts of the world not already under Washington's sway . . . and—grail of holy grails—access to the fabulous non-OPEC oil and gas wealth of central Asia."[67]

William Appleman Williams proposed long ago that the United States combined rhetorical anticolonialism with actual imperialism, rendering its own history invisible to itself. The concept of "limited sovereignty," as described by Richard Haass to Nicholas Lemann, is a good way to characterize how imperialism and colonialism have always operated. Depending on the political economy and culture of the colonial state, colonized people often exercised limited rights of sovereignty. Haass was not deaf to the implication but insisted there was "a big difference between being imperial and imperial*ist*." In this, he was firmly in the American tradition. Even so, until recently, only the left named America imperial. Now, by contrast, according to Charles Krauthammer, "people are . . . coming out of the closet on the word empire." Emily Eakin tracked the change for the *New York Times:* "Americans are used to being told—typically by resentful foreigners—that they're imperialists. But lately some of the nation's own eminent thinkers are embracing the idea. More astonishing, they are using the term with approval."[68]

Stephen Peter Rosen, director of the Olin Institute for Strategic Studies and a professor in the government department at Harvard University, is an example of the trend. "A political unit that has overwhelming superiority in military power, and uses that power to influence the internal behavior of other states, is called an empire. . . . [W]e are an informal empire, to be sure, but an empire nonetheless. If this is correct, our goal is not combating a rival, but maintaining our imperial position, and maintaining imperial order." Imperial wars, Rosen observes, are different from conventional wars, which end with the troops coming home. "Imperial wars end, but imperial garrisons must be left in place for decades to ensure order and stability." Moreover, imperial strategy requires preventing the emergence "of powerful, hostile challengers to the empire: by war if necessary, but by imperial assimilation if possible." Rosen does not shrink from the prospect.[69]

Again, an issue in these new developments is the relation between continuity and change. Although Eakin and the thinkers she consulted describe the new American empire in terms of its contemporary military and economic power, the imperial stance has been characteristic of the United States. The choice between "isolationism," a euphemism for unilateralism, and internationalism is about the best means to attain American ends. Anthony Lake, Clinton's national security adviser, captured the point perfectly: "We should act multilaterally where doing so advances our interests—and should act unilaterally when that will serve our purpose."[70]

The tension between Europe and the United States, Richard Kagan, senior associate at the Carnegie Endowment for International Peace, argues, "is not a George Bush problem. It is a power problem. American military strength has produced a propensity to use that strength. Europe's military weakness has produced a perfectly understandable aversion to the exercise of military power." Kagan is forgiving of the Europeans. In contrast to the standard view that the United States operates in a transcendent, ahistorical realm, he sees an America "mired in history," living and struggling in a Hobbesian jungle so that Europeans may lead a privileged life of "laws and rules and transnational negotiation and cooperation." To the extent that law regulates international behavior, it is because "a power like the United States defends it by force of arms." However, in order to do so, the United States "must refuse to abide by certain international conventions that may constrain its ability to fight." This is a contradiction only if one fails to believe that such a double standard "may be the best means of advancing human progress—and perhaps the only means."[71]

At once universal and exceptional, America, Anders Stephanson wrote, "was (and is) a world empire. Like Rome, it is in principle the world, or the world to be. There is an outside, to be sure, but it is intrinsically not an equal. . . . The outside is either evil or simply an undifferentiated, amorphous mass to be acted upon in some manner or other."[72] It is for this reason that Secretary of Defense Donald Rumsfeld can speak of "projecting American power into any corner of the world." Stephanson analyzes the consequences of America's self-understanding in terms of its approach to war. War "can scarcely be grasped as a simple instrument of statecraft and grand strategy." It is seen either as "a crusade to end all wars or, more frequently, as policing operations designed to punish perceived criminality and transgressions against an always already existing natural order of law and norms." From 1945 to the present, U.S. wars, none of them declared by Congress, have combined the two: they have been crusades to police the world. Madeline Albright said it clearly in 1998 with respect to the ongoing bombing of Iraq: "If we have to use force it is because we are America. We are the indispensable nation. We stand tall. We see farther into the future."[73] The collapsed towers have provided a platform for a tall nation.

The neoconservative journal the *Weekly Standard* outdoes Albright, dropping the conditional ("if we have to use force") in favor of a forthright celebration of violence. Bush's "emergence as a full-blown war president" has given him the "luxury of defining his presidency, deciding exactly what he wants it to be about. And now we know: It's about war and security and sustaining the spirit of America produced by the Sept. 11 terrorist attacks." According to one of the journal's editors, September 11 has meant the transformation of Bush's presidency from one of "school uniforms and wars on tobacco" to "the presidency of Special Forces uniforms and shooting wars. . . . There is no issue more basic than life and survival; nothing bigger than this around-the-world war. The presidency is back at the center of things."[74] The days of peace and sloth are over.

Perhaps, as the political scientist John J. Mearsheimer argues, all that is new is that the United States "has actually acknowledged what it does, rather than gussy up its impulses with liberal rhetoric."[75] Still, there is a new fear of the United States abroad in the world, especially among America's allies. Anatol Lieven writes of the United States as "a great country, with noble impulses . . . which has become a menace to itself and mankind." Tony Judt worries about the damage that is being done to the "postwar North Atlantic community of interest and mutual friendship" and observes that America's lack of trust in the intentions of others to deal fairly, as expressed in its rejection of the International Criminal Court, may result in its losing the trust of others.[76] The insistent exemption of the United States from the emerging body of international law has first puzzled and then outraged the international elites on whom, for all its military power, the United States must ultimately rely.[77]

The meaning of September 11 for most people seems to be that the world is a dangerous place and that the government of this country, by a careful examination of its own policies and behavior, might contribute to making it a marginally less dangerous place. The meaning of September 11 for the Bush administration, by contrast, seems to be the conviction that it can control the world. The language is imperial: the president "expects" this leader or that to do what the United States wishes to be done, the expectation, absolute security, being divine. J. M. Coetzee captured its spirit in his novel *Waiting for the Barbarians:* "Empire dooms itself to live in history and plot against history. One thought alone preoccupies the submerged mind of Empire: how not to end, how not to die, how to prolong its era. By day it pursues its enemies. It is cunning and ruthless, it sends its bloodhounds everywhere. By night it feeds on images of disaster: the sack of cities, the rape of populations, pyramids of bones, acres of desolation. A mad vision yet a virulent one." "To the last," Coetzee's narrator reflects, "we will have learned nothing. In all of us, deep down, there seems to be something granite and unteachable."[78] The hard unteachability of this administration is fearful. It seems unlikely its ambition can be fulfilled, but it is certain that the cost of either success or failure would be terrible.

Postscript

This essay was written close to September 11, 2001. I reviewed the copy-edited version during the forty-eight-hour ultimatum President Bush imposed on Saddam Hussein, at the beginning of a U.S. "preemptive war" against Iraq in March 2003. In the time between, the tendencies to which I point in the essay have intensified: restrictions on civil rights; a crackdown on immigrants; war and threats of war against a series of enemies; the dominance of the right wing in all branches of government. The Bush administration's plot against history, its ruthless cunning, is demonstrated everywhere: in an attorney general who insists on the death penalty even in cases in which the prosecution itself rejects it; in a lie told so regularly by the administration and a subservient media that a majority of Americans repeat it as gospel, namely the link between Iraq and Al Qaeda; in a military tactic designed to terrorize the population of an adversary and named, in puerile arrogance, "shock and awe." The list will grow, as long as this administration remains in power. The attorney general, John Ashcroft, has composed a song he calls "Let the Eagles Soar," which he performs for selected audiences. "Let the mighty eagle soar," Ashcroft sings out. "She's not yet begun to fly. Let the mighty eagle soar, like she's never soared before."[79] The attachment of the Bush cabal to the national bird of prey is ferocious, and frightening.

Notes

1. For an interesting cultural history of the war against terrorism, see Melani McAlister, "A Cultural History of the War without End," *Journal of American History* 89 (2) (September 2002): 439–55.

2. At the time, Robert Fisk, the Middle East correspondent for the London *Independent,* observed that Clinton's bombing raids were exactly what bin Laden wanted. "He can count on the support of millions of Muslims who will never believe that the strikes against Afghanistan and Sudan were anything but a cynical ploy to distract attention from Mr. Clinton's sexual adventures." See Robert Fisk, "Bin Laden Will Take His Revenge," *Independent,* August 28, 1998; see also Eric Margolis, "US-Russian Crusade against Osama bin Laden," *Toronto Sun,* December 4, 2000; Dick Polman, "Sept. 11 May Taint Clinton's Legacy," *Philadelphia Inquirer,* January 14, 2002.

3. Clinton speech, December 16, 1998. Transcript available from Carnegie Endowment for International Peace Web site, http://www.ceip.org.

4. Jonathan Schell, "Letter from Ground Zero: The Power of the Powerful," October 15, 2001, http://www.thenation.com.

5. See, for example, PBS, "America Responds," http://www.pbs.org/americaresponds. In a speech to the Aviation Security Conference in 2002, Senator John D. Rockefeller IV spoke of the "loss of innocence—an innocence we didn't even know we had until it was so brutally taken from us." The examples are legion—check your favorite search engine.

6. See Corey Robin, "Remembrance of Empires Past: 9/11 and the End of the Cold War," in the forthcoming volume tentatively titled *Victor History: Cold War Triumphalism and America's Recent Past,* ed. Maurice Isserman and Ellen Schrecker (New York: New Press, 2003).

7. David Lightman, "Lieberman's Foreign Policy: Propagate U.S. Values," *Hartford Courant* online service, January 14, 2002, http://www.hartfordcourant.com.

8. Jim Rutenberg, "Hollywood Seeks Role in the War," *New York Times,* October 20, 2001, sec. B, p. 9.

9. Provisions include indefinite detention of noncitizens on minor visa violations, reduced judicial supervision of the monitoring of telephone and Internet communications, and granting to the attorney general and the secretary of state the power to label domestic groups terrorist organizations and deport noncitizen members. In general, the act "significantly boosted the government's law enforcement powers while continuing a trend to cut back on the checks and balances that Americans have traditionally relied on to protect individual liberty." See American Civil Liberties Union, "USA Patriot Act Boosts Government Powers," http://www.aclu.org.

10. See Andy Newman, "Citizen Snoops Wanted (Call Toll-Free)," *New York Times,* July 12, 2002, sec. 4, p. 1. See also http://www.citizencorps.gov. Protest against Operation TIPS has been vigorous. See unsigned editorial, "Ashcroft vs. Americans," *Boston Globe,* July 17, 2002, sec. A, p. 22: "Ashcroft's informant corps is a vile idea. . . . Operation TIPS should be stopped because it is utterly anti-American. It would give Stalin and the KGB a delayed triumph in the Cold War."

11. Ibid.

12. "Citing Fear, Man Shoots at Helicopter," *New York Times,* July 21, 2002, 18.

13. Newman, "Citizen Snoops Wanted."

14. Ibid. In New York, the plane carrying an Indian movie star and her family to the city for a tour was accompanied to LaGuardia Airport by fighter jets, and the family was detained after passengers reported their "suspicious behavior" to the airline stewards. Lydia Polgreen, "Bollywood Farce: Indian Actress and Family Are Detained," *New York Times,* July 18, 2002, sec. B, p. 1. Apparently family competition for the window seat frightened their fellow passengers.

15. Stuart Eskenazi, "Academic Freedom Is under Attack," *Seattle Times,* December 16, 2001, http://www.seattletimes.com; Matthew Rothschild, "McCarthyism Watch: Student Teacher Canned for Teaching Islam," *Progressive,* March 23, 2002, http://www.progressive.org. When the intern asked the class what they thought Islam was, they responded: "crazy, terrorist, uneducated, poor, dirty, oppresses women." On AVOT, see Jim Lobe, "Bill Bennett Organizes Neo-Cons against Dissent," *Foreign Policy in Focus,* March 15, 2002, http://www.foreignpolicy-infocus.org.

16. For one of many accounts of the ordeals experienced by immigrants, see Matthew Brzezinski, "Hady Hassan Omar's Detention," *New York Times Magazine,* October 27, 2002, 50–55.

17. The revelations about what the government knew in August also bring to mind Pearl Harbor, albeit not in the way Bush intended.

18. Paul R. Kennedy, "Truman Calls Reds Present-Day Heirs of Mongol Killers," *New York Times,* December 24, 1950, 1. Though wordier than President Bush, Truman drew the line of global division just as sharply: "Those people who believe in ethics, morals and right associate themselves together to meet those who do not believe in ethics, morals and right, who have no idea of honor or truth."

19. Nicholas Lemann, "The Next World Order," *New Yorker,* April 1, 2002, 42. Seymour Hersh puts it a little differently: "In the old days, the way it worked was, anybody, any despot, any fingernail-puller, that was against the Communists was our man. . . . Now we've got the same standard. If you are willing to join the fight against terrorism, why, you're our

boy." Quoted in Steve Rhodes, "Sy Hersh Unbound," *Chicago Magazine,* May 2, 2002, http://www.chicagomag.com.

20. "Next Stop, Iraq," Remarks of the Hon. Richard Perle at the Foreign Policy Research Institute, Philadelphia, Pa., November 30, 2001.

21. Zalmay M. Khalilzad, *From Containment to Global Leadership? America and the World after the Cold War* (Santa Monica, Calif.: Rand, 1995): 41, ix. Khalilzad believed that 1995 was the year of decision, "an opportunity the nation may never see again. . . . Should the United States fail to seize this historic moment, over time its relative position is likely to decline, and the world is likely to become a balance-of-power multipolar system—and become more dangerous for the United States." Ibid., 41.

22. Quoted in Benjamin Schwarz and Christoper Layne, "A New Grand Strategy," *Atlantic Monthly,* January 2002, http://www.theatlantic.com. For a history of the transformation of the Defense Planning Guidance of 1992 into the National Security Strategy of 2002, see David Armstrong, "Dick Cheney's Song of America: Drafting a Plan for Global Dominance," *Harper's Magazine,* October 2002, 76–83.

23. Schwarz and Layne, "A New Grand Strategy."

24. In Indonesia, the Clinton administration cut off all military aid after the attacks against East Timor. In December 2002, a $17.9 million "Regional Counter-Terrorism Defense Fellowship Program" was approved under which Indonesian military personnel will be brought to the United States for training. See Center for Defense Information, April 8, 2002, http://www.cdi.org. Note, too, that the task of training foreign militaries has created a boom industry in private military firms to which much of the work is contracted out. See Esther Schrader, "U.S. Companies Hired to Train Foreign Armies," *Los Angeles Times,* April 14, 2002.

25. Here too, the antidrug war has been conflated with counterinsurgency. " 'You have to understand,' a Bolivian officer attached to the Expeditionary Task Force explained, 'we are dealing with something like the Soviet Union in the 1930s. . . . These are Marxists and Communists, they are dangerous for both [the United States] and Bolivia.' " See Anthony Faiola, "U.S. Draws Fire over Hired Bolivians in Anti-Coca Force," *International Herald Tribune,* June 25, 2002, 2.

26. McNair Paper Number 41, "Radical Responses to Radical Regimes: Evaluation of Preemptive Counter-Proliferation," May 1995, Institute for National Strategic Studies, http://www.fas.org/spp/starwars/program/docs/m41cont.html.

27. Anatol Lieven, "The Push for War," *London Review of Books,* October 6, 2002, http://www.lrb.uk.co.

28. *The National Security Strategy of the United States of America,* September 17, 2002, p. 1, available at http://www.whitehouse.gov/nsc. See David Armstrong, "Dick Cheney's Song of America: Drafting a Plan for Global Dominance," *Harper's,* October 2002, 76–83, for an interesting account of this document in comparison to earlier versions under discussion since 1992.

29. *The National Security Strategy of the United States of America,* 3, 11, 12.

30. Ibid., 10, 11.

31. Ibid., 20, 3.

32. Interview with Margaret Warner on *The NewsHour with Jim Lehrer,* October 25, 2002, http://www.pbs.org.

33. See National Security Archive, November 28, 2001, http://www.gwu.edu/~nsarchiv/news/20011128.

34. See Terje Langeland, "The Final Frontier: The U.S. Military's Drive to Dominate Space,"

Colorado Springs Independent, December 13, 2002, http://www.csindy.com; John Diedrich, "Military Explores Space Planes," *Colorado Springs Gazette,* April 10, 2002, http://www.gazette.com.

35. Walter Pincus, "U.S. Nuclear Arms Stance Modified by Policy Study: Preemptive Strike Becomes an Option," *Washington Post,* March 23, 2002, sec. A, p. 14.

36. Lemann, "The Next World Order," 45.

37. Ibid., 46.

38. If we add terrorists to the category of international criminals resident in the United States, the list is very long indeed. The INS itself estimated that between 800 and 1,000 "human rights abusers" are living in the United States. See William J. Aceves, "United States of America: A Safe Haven for Torturers," *Amnesty International USA Publications* (2002): 24.

39. Duncan Campbell, "Friends of Terrorism," *Guardian* (London), February 8, 2002. See also William Finnegan, "Castro's Shadow," *New Yorker,* October 14–21, 2002, 101–13. The recess appointment expired when Congress adjourned in November 2002. Currently Reich is a special adviser to Colin Powell.

40. Christopher Marques, "U.S. Cautioned Leader of Plot against Chavez," *New York Times,* April 17, 2002, sec. A, p. 1. Already, there are indications that Elliott Abrams directly "gave the nod" to the plotters. Otto Reich personally received Venezuelans implicated in the plot, including Carmona, in the months leading up to the coup. According to sources in the Organization of American States, the coup "was discussed in some detail, right down to its timing and chances of success, which were deemed to be excellent" (Ed Vulliamy, "Venezuela Coup Linked to Bush Team," *Observer* [London], April 21, 2002, http://www.observer.co.uk). Information on links between the coup leaders and the United States continues to be uncovered: two of the generals involved were trained at the U.S. Army School of the Americas; the television station that gleefully announced the coup is owned by Gustavo Cisneros, a friend of the senior George Bush. See Duncan Campbell, "Bush's Bay of Piglets," *Guardian,* April 24, 2002, http://www.guardian.co.uk. According to Campbell, "hundreds of thousands of dollars in grants" has been given to groups opposed to Chavez through the National Endowment for Democracy. In addition, American military attachés are said to have been in touch with members of the Venezuelan military about the possibility of a coup. See "American Navy 'Helped Venezuelan Coup,'" *Guardian,* April 29, 2002, http://www.guardian.co.uk. The latest revelation in this regard is an account by *Guardian* reporter Greg Palast, who writes that Chavez was warned of a coup possibility by a tip from OPEC headquarters in Vienna, allowing Chavez to take military measures that ensured his quick return to power, though they did not entirely avert the coup. "The American government's panic over the looming calls for an oil embargo, made public by Iraq and Libya," Palast writes, "also explains the U.S. State Department's ill-concealed and clumsy support for the coup attempt" (Greg Palast, "OPEC Chief Warned Chavez about Coup," *Guardian,* May 13, 2002, http://www.guardian.co.uk).

41. Poindexter's conviction was overturned on a technicality.

42. See Larry Boyd, "Honduras under Pressure," *Christian Science Monitor,* September 27, 1982, http://www.csmonitor.com; Raymond Bonner, "All of a Sudden, Honduras Has Gone on War Footing," *New York Times,* August 15, 1982, http://www.nytimes.com.

43. Stephen Kinzer, "Our Man in Honduras," *New York Review of Books,* August 21, 2001, 41.

44. Gary Cohn and Ginger Thompson, "Unearthed: Fatal Secrets," *Baltimore Sun,* June 11, 1995, http://www.baltimoresun.com.

45. Kinzer, "Our Man in Honduras," 42. Writing in August 2001, Kinzer was certain the hearings on Negroponte's appointment would be "anything but routine."

46. George Monbiot, "America's Bioterror," *Guardian,* April 6, 2002, http://www.guardian.co.uk.

47. In the event, after three weeks of intense negotiations, a compromise was reached: U.S. soldiers would be exempt from the court for one year, a provision that would be renewable.

48. George Monbiot, "Chemical Coup d'Etat," *Guardian,* 16 April 2002; George Monbiot, "Diplomacy, U.S. Style," *Guardian,* April 23, 2002, http://www.guardian.co.uk.

49. Walter Pincus and Colum Lynch, "U.S. Probed Record of un Arms Inspector," *Washington Post,* April 16, 2002, http://www.washingtonpost.com.

50. "U.S. Scientist Booted Off Climate Panel," cbs News, April 19, 2002, http://www.CBSNews.com.

51. Reagan proclaimed March 21, 1983, to be Afghanistan Day, an occasion for Americans to "reflect on the events in Afghanistan, to think about the agony which these brave people bear, [to] recall for all the world America's unflagging sympathy for a determined people."

52. John F. Burns, "U.S. Leapt before Looking, Angry Villagers Say," *New York Times,* February 17, 2002, sec. 1, p. 18; Zalmay Khalilzad, quoted in Ahmed Rashid, "Afghanistan: Great Leap Backwards," *Far Eastern Economic Review,* April 18, 2002, http://www.feer.com.

53. For a good account of the impact in one area, see Barry Wain, "Southeast Asia: Wrong Target," *Far Eastern Economic Review,* April 18, 2002, ibid. According to Wain, the war against terrorism has led the United States into complex local politics of which it has little knowledge; its interference in the name of antiterrorism is "in danger of doing as much harm as good." The violence of Islamic militants in Southeast Asia is over "home-grown political concerns that long predated September 11 and are likely to continue despite the U.S. crackdown on terror."

54. Quoted in Jim Lobe, "One, Two, Many Afghanistans," *Asia Times,* March 5, 2002, http://www.atimes.com. The Bush administration is pressuring Congress to lift the ban against funding the counterinsurgency effort on grounds of the military's violation of human rights. Funds were to be used only to fund the drug war. The distinction has never been entirely clear and recently released classified documents obtained by the National Security Archives indicates the restriction has been regularly violated since its inception. See Michael Evans, editor, "War in Colombia: Guerillas, Drugs, and Human Rights in U.S.–Colombia Policy, 1998–2002," National Security Archives Electronic Briefing Book, no. 69, May 3, 2002, http://www.nsarchive.org.

55. Quoted in Lobe, "One, Two, Many Afghanistans."

56. Peter Beaumont and Ed Vulliamy, "Is America Too Powerful for Its Own Good?" *Observer,* February 10, 2002, http://www.observer.co.uk.

57. Paul-Marie de la Gorce, "Offensive New Pentagon Defence Plan" (trans. Barry Smerin), *Le Monde Diplomatique,* March 2002, http://www.monde-diplomatique.fr.

58. Quoted in Scott Peterson, "Terror, War and Oil Expand U.S. Sphere of Influence," *Christian Science Monitor,* March 19, 2002, http://www.csmonitor.com. For an excellent review of the changes in the U.S. defense posture, see Michael Klare, "Endless Military Superiority," *Nation,* July 15, 2002, http://www.thenation.com.

59. Thomas Graham and Leonor Tomero, " 'Obligations for Us All': nato and Negative Security Assurances," *Disarmament Diplomacy,* no. 49, http://www.acronym.org.uk/index.htm (Acronym Institute for Disarmament Diplomacy).

60. Quoted in Bill Arkin, "The Last Word," *Bulletin of Atomic Scientists* 54 (May/June 1998): 3.

61. Eric Margolis, "Old Dreams of Empire Dance in Blair's Head," *Toronto Sun,* March 31, 2002, http://www.torontosun.com.

62. Quoted in Nicholas Kralev, "U.S. Drops Pledge on Nukes," *Washington Times,* February 22, 2002, http://www.washtimes.com.

63. David Corn, "Bush's New Nuclear Weapons Plan: A Shot at Nonproliferation," *Nation,* March 11, 2002, http://www.thenation.com.

64. U.S. Nuclear Posture Review Factsheet, Physicians for Social Responsibility, March 31, 2002, http://www.psr.org. John Bolton recently added Cuba to the list of those "rogue states" seeking weapons of mass destruction—in this case biological; see "Beyond the Axis of Evil: Additional Threats from Weapons of Mass Destruction," Remarks to the Heritage Foundation, Washington, D.C., May 6, 2002.

65. Jonathan Schell, "The Disarmament Wars," *Nation,* February 10, 2002, http://www.thenation.com.

66. U.S. Congress, House Committee on International Relations, Subcommittee on Asia and the Pacific, Unocal Testimony, 107th Congress, 1st session, February 12, 1998.

67. Simon Tisdall, "In Return for Security in the Region, the U.S. Will Snap Up Central Asia's Oil," *Guardian,* January 16, 2002, http://www.guardian.co.uk. See also Michael Klare, "Bush's Master Oil Plan," *Pacific News Service,* April 23, 2002, http://www.pacificnews. org. The merging of the war against terrorism with the effort to expand U.S. access to oil is succinctly reviewed by Michael Klare in "Oil Moves the War Machine," *Progressive Magazine,* June 2002, http://www.progressive.org. Klare notes the role of oil policy in Colombia as well as in the more familiar regions of Central Asia and the Middle East. The war on terror, he concludes, is a "convenient rationale for extending U.S. military involvement into areas that are of concern to Washington primarily because of their role in supplying energy to the United States."

68. Emily Eakin, "All Roads Lead to D.C.," *New York Times Magazine,* April 1, 2002, http://www.nytimes.com.

69. Stephen Peter Rosen, "The Future of War and the American Military," *Harvard Magazine,* May/June 2002, 30–31.

70. Quoted in Robin, "Remembrance of Empires Past." See also Perry Anderson, "Internationalism: A Breviary," *New Left Review,* March/April 2002, 14.

71. Robert Kagan, "Power and Weakness," *Policy Review* 113 (June/July 2002), http://www. policyreview.org. There is a sense in which Kagan is right. The United States and Europe do live in different worlds. These are defined not, as Kagan would have it, by European military weakness and American military strength but rather by a sharp difference in values and in the way people live. As Tony Judt pointed out in a recent essay, rates of poverty are consistently and considerably higher in the United States than in Europe, as are infant mortality rates and income disparities. European economies are more productive; the economic security and health of its population, greater by far. There is little to attract Europeans to the American model, which, Judt concludes, "is unique and not for export." See Tony Judt, "Its Own Worst Enemy," *New York Review of Books,* August 15, 2002, http://www.nybooks.com.

72. Anders Stephanson, "War and Diplomatic History," *Diplomatic History* 25 (3) (summer 2001): 401.

73. Secretary of State Madeline Albright, *Today Show,* NBC, February 19, 1998.

74. Quoted in Richard Reeves, "President Bush: The King of the World," February 19, 2002, http://www.richardreeves.com.
75. Quoted in Judith Miller, "Keeping U.S. No. 1: Is It Wise? Is It New?" *New York Times*, October 26, 2002, sec. B, p. 10.
76. Lieven, "The Push for War"; Judt, "Its Own Worst Enemy."
77. See Paul Rogers, "The Coup in America," October 9, 2002, http://www.opendemocracy. net. Rogers reports on a number of international gatherings at which he became aware of a "palpable sense of unease" about American policies. "What struck me most was a sense of dismay, sometimes almost bordering on depression, and this was particularly noticeable in some of the senior international civil servants. At the root of this was an uncomfortable recognition that the Bush administration has, in less than two years, un- done most of the multilateral progress of well over a decade and, at the same time, has simply shattered the much deeper multilateral consensus that had taken even longer to develop."
78. J. M. Coetzee, *Waiting for the Barbarians* (New York: Penguin, 1982), 133, 143. Compare Rosen, "The Future of War," 31: "As Pericles pointed out to this fellow Athenians, they might think it a fine thing to give up their empire, but they would find that empires are like tyrannies: they may have been wrong to take, but they are dangerous to let go."
79. The attorney general's rendition of his composition before a North Carolina Seminary audience on February 25, 2002, can be accessed at http://www.cnn.com/video/us/2002/ 02/25/ashcroft.sings.wbtv.med.html.

Echoes of the Cold War:
The Aftermath of
September 11 at Home

ELAINE TYLER MAY

"The world will never be the same again," observers proclaimed on September 11, 2001, when hijacked airliners plowed into the World Trade Center, the Pentagon, and a Pennsylvania field. There seemed to be no way to describe the attacks in any familiar context. However, before the sun set on that horrible day, witnesses and journalists were already reaching into historical memory in order to make sense of what happened. They harked back to Pearl Harbor, described the sites of death and destruction as "ground zero," and characterized the situation as "war." Commentators wrote that the attacks were unprecedented. But at the same time, they searched for precedents. The terrorist attacks on that day were the most deadly and destructive assaults by foreign foes on the continental United States in the nation's history. Lacking a vocabulary as well as any historical precedents to place an event of this magnitude in some familiar and manageable context, the nation's leaders, pundits, and large numbers of citizens struggled to find reference points and searched for something familiar to draw out of historical memory. Almost immediately, they found those reference points in World War II and the Cold War. On one level, these responses seem unremarkable and even natural under the circumstances. But were they appropriate or even useful? Were there no other historical precedents or familiar markers to shape the response to September 11? This essay explores the impact of September 11 in terms of these historical reference points, and it raises some questions about other possible precedents that might have led to different responses.

Cultural critic Kenneth Burke describes moments of historical crisis as calling for "frames of acceptance," in which new situations are met with old frames. Although Burke derived his model from the Christian frame of acceptance utilized by the medieval Church, the model is suggestive for post-9/11 America. According to Burke, the old frame provides the parameters of response to a new crisis. Although "new factors . . . bewilder the old frame, which is not designed to encompass them," the frame "will be extended to meet the new necessities by casuistic stretching."[1] Although previous terrorist attacks and other national emergencies offered a variety of frames to choose from, immediately after September 11 the Cold War provided the frame of acceptance. But the Cold War itself emerged from a World War II frame of acceptance, particularly the lessons of Pearl Harbor.

These historical frames of acceptance had immediate resonance in the wake of September 11. The memory of Pearl Harbor evoked the surprise attack that caused massive death and destruction and drew the United States into World War II. The references to "ground zero" recalled the apocalyptic nightmares of the atomic age, long dormant but now revived, complete with visions of civilians going about their daily business snuffed out in an instant. Snippets from the press on September 12 suggest how quickly these frames of reference reappeared in the national vocabulary. The *Baltimore Sun* quoted Neil Hare, a lawyer for the U.S. Chamber of Commerce who works near the White House: "I think we're at war . . . I'm running. This is probably ground zero, and I don't want to be anywhere near here." The *Boston Herald* described the site of the World Trade Center as "ground zero of the worst terrorist attack in American history." The *Boston Globe* noted that people in Washington, D.C., "live with the nightmare that their city is ground zero for a major terrorist attack." But September 11 was not an atomic attack. Nor was it another Pearl Harbor, where an identifiable enemy nation attacked a military base. September 11 was something new. As Americans struggled to make sense of what happened, they reached into their collective historical memories.[2]

The immediate response in the press reflects this effort to meet the unfamiliar with the familiar, marking the event as both unprecedented and precedented. In a typical news report, Rosie DiManno wrote in the *Toronto Star* that on September 11

> the heart of the American empire was Ground Zero. . . . Now U.S. fighter jets buzz overhead in a surreal tableau of war. . . . This is terrorism in the 21st century; faceless, pointless, fanatical and cowardly. But most alarmingly, it is unpredictable and it cannot be defended against. If the mightiest nation in the world was caught un-

awares, so piteously vulnerable to the whims of madmen, then there is no hope and sanity is doomed.... The world will never be the same again. . . . All that steel and concrete convulsing, shuddering, reduced in seconds to a mountain of debris and a mushrooming cloud of smoke and dust. . . . defense officials were herded into secured bunkers deep inside the earth. . . . How could this happen? Who is doing this to us? . . . For Americans, the infliction of terror and bloodshed was the worst single incident calamity since Pearl Harbor. That was an act of war, drawing the U.S. into a global conflict. But at least they knew their enemy then, how to retaliate, how to avenge their losses, and how to affirm their power. But what is this, whose outrageous crime, who to punish? . . . The flexing of U.S. military might is what [Americans] crave, the annihilation of those who perpetrated this grotesquerie. And who can blame them for wanting blood? But vengeance and retribution will not give back to America, to the entire world, any sense of safety, of invincibility. There is no place safe from the bedlam of madness and mania.[3]

In this one account, a journalist notes that the attacks were without precedent. Yet she draws on historical references: ground zero, the "tableau of war," the "mushrooming cloud of smoke and dust," and the memory of Pearl Harbor. She also asserts that Americans crave "blood" and "revenge" and the "flexing of U.S. military might." But when this article went to press to appear on September 12, there were no polls to substantiate those assertions. The nation's leaders and the press nevertheless quickly adopted the same assumptions, and soon the people accepted them, too.

This response went far beyond symbols, language, and vocabulary. Plans drawn up in an earlier era as preparedness for a very different sort of attack immediately went into effect. Taking cues from Cold War atomic age emergency procedures, the president remained mostly airborne and flitted from one small city to another, drawing widespread criticism for his apparent flight in the face of danger. The defense establishment retreated to "secured bunkers deep inside the earth," into fallout shelters constructed during the early years of the Cold War. And everyone talked about war, even though there was no identifiable enemy. Responding to frames of reference dating back half a century, the nation mobilized for battle.

As Americans struggled to come to terms with the shock and horror of the events of September 11, the president declared war and quickly deployed troops. As in the case of all wars waged by the United States since World War II, Congress did not declare this war. But few politicians or commentators questioned the president's unofficial declaration of war. Three days after the attack, Congress overwhelmingly passed a resolution authorizing the president to use "all necessary and appropriate force" against the terrorists and the nations that sponsor or protect them.[4] The nation had been attacked. Thousands of Americans were killed. War seemed the most appropriate definition of the situation. Declaring war provided a blueprint for action.

But was war the only option? What other historical frames of reference were available to shape the national response? The attacks were unprecedented in many ways. Never before had terrorists used such methods: transforming commercial airliners into weapons of mass destruction, hijacking planes with the intention of suicide missions, living and working within the nation for years in order to conspire, plot, and plan the attacks. The ghastly scale of death and destruction, the vast network of participants, the carefully coordinated suicide missions—all added up to a deed so cunning and vile that it almost defied definition.

Nevertheless, there were precedents. This was the worst, but not the first, terrorist attack on the nation. There have been many terrorist attacks, most of them domestic. Domestic terrorist attacks include the bombing of the federal building in Oklahoma City, the murders of abortion providers and attacks on clinics, and the Unabomber's murder-by-mail. There have also been attacks on the nation by international terrorists. Many of these attacks occurred outside the United States. In June 1996 a truck bomb killed nineteen U.S. airmen in Dhahran, Saudi Arabia. Two years later, bombs exploded at two U.S. embassies in East Africa, killing 224 people in Nairobi, Kenya, and Dar es Salaam, Tanzania. Four men were convicted of conspiracy in the terrorist attacks. They were identified at the time as followers of Islamic militant Osama bin Laden, who was also indicted in connection with the embassy bombings. Bin Laden, originally from Saudi Arabia, was living in Afghanistan under the protection of the fundamentalist Taliban regime, and remained a fugitive. He was known to be the leader of the Al Qaeda terrorist network operating in several countries throughout the Middle East. On October 12, 2000, a small boat pulled up next to the destroyer USS *Cole* in Yemen's port of Aden. A bomb exploded and ripped a hole in the destroyer, killing seventeen Americans and wounding thirty-nine others. Two suicide bombers carried out the attack. U.S. officials believed that they, too, were associated with Osama bin Laden. But nobody declared war.

International terrorist attacks also occurred on American soil, including the World Trade Center nearly a decade earlier. What distinguished this previous attack from the one on September 11 was its conventional method and the relatively minor damage it caused—minor only by comparison to September 11. On February 26, 1993, a bomb exploded in the parking garage underneath the World Trade Center. Five people were killed and more than a thousand were injured. The *New York Times* reported that the explosion "destroyed a multistoried parking garage under the trade center, knocked out power to the center and touched off fires that sent smoke billowing up through its 110-story twin towers and forced 50,000 people into a nightmarish evacuation that took all day and half the night." President Clinton tried to quell the fears of the nation in the face of what appeared to be an act of international terrorism. "Working together, we'll find out who was involved and why this happened," the president declared. "Americans should know we'll do everything in our power to keep them safe in their streets, their offices and their homes."[5] But he did not declare war on terrorism. Shortly thereafter, investigators discovered a plot to blow up the tunnels and bridges leading into New York. That plot was foiled, but had it succeeded, it would have wreaked unprecedented devastation.

The responses to these earlier terrorist attacks were dramatically different from the response to September 11, and they had vastly different consequences for the nation. The attacks were considered crimes, and the perpetrators were treated as criminals. The criminal investigative apparatus of the nation moved into high gear to track down and prosecute the offenders. Although in a few cases of international terrorism the United States launched retaliatory military strikes on sites of suspected terrorist operations, there was no talk of war. In these earlier cases, the president promised swift and thorough action against the perpetrators, denounced the violent and ruthless acts, promised to provide security and called for calm. For Americans who were not immediately affected, life went on as usual.

After September 11, of course, life did not go on as usual. The sight of hijacked airliners exploding into buildings, the sheer magnitude of the attack, the collapse of the mighty trade towers, the crumpled walls of the Pentagon, the thousands dead, all gave rise to shock and horror. Nevertheless, these were the same sorts of crimes as the earlier attacks, although vastly more efficient and successful. They, too, might have been handled as the previous attacks had been: through the investigative processes of the criminal justice system. But the immediate response was to declare war, not to launch a criminal investigation.

Declaring war has a number of immediate consequences. One is that it elevates the criminals to the level of a legitimate enemy and recognizes their authority as leaders. It provides an opportunity for those who oppose U.S. policies to join armies to fight against us, making them soldiers for a cause rather than accomplices to a crime. In the case of an act of criminal terrorism, this strategy is problematic. U.S. officials immediately identified Osama bin Laden as the mastermind behind the plot and declared war on his Al Qaeda network as well as any government that tolerated terrorists within its borders. President Bush then declared, in classic Cold War terms, that those who were not "with us" in this war against terrorism were "against us"—both at home and abroad.[6]

Internationally, this declaration had important consequences, forcing nations to be either our allies or our enemies. Within the United States, a declaration of war allows the government to compromise and constrict the normal workings of a democratic society in the name of national security. Most citizens willingly complied and rallied around their leaders. Trust in the federal government reached levels not seen since the early 1960s. Since 1958, the Gallup Poll has asked Americans, "How much of the time do you think you can trust government in Washington to do what is right?" The percentage of those who answered "most of the time" peaked in 1963 at 75 percent, fell to 25 percent in 1979, and hit its lowest point in 1994 at about 18 percent. The percentage climbed after that, reaching above 40 percent in July 2000, and then leapt to 60 percent a month after 9/11—the highest point in more than thirty years. "Not since the Cold War has the government had such an important mission," said Carroll Doherty, a political analyst at the Pew Research Center for the People and the Press. "So this trust is not so much a reflection of what government has done, but a hope for what government can accomplish."[7]

The September 11 attacks gave George W. Bush new stature as president of the nation in a way that the problematic election of 2000 did not. Taking office without a mandate, failing to win a majority of the popular vote and without a clear victory in the Electoral College, Bush's presidency lacked legitimacy. By declaring war against terrorism immediately after the September 11 attacks, Bush became the leader of a nation at war. War, if it has widespread support, has always contributed to the popularity of presidents. Crime has done just the opposite. Declaring the attacks an act of war, rather than a crime, elevated Bush's stature and boosted his sagging popularity. Within a month of the attacks, a president who had not been elected with an electoral majority achieved an approval rating above 80 percent.

Echoes of World War II and the Cold War

Pearl Harbor caught the nation by surprise and led to an official preoccupation with preparedness and national security, which outlasted World War II and shaped much of the domestic response to the Cold War. After September 11, the Pearl Harbor frame of reference emerged immediately and reverberated for days and months to remind Americans that war is the appropriate response to the attack. On September 12, 2001, Carl J. Calabrese, from Buffalo, New York, spoke for many when he said, "I finally know how my parents felt when Pearl Harbor was bombed in 1941. This is a calculated, focused attack on our nation. There's this tremendous sense of fear. But we have to do all we can to keep things operating." President Bush also invoked Pearl Harbor to rally the nation for the war on terrorism. On December 7, 2001, the sixtieth anniversary of the Japanese attack on Pearl Harbor, the president spoke from the deck of the aircraft carrier *Enterprise,* which had just returned from the North Arabian Sea after commencing the first bombing runs over Afghanistan. Using the language of World War II, Bush said, "Like all fascists, the terrorists cannot be appeased. They must be defeated. This struggle will not end in a truce or a treaty." Pearl Harbor, he said, was the start of a "long and terrible" war for America, yet out of that attack grew the most powerful navy in the world and a "steadfast resolve" to defend freedom. "And that mission, our great calling, continues to this hour, as the brave men and women of our military fight the forces of terror in Afghanistan and around the world. . . . Many of you in today's Navy are the children and grandchildren of the generation that fought and won the Second World War. Now your calling has come." The *Washington Post* also made a direct comparison to Pearl Harbor, noting the similarities: "After the sneak attack, crowds gathered outside the White House and sang 'God Bless America.' Soldiers armed with machine guns guarded government buildings. The FBI began rounding up suspicious foreigners. And the head of the Secret Service stared nervously at the sky, watching for suspicious aircraft. It was Dec. 7, 1941, 60 years ago today. Japanese planes had bombed Pearl Harbor, and the West Coast was in a state of panic."[8]

Michael Sherry, in his ambitious synthesis of the last half of the twentieth century, *In the Shadow of War,* notes that militarization shaped

American life after World War II. Virtually every national crisis, from the War on Poverty to the War on Drugs, brought forth a new war metaphor, if not a new war. During the Cold War, the apparatus of wartime became a permanent feature of American life. Sherry writes:

> National security assumed permanent and paramount importance in American life, so that much of the nation's treasure was devoted to it, its armed forces spread over much of the globe, and its science and industry were profoundly reoriented. . . . [W]ar defined much of the American imagination . . . to the point that Americans routinely declared "war" on all sorts of things that did not involve physical combat at all. Thus, militarization reshaped every realm of American life—politics and foreign policy, economics and technology, culture and social relations—making America a profoundly different nation. To varying degrees, almost all groups were invested in it and attracted to it—rich and poor, whites and nonwhites, conservatives and liberals (the last more so than is usually recognized today). Certainly, all were changed by it.[9]

Sherry's insights help explain why, in a situation so unpredictable, the national response was remarkably predictable, on the part of leaders as well as citizens. When the president declared "war on terrorism" immediately after the September 11 attacks, he announced that this would be a "new" type of war. But the war he initiated was not really a new type of war. It was modeled on older wars—not on World War II, but on the various military actions of the Cold War. It was the Cold War that echoed most loudly across the post-9/11 landscape. The terrorists seemed to have brought into reality national nightmares that dated back more than half a century. Although the weapons they used were not nuclear bombs—they were in fact remarkably low-tech instruments such as box cutters—the villains seemed to personify the characteristics of the Communist threat: foreigners who infiltrated the nation, studied our technology, and used our own power against us. They blended into society, plotting against us while enjoying the good life they professed to disdain. They turned our own proud monuments of postwar technological and consumer triumph, commercial airliners and towering skyscrapers, into the means of our destruction. Like the suspected Communist spy, they represented the enemy within, loyal to a foreign foe. The worst Cold War fears seemed to have become a reality, more than a decade after the end of the Cold War. The Bush administration responded in Cold War fashion: increasing the defense budget by $48 billion (a sum larger than the entire defense budget of any other nation) and developing new nuclear weapons, according to a secret Pentagon report. The president also insisted on continued funding for the "Star Wars" missile shield, which would be useless as a defense against terrorist attacks.[10]

In terms of the politics of the Cold War, the war on terrorism holds some irony. Cold War priorities prompted the United States to oppose the Soviet invasion of Afghanistan when Jimmy Carter was president. At that time, the United States supported the Taliban against the Soviets, and Osama bin Laden was our ally. That relationship persisted for decades. As recently as the spring of 2001, the United States gave millions of dollars to the Taliban to help in the War on Drugs, to support a poppy eradication program in Afghanistan. Only the political satire magazine the *Onion* dared to raise the issue: "Former president George Bush issued an apology to his son Monday for advocating the CIA's mid-'80s funding of Osama bin Laden, who at the time was resisting the Soviet invasion of Afghanistan. 'I'm sorry, son,' Bush told President George W. Bush. 'We thought it was a good idea at the time because he was part of a group fighting communism in Central Asia. We called them "freedom fighters" back then. I know it sounds weird. You sort of had to be there.'"[11]

In its domestic ramifications, the waging of the war against terrorism resembled the waging of the Cold War more than it did World War II. Although Pearl Harbor served as a frame of reference, there were few domestic responses to September 11 comparable to World War II, when the nation went to war against an identifiable enemy. Perhaps the only similarity to World War II home-front practices is the treatment of people of Arab descent. Vigilante activity resulted in a burst of violence as Muslims became the targets of hostility, threats, racist slurs, assaults, and even murder. President Bush called for tolerance toward Muslims and noted, "We welcome legal immigrants but we don't welcome people who come to hurt Americans." Yet post-9/11 antiterror strategies targeted people of Middle Eastern descent. Government policies, although not as draconian as the internment of people of Japanese ancestry during World War II, resulted in the roundup of people of Arab descent for questioning and incarceration without charging them with any crime. Since September 11, the Justice Department has detained more than 900 people in connection with the attacks. On November 9, 2001, the State Department announced it would subject to special scrutiny male visa applicants aged sixteen to forty-five from twenty-six nations in the Middle East, South Asia, Southeast Asia, and Africa. Students were particularly at risk of investigation. In the first two months after September 11, federal investigators questioned students from Middle Eastern countries at more than 200 college campuses. The students were asked about the subjects they were studying, their academic achievement, where they lived, and their opinions of Osama bin Laden. College administrators said that this type of investigation of campuses has not been seen since the Cold War. Yet in nearly every case, the colleges cooperated with the investigations.[12]

Aside from racial profiling measures, there are few similarities to wartime home-front policies. During World War II, the nation's leaders asked the people to make sacrifices. The government drafted men to fight, rationed foods and other goods, converted consumer industries into war industries, and asked citizens to support the war effort by buying war bonds, planting "victory gardens," and conserving everything useful. Since the onset of the war on terrorism, the nation's leaders have asked the people to do just the opposite: take trips, spend money, enjoy leisure time, and buy consumer goods. President Bush urged Americans to "fly and enjoy America's great destination spots. . . . Get down to Disney World in Florida. Take your families and enjoy life the way we want it to be enjoyed." The government called up its volunteer army but did not draft anyone. It gave back tax dollars for people to spend, rather than asking citizens to invest or save.[13]

Government policies went counter to all efforts to conserve resources of any kind. President Bush opposed efforts to promote energy efficiency for cars or industries and did nothing to minimize the nation's dependence on oil from the Middle East. The Bush administration proposal to drill for oil in the Arctic National Wildlife Refuge would reduce oil imports from the Middle East by only 4 to 5 percent, and not for at least ten years.[14] These policies were not wartime policies, but they did echo the emphasis on consumer freedom and the "American way of life" that was central to Cold War propaganda. As Vice President Richard Nixon emphasized in the 1959 "kitchen debate" in Moscow, consumerism was the real stealth weapon that would trump the Soviets and win the Cold War.[15]

Unfortunately, the aspects of the Cold War that forced American leaders to adopt progressive measures are not present in the war against terrorism. We no longer have Communist leaders taunting the United States into improved race relations. As Mary Dudziak and Thomas Borstelmann have shown, the United States promoted the Civil Rights Movement at home to help fight the Cold War in the Third World, in an effort to win the hearts and minds of people of color as they threw off the shackles of white colonial rule.[16] The Communists also promised impoverished people a redistribution of wealth, encouraging American leaders to provide workers with the fruits of affluence through home mortgages and education grants, and by mitigating the impact of poverty through the continuation of the New Deal welfare state. In the name of classlessness and prosperity, cold warriors hoped to avoid a Communist-inspired uprising of poor people at home and abroad. These Cold War pressures are absent now.

It might have been otherwise. Immediately after September 11, many people asked the question, "Why do they hate us?" That question sparked an initial outpouring of teach-ins on college campuses, thoughtful editorials in the press, and vastly increased coverage of the Arab world in the media. It appeared as though, perhaps for the first time, Americans were genuinely interested in learning something about other countries, and about the role of the United States in the world. But that initial impulse withered quickly as President Bush whipped up the rhetoric of war. There were good Arabs and bad Arabs, and all we needed to know was if they were "on our side." Because President Bush adopted a posture of good versus evil, the opportunity for national soul-searching about the American presence in the Arab world rapidly withered.[17]

Homeland Security

The war against terrorism, like the struggle against Communism, defines the enemy as a worldwide conspiracy, with cells operating in many countries around the world and with operatives infiltrating the United States as well. The Bush administration has borrowed language as well as policies from the days of the Cold War. The clever term "axis of evil" fuses the World War II memory of the Axis powers to Ronald Reagan's Cold War description of the Soviet Union as the "Evil Empire." The establishment of the Office—and then Department—of Homeland Security echoes the civil defense bureaucracy set up during the Cold War to bolster morale and develop visible security measures that would offer the illusion of safety against an unpredictable enemy with access to weapons of mass destruction.

Creating a sense of security after an attack of the magnitude of September 11 is virtually impossible, just as it was impossible to reassure a nation about the danger of an atomic attack after the world had witnessed the effects of an atomic bomb. In the early years of the Cold War, civil defense measures such as teaching housewives how to stock a fallout shelter, or training children to "duck and cover" in their school classrooms, offered the illusion that survival was possible in the event of a nuclear attack.[18] Similar efforts to reassure a nervous public have emerged in the wake of September 11.

The most obvious of those are the attempts to achieve airport security. When the public learned about the minimal training and low pay of airport security guards employed by airlines trying to pinch pennies, people were justifiably outraged. After much clamor, the government took over the task, so now the poorly trained and underpaid airport security guards work for the government, under the watch of military personnel who now roam the airports in uniform, armed with menacing weapons. Most Americans and foreign visitors have patiently accepted the long waits in security lines at airports, the frequent checking of documents, the intrusions into their privacy as a result of random baggage checks, and the affronts to their bodies in routine pat-down searches. These measures give the illusion of security, as did the home bomb shelters and "duck and cover" campaigns of the early Cold War years. But just as the civil defense campaigns did nothing to minimize the danger of death from an atomic attack in the midst of an escalating arms race, these highly visible but feeble efforts at airport security offer little protection. Confiscating nail clippers and providing plastic knives with in-flight meals offer meager, perhaps even useless, safeguards against terrorism.[19] More to the point, airport security is a Band-Aid approach to a problem that will continue to grow as long as anger against the United States festers around the world. The policies enacted in the wake of September 11—especially the military deployments—have done nothing to diminish that anger, and they have done much to intensify it. Polls taken in the Muslim world show that vast majorities of civilians harbor hostility to the official policies of the United States.[20] Like fallout shelters, airport security measures offer the illusion of protection; but they will not provide safety. Safety will come only in the de-escalation of international tensions.

Patriotism as Consumerism

Patience at airports was only one of many ways that citizens expressed their acquiescence to wartime conditions. Americans seemed to forget their political differences and their culture wars to rally around the flag, quite literally. Patriotic symbols, proliferating instantly after the attack, became ubiquitous around the country and sparked a new market for patriotic consumer goods. Flags appeared on houses and in public spaces, on lapels, bags, bumper stickers, and billboards. Foreign journalists noted this patriotic spending frenzy. On September 29, 2001, the London *Guardian* described the scene at the Mall of America in Bloomington, Minnesota:

> You are never far from a flag in the Mall of America. All four miles of walkway are bedecked with red, white and blue banners, hammer-

ing home the warlike mantra "United We Stand." The country's biggest indoor shopping centre, on the outskirts of Minneapolis, reflects the patriotic fervour now in evidence across the stunned US. . . . Patriotism seems to go hand-in-hand with the shopping. A choice of how to spend money is one of the great "freedoms" cited by many in the mall as American characteristics. "I'm proud of our freedoms—perhaps we've even got too many—that's why all this has been allowed to happen," says Elizabeth Smith, 69, from Seattle. "We have so much more freedom here than in other countries." Mike Wilson, a factory electrician from Muncie, Indiana, echoes this: "If you're proud of your country, you need to show it all the time. I served in the military—I love my country."[21]

Topps, the bubble gum company that invented baseball trading cards in the 1950s, quickly produced and marketed "Enduring Freedom" card packets immediately after September 11. The cards, which came in several different sets, included a "God Bless America" sticker picturing the American flag, along with cards commemorating the war on terrorism, designed to educate and inspire support for the campaign. One card pictures "Army Paratroopers Boarding an Aircraft," and quotes Bush on the back: "This war will not be like the war against Iraq a decade ago, with a decisive liberation of territory and a swift conclusion." Another card pictures Bush with Federal Emergency Management Agency (FEMA) director Joe M. Allbaugh and quotes Allbaugh praising all the federal, state, and local agencies for their cooperation and professionalism. Another shows Bush speaking to Muslims and quotes him on September 17 attempting to quell the growing anti-Muslim sentiments and violence. Another depicts Russian president Vladimir Putin offering sympathy for the United States. Other cards contain images and descriptions of warships and fighter planes.[22] Consumer items such as these provide effective propaganda to build support for the war against terrorism.

"Enduring Freedom" trading cards may seem innocuous. But when citizens can buy patriotism, the essence of citizenship withers. Flags flew across the land at the same time that lawmakers debated and enacted legislation that included some of the most serious threats to civil liberties since the draconian measures of the McCarthy era. Less than two months after September 11, Congress passed the USA Patriot Act, authorizing new powers for law enforcement agencies. The bill granted federal agents access to e-mails and voice mails of suspected terrorists and allows for the prosecution of hundreds of people detained after 9/11 for immigration violations. The law expands the authority of the federal government to conduct electronic surveillance and wiretaps, screen computers, and access private records. It permits the detention of immigrants suspected of supporting terrorism for as long as a week without charging them with a crime or immigration violations. American Civil Liberties Union lawyers expressed concern that the law will harm civil liberties and give the federal government "unchecked powers." But there was little public outcry. By strategically naming the bill the "Patriot Act," political leaders benefited from the consumption of patriotism, by symbolically wrapping themselves in the flag.[23]

In addition to national legislation, across the country state legislatures debated measures that would require citizens to express their patriotism, reminiscent of the loyalty oaths of the early Cold War. In Minnesota, for example, legislators passed by a huge margin a bill that requires schoolchildren to recite the pledge of allegiance. Students and teachers may opt out, but they will then be singled out as dissenters. An editorial in a Minneapolis paper asked, "Should government *mandate* demonstrations of patriotism? Or is love of country something that occurs when government serves people well and protects the freedom to disagree?" With this bill, Minnesota became the twenty-sixth state to require the pledge of allegiance.[24]

One of the most disturbing political casualties of 9/11 was the stifling of public debate and the emergence of a new political consensus. According to political scientist Lawrence Jacobs, "There's a real conformitarian spirit in America right now. . . . [I]t's flipped gradually into an expectation that you won't raise critical issues, that you'll fall into line. It's the new 1950s."[25] As in the Cold War, Democrats and Republicans closed ranks, and few if any dared to question the president or the administration. Republicans were quick to brand anyone who criticized the administration as "giving aid and comfort to our enemies." When Senator Tom Daschle opposed drilling in the Arctic National Wildlife Refuge, the Family Research Council compared Daschle to Saddam Hussein. When he raised questions about the military campaign, Trent Lott scolded, "How dare Senator Daschle criticize President Bush while we are fighting our war on terrorism?"[26] Along with politicians, journalists, academics, and even entertainers faced censure for criticizing the nation's leaders. Tom Guttig of the *Texas City Sun* and Dan Guthrie of the *Grants Pass Daily Courier* (Oregon) were fired for suggesting that President Bush should have returned immediately to the White House after the September 11 attacks, rather than dart furtively around the country. Several television stations suspended ABC's *Politically Incorrect* when comedian Bill Maher questioned Bush's characterization of the terrorists as "cowards." Maher was forced to make a public apology for saying, "We have been the cowards, lobbing cruise missiles from 2,000 miles away. That's cowardly. Staying in the airplane when it hits the building, say what you want about it, it's not cowardly." The *Washington Post* noted that the networks caved in to pressure when White House spokesman Ari Fleisher denounced Maher, saying that Americans "need to watch what they say."[27]

Academic freedom also came under siege, reviving disturbing memories of the McCarthy era. On November 11, the American Council of Trustees and Alumni (ACTA), founded in 1995 by former National Endowment for the Humanities (NEH) chair Lynne Cheney and Senator Joseph Lieberman, released a report that included a list of names of academics who had made public statements that questioned aspects of the war on terrorism. Evoking McCarthyite tactics, the report stated that college and university faculty "have been the weak link in America's response to the attack," and urged alumni to express their displeasure to university administrators. On December 6, Attorney General John Ashcroft told the Senate Judiciary Committee that those who criticize the post-9/11 curtailment of civil liberties "aid terrorists . . . erode our national unity and diminish our resolve." Even the normal functioning of the judicial system was compromised in the name of national security. The establishment of military tribunals to try suspected terrorists moves the process farther from the system of criminal justice and closer to secret trials that do not respect due process.[28]

Domestic Security

Along with the invigorated stature of public officials, security concerns created new heroes among fire fighters and law enforcement officers, who suddenly achieved a newly exalted stature. The New York City police, who faced severe public condemnation in recent years for acts of brutality against racial minorities, rose above criticism as quickly as smoke rose above the twin towers. Since 9/11, the nation's police and security forces have gained a panache not equaled since the heyday of the FBI "G-man" during the early years of the Cold War. Even after the revelations of serious problems of communication, discipline, and turf wars within and between the police and fire departments that led to catastrophic results on September 11, the stature of these agencies and their members did not diminish.[29]

Men in uniform—and they were almost all men—gained public reverence, while women faded into the background. Although many of the law enforcement officers were women, along with powerful women leaders, the names in the headlines were all powerful men, from the terrorists to the heroes: the hijackers, Osama bin Laden, George W. Bush, Dick Cheney, Tony Blair. As in the Cold War, the time had arrived for an image of reinvigorated manhood. Powerful men appeared as the major players on both sides of the "good" and "evil" equation, while women and children seemed vulnerable, in need of protection, whether it was the widows of 9/11 firefighters or the women of Afghanistan. Of course, these women and children did need support and protection. But the framing of the media images, focusing on heroic men and dependent women, reinforced gender constructions that date back half a century.

Meanwhile, Bush and the Office of Homeland Security urged citizens to become "citizen-sentinels" and create a "national neighborhood watch" to become vigilant in spotting terrorist threats. Using the language of the Cold War era when "communist infiltration" was the prevailing fear, the government called for "improved domestic preparedness," as the *Christian Science Monitor* noted, in order "to let people know what it really means to be prepared—to be vigilant," so that "Americans can better provide for their common defense."[30] In July 2002 the Bush administration called for the establishment of the TIPS program, which would recruit volunteers among delivery people, utility workers, and others whose jobs bring them into people's homes to snoop on their fellow citizens. The plan evoked visions of the excesses of the Cold War anti-Communist crusade when "naming names" of possible subversives was a sign of patriotism and schoolchildren viewed propaganda films in which patriotic youngsters turned in their parents to authorities.

Whether or not they considered themselves "citizen sentinels," most Americans followed their leaders uncritically and sought their own security in personal life. This response also echoes the behavior of Americans in the early years of the Cold War, when men and women sought security within the intimate realm of marriage and the family. After 9/11, Americans also turned to each other for solace and comfort. "Many people are looking around after these events and feeling like they want to get closer to the people they care about," noted the Montreal *Gazette*. As one single woman noted, "Somehow, people want to connect." Many New Yorkers interviewed after the attacks expressed their immediate desire to get close to another person on an intimate level. Newspapers reported "quickly kindled romances and rampant post-disaster intimacy." In Denver, requests for marriage licenses went up 10 to 15 percent after 9/11. The proprietor at the Chapel of Love in the Mall of America in Bloomington, Minnesota, noted that while most of the mall's shops went begging for customers, her business boomed. Couples rushed to the chapel to get married in a hurry. Some observers predicted that there might be a baby boom nine months after September 11.[31]

Articles in the *New York Times,* the *Los Angeles Times,* and elsewhere noted the sudden outpouring of neighborliness and kindness among strangers and within communities. Spontaneous acts of generosity, a spirit of voluntarism and charity, and a coming together in the face of tragedy permeated the country. People reached out to their family members across the country and the world, contacted friends and kinfolk, offered assistance to people they hardly knew, donated generously to charities to help the families of victims. Political scientist Robert Putnam, author of *Bowling Alone,* in which he documented a drastic decline in community and civic life in recent decades, conducted a survey after 9/11. He concluded that in response to the tragedy, "almost instantly, we rediscovered our friends, our neighbors, our public institutions, and our shared fate."[32] This outpouring of community spirit saturated the media, the press, and the airwaves, garnering so much attention that it seemed to suggest that Americans normally behaved with selfishness and hostility toward one another. The phenomenon prompted the *Onion* to quip, "Hugging up 76,000 Percent . . . Rest of Country Temporarily Feels Deep Affection for New York," and to publish mock interviews with New Yorkers who couldn't wait for life to return to normal so they could be mean and selfish again.[33]

Despite the media fanfare, the quest for security was not all loving and sharing. In the first six months after September 11, the FBI conducted 455,000 more background checks for gun purchases than during the same period the previous year. The FBI also handled 130,000 more applications to carry concealed weapons. Gun ownership has also spread to new groups. For the first time, the Second Amendment Sisters, a national women's pro-gun group, formed a chapter on a college campus. About fifty women at Mount Holyoke have joined the new chapter. One new member boasted, "One of my guy friends said, 'You're a chick with a gun—I'm scared.'" Women's gun organizations have also proliferated, such as Mother's Arms and Armed Females of America. Drawing a rather illogical connection to September 11, the Web site for Armed Females of America asserts, "Those who push for 'gun control' are of the same mindset as Palestinian suicide-bombers and the Taliban who kidnap women for rape and sex-slave trade. Both don't like the possibility of armed citizens, in these cases, especially armed *Women*."[34]

The idea of "chicks with guns" may not be the most reassuring thought in the wake of 9/11. But we should remember that in the early years of the Cold War homemakers who stocked makeshift fallout shelters in their basements also served as visible icons of women doing their part to protect themselves and their families from danger. As in the Cold War, Americans have again embarked on political and cultural strategies in the name of national security that offer little protection, while enacting policies that escalate conflict and create more danger.

Conclusion

Kenneth Burke's notion of "frames of acceptance" helps to explain the ways in which historical memories of World War II and the Cold War shaped official U.S. responses to September 11 and promoted the acquiescence of the American public. Those previous national crises provided precedents that allowed policy makers and citizens, consciously or not, to react to an unfamiliar situation in familiar ways. But these frames of acceptance may not have been appropriate. Thwarting political debate and stifling free speech in the name of national security and antiterrorism threaten the democratic values that we are presumably fighting to protect. Saber-rattling rhetoric, dividing the world into "good" and "evil," censoring criticism of the nation's leaders, embarking on murky military campaigns across the globe, inflating the defense budget, and folding political differences into a rigid consensus did not serve the country well in the Cold War, and will not serve the nation well now. Trumpeting consumerism, fawning over law enforcement officials, demanding displays of patriotism, retreating into the private world of family and sex, and creating the illusion of safety through visible but largely useless performances of security did not bring about the end of the Cold War and will not likely hasten the end to this crisis either. The Cold War consensus finally broke when the nation became embroiled in a tragic and unwinnable war that became so unpopular that a fierce and divisive national political debate eventually emerged. But it took the loss of many more thousands of lives, and many decades, before the Cold War finally ended. The United States may have "won" the Cold War, but it lost quite a bit in the process. Hopefully, the tragic consequences of Cold War policies and practices will evoke historical memories that yield a different frame of reference, so that the disasters of the Cold War era will not be repeated at the dawn of the twenty-first century.

Notes

1. Kenneth Burke, *Attitudes toward History*, 3d ed. (Berkeley and Los Angeles: University of California Press, 1984), 132–33.

2. Susan Baer and Ellen Gamerman, "Terrorism Strikes America," *Baltimore Sun,* September 12, 2001, sec. A, p. 12; Laurel J. Sweet and Kay Lazar, "Attack on America," *Boston Herald,* September 12, 2001, p. 32; Mary Leonard, "Attack on America / Washington, D.C.: Center of Government Becomes a Ghost Town," *Boston Globe,* September 12, 2001, sec. A, p. 2.

3. Rosie DiManno, "A Nation's Confidence Is among the Casualties," *Toronto Star,* September 12, 2001, sec. B, p. 1.

4. Unsigned editorial approving the action, "Fighting Back: Congress Acts Quickly in War on Terror," *San Diego Union-Tribune,* September 15, 2001, sec. B, p. 10.

5. Tom Mashberg, "Terrorism Suspected in N.Y. Blast," *Boston Globe,* February 28, 1993, sec. A., p. 1.

6. See Marc Howard Ross, "The Political Psychology of Competing Narratives," Social Science Research Council, *After September 11 Archive,* http://www.ssrc.org/sept11/essays.

7. Quoted in Kevin Diaz, "Cynicism Is Out, Trust in Government Is In," *Minneapolis Star Tribune,* October 23, 2001, sec. A, p. 11.

8. Dan Herbeck, "WNY Feels the Impact: Closings and Security Alerts Add to the Day's Tension," *Buffalo News,* September 12, 2001, sec. C, p. 1; Elisabeth Bumiller, "Remembering Pearl Harbor, Bush Ties It to the Current Campaign," *New York Times,* December 8, 2001, sec. B, p. 1; Peter Carlson, "America Gamely Stumbled Off to War," *Washington Post,* December 7, 2001, sec. A, p. 1.

9. Michael S. Sherry, *In the Shadow of War* (New Haven: Yale University Press, 1995), x.

10. Frank Rich, "The Wimps of War," *New York Times,* March 30, 2002, sec. A, p. 15; Michael R. Gordon, "U.S. Nuclear Plan Sees New Weapons and New Targets," *New York Times,* March 10, 2002, sec. A, p. 1.

11. "Bush Sr. Apologizes to Son for Funding Bin Laden in '80s," *Onion,* September 26, 2001, http://www.theonion.com/archive_37.html.

12. Aristide Zolberg, "Guarding the Gates in a World on the Move," Social Science Research Council, *After September 11 Archive,* http://www.ssrc.org/sept11/essays; Ann McFeatters, "Bush Signs Anti-Terror Bill; Says Tough Law Will Preserve Constitutional Rights," *Pittsburgh Post-Gazette,* October 27, 2001, sec. A, p. 6; Jacques Steinberg, "A Nation Challenged: The Students; U.S. Has Covered 200 Campuses to Check Up on Mideast Students," *New York Times,* November 12, 2001, sec. A, p. 1.

13. Carlson, "America Gamely Stumbled Off to War."

14. Frank Rich, "The Bush Doctrine, R.I.P.," *New York Times,* April 13, 2002, sec. A, p. 17.

15. See Elaine Tyler May, *Homeward Bound: American Families in the Cold War Era* (New York: Basic Books, 1999), 10–13, 145–47.

16. Mary L. Dudziak, *Cold War Civil Rights: Race and the Image of American Democracy* (Princeton: Princeton University Press, 2000); Thomas Borstelmann, *The Cold War and the Color Line: American Race Relations in the Global Arena* (Cambridge: Harvard University Press, 2001).

17. See Ross, "The Political Psychology of Competing Narratives."

18. See May, *Homeward Bound,* 90–94.

19. See, e.g., Steve Samuel, "A Weak Spot: The Luggage Hold," *New York Times,* October 11, 2001, sec. A, p. 25.

20. Jim Vandehei, "Islam's Split-Screen View of the U.S.," *Wall Street Journal,* April 11, 2002, sec. A, p. 15. The article notes that a "survey of Muslims in five Arab and three non-Arab countries . . . finds widespread approval of U.S. consumer products, movies and television programs but disapproval of U.S. policies toward Arab states and Palestinians."

21. Andrew Clark, "When Sales Start to Flag: The American Consumer," *Guardian* (London), September 29, 2001, 32.

22. Topps Enduring Freedom card packet, distributed by the Topps Company, Inc., Duryea, Pa.

23. McFeatters, "Bush Signs Anti-Terror Bill."

24. Unsigned editorial, "Pledge of Allegiance—Mandatory Recitation Unnecessary," *Minneapolis Star Tribune,* March 18, 2002, sec. A, p. 12; Anthony Lonetree and James Walsh, "State Senate Backs Pledge Bill," *Minneapolis Star Tribune,* April 26, 2002, sec. A, p. 1.

25. Quoted in Diaz, "Cynicism is Out," 11.

26. Quoted in Rich, "The Wimps of War," 15.

27. Cynthia Billhartz, "Maher's Comments Lead to Show's Suspension," *St. Louis Post Dispatch,* September 22, 2001, p. 15; Sheryl McCarthy, "City College Officials Need an Education on Freedom," *Newsday,* October 11, 2001, sec. A, p. 48; Editorial, *Washington Post,* September 29, 2001, sec. A, p. 26.

28. Martin J. Sherwin, "Tattletales for an Open Society," *Nation,* January 21, 2002, 40.

29. Kevin Flynn and Jim Dwyer, "Fire Dept. Lapses on 9/11 Are Cited," *New York Times,* August 3, 2002, sec. A, p. 1; Jim Dwyer, Kevin Flynn, and Ford Fessenden, "9/11 Exposed Deadly Flaws in Rescue Plan," *New York Times,* July 11, 2002, N.Y. Region, 1. These stories note that at least 121 firefighters in striking distance of safety died as a result of a lack of communication between the police and fire departments and within the fire department.

30. Editorial, "Closing the Safety Gap," *Christian Science Monitor,* October 11, 2001, 8.

31. Donna Nebenzahl, "Getting Closer: Sept. 11 Affecting Personal Relations," *Gazette* (Montreal), October 11, 2001, sec. D, p. 1; Courtney Lingle and John Libid, "Marriage-License Requests Up," *Denver Post,* October 10, 2001, sec. A, p. 12; Michael E. Ruane, "A Wedding Out of Mourning: Like Many Touched by Attacks, Couple Changed Approach to Life after Sept. 11," *Washington Post,* October 10, 2001, sec. B, p. 3.

32. Robert D. Putnam, "Bowling Together," *American Prospect,* February 11, 2002, http://www.prospect.org/print/V13/3/putnam-r.html.

33. "Hugging up 76,000 Percent," *Onion,* September 26, 2001, http://www.theonion.com/archive_37.html.

34. Nicholas D. Kristof, " 'Chicks with Guns,' " *New York Times,* March 8, 2002, sec. A, p. 23.

Homeland Insecurities:
Transformations of Language and Space

AMY KAPLAN

Since September 11, 2001, new words have entered our everyday lexicon as though they have always been there. "Ground zero" and "homeland" are especially salient and evocative spatial metaphors, which in public discourse do not appear metaphoric at all but as literal descriptions of actual places. I am interested in how these words frame, interpret, and produce meanings—and preclude other meanings—both for the events that have come to be known as "9/11" and for changing images of U.S. nationhood and its relation to the outside world. In contrast to the highly charged—perhaps even sacralized—spaces of "ground zero" and "the homeland," there are key locations around the globe that have new political uses and meanings, but they are ones for which there seems to be a dearth of public discourse and language. One of these locations is Guantánamo Bay, Cuba. I am interested in how these three spaces— ground zero, the homeland, and Guantánamo Bay—are represented and what the relations among them might be. My reflections explore the relationship between language and space, how words are mapping, blurring, and reconstructing the conceptual, affective, and symbolic borders between spheres once thought of as distinctly separate, as either national or international, domestic or foreign, "at home" or "abroad."

Ground Zero

Let me start at ground zero—not with the site of carnage in lower Manhattan, but with the meaning of the words, which have a temporal as well as a spatial dimension. Like the use of "9/11," "ground zero" is a highly condensed and charged appellation that has come to represent the terrorist attacks on the World Trade Center, the physical location itself, the experience of untold suffering, and the absence of the twin towers, the people, and the corpses to bury. We can learn something about the usage of this term before September 11 from the *Merriam-Webster Dictionary*. First, the date it entered the English language: 1946. Then, "1. the point directly above, below, or at which a nuclear explosion occurs; 2. the center or origin of rapid, intense, or violent activity or change." The latter definition, more metaphorical than the first, moves from a single point of spatial impact to the unleashing of vast repercussions over time. Definition 3: "the very beginning, *Square One*."[1] We often use "ground zero" colloquially to convey the sense of starting from scratch, a clean slate, the bottom line. This meaning resonates with the often-heard claim that the world was radically altered by 9/11, that the world will never be the same, that Americans have lost their former innocence about their safety and invulnerability at home. This way of thinking might be called a narrative of historical exceptionalism, almost an antinarrative that claims that the event was so unique and unprecedented as to transcend time and defy comparison or historical analysis. Even though it describes cataclysmic change, it also conveys a traumatic sense of time standing still, which denies the reality of change, that is, if we think of change as a process of transformation with both continuity with and discontinuity to what came before and after. Furthermore, another political implication of "ground zero" as the point of origin is that the illimitable response to terrorism must itself start from square one, from this original perpetration of evil, and the response must match the full power of this traumatic rupture, for which no prior guidance, historical limits, or wider political context is appropriate.

As Marita Sturken has shown, this narrative of unprecedented trauma in fact has many precedents; it is an oft-told story of America's fall from innocence, one that in its repetition reaffirms a double meaning of innocence as not guilty and as naively trusting.[2] (Thomas Friedman has even attributed the colossal failure of U.S. intelligence prior to September 11 to the trusting good nature of the American character that could not conceive of such evil).[3] Historical exceptionalism, I would argue, is intimately related to a long-standing tradition of American exceptionalism, a story about the nation's uniqueness in time and place. The historical exceptionalism implicit in the appellation "ground zero" is belied by the history of the term itself that started with the first use of the nuclear bomb. It was coined to describe the nuclear strikes on Hiroshima and Nagasaki. Yet the wholesale adoption of the name "ground zero" for the destruction in New York has not prompted any overt comparisons to Hiroshima and Nagasaki; September 11 was not compared to August 6. Instead the analogy we heard over and over again was to Pearl Harbor, December 7, even though the experience of a sudden horrific attack on civilians in an urban center seemed more like the events of September 11 than the military attack on a naval base. The repeated overemphasis on the one event worked to disavow the obvious connections to the other.

The term "ground zero" both evokes and eclipses the prior historical reference in using it as a yardstick of terror—to claim that this was just like the horrific experience of a nuclear bomb, while at the same time consigning this prior reference to historical amnesia. "Ground zero" relies on a historical analogy that cannot be acknowledged because to do so would trouble the very binary oppositions and exceptionalist narratives erected on that ground, between before and after, between being with us or with the terrorists, between the American way of life and the "axis of evil." Instead, the use of "ground zero" in this context implies that only terrorists could inflict such a level of untold suffering on a civilian population. Thus historical exceptionalism contributes to what writer Ariel Dorfman has discussed as the exceptionalism of North American suffering, "that attitude which allowed citizens of this country to imagine themselves as beyond the sorrows and calamities that have plagued less fortunate people around the world."[4]

My point is not to enter into a debate about the comparative measurement of immeasurable human suffering. Nor is it to offer a cause-and-effect narrative—that the terrorism of 9/11 was an indirect blowback of earlier U.S. imperial designs at the end of World War II. Rather, it is to highlight the importance of language in giving meaning to an event that seems to defy meaning, and to suggest that narratives and metaphors bear the traces of history that our current usage disavows. In the use of "ground zero" to express the unprecedented nature of recent terrorist attacks, we can hear the echoes of earlier forms of terror perpetrated by the United States, which locates us in world history rather than as an exception to it.

Ground zero might be thought of as an uncanny location, not only because of the thousands of unburied dead that haunt it. According to Freud, the uncanny derives its terror not from the alien and the unknown but from "something which is familiar and old-established in the mind and which has become alienated from it only through the process of repression."[5] The uncanny entails the return of the repressed as something at once threatening, external, and unrecognizable, yet strangely familiar and inseparable from our own pasts. Perhaps a political sense of the uncanny might be a way of combating the perils of American exceptionalism, of acknowledging what W. E. B. Du Bois learned from what he called the "awful cataclysm" of World War I: "That the United States was living not to itself, but as part of the strain and stress of the world."[6]

The Homeland

As plans for rebuilding on ground zero get underway, an important ideological edifice has also been under construction: the concept of homeland security. Public discussions about the creation of the Department of Homeland Security rarely touched on the meaning of the word "homeland." If "ground zero" implies starting anew from the point of total annihilation, "homeland" connotes an inexorable connection to a place deeply rooted in the past. George W. Bush first used the term in a speech on September 20, 2001. It struck a jarring note as an unfamiliar way of referring to the American nation, an idiom not found in the traditional political vocabulary that includes "national security," "domestic security," and "civil defense." Few Americans refer to their nation as the homeland, even in the heat of fervent patriotism. Indeed many may express allegiance to their country as home, while they think of places elsewhere as their historical, ethnic, or spiritual homeland.

Referring to the nation as a home, as a domestic space through familial metaphors, is commonplace, probably as old as the nation form itself. Yet, although "homeland" has the ring of ancient loyalties, it is in fact a recent term in the American lexicon. Presidents before Bush never used the word to refer to the United States during periods of world crisis.[7] In World War II there was the "home front," a metaphor that by asserting a similarity also underlined the gap between the battlefields abroad and an entire national territory unscathed by war's violence. Neither Roosevelt nor Truman referred to the United States as the homeland; they only used the term to refer to other countries under the threat of invasion (Holland, Russia, and Japan). Perhaps "homeland" was evocative of the German fatherland and the sinister identification of *Heimat* with fascist ideologies of racial purity, and maybe it also called to mind the German home guard and homeland defense (*Heimwehr, Heimatschutz*). "Homeland" did not enter the Cold War vocabulary either, despite the obsession with the Communist menace within. Perhaps "homeland" then evoked the Russian motherland used especially to describe the sacrifices of World War II. The domestic response to nuclear threat during the Cold War was called "civil defense," not "homeland defense." During World War I, Wilson did not refer to America as the "homeland," but that word was attached by many international groups to his support of self-determination for aspiring nations, popularized especially by the Zionist rhetoric of the Jewish homeland.

Since September 11, official rhetoric has transformed the United States into the homeland, a word that bears cultural connotations, affective meanings, and ideological implications. While the attack on the twin towers and the Pentagon radically exposed the permeability of national borders that had been eroded by the forces of globalization, the administration has gone through great lengths to tighten and shore up those borders, legally, politically, and militarily. This reconstruction of national boundaries relies on linguistic work as well in the battle over what has been called "protected zones of language."[8] The word "homeland" contributes to the cultural work of securing national borders, while it also produces a sense of radical insecurity. Even though it is being represented as a return to a fundamental notion of patriotism—the love of one's country and the desire to protect it—the naturalization of this term may indicate a transformative moment for American nationalism. For one, the usage always entails the definite article (*the* homeland), indicating its unitary meaning, as opposed to pluralistic definitions of national identity.

The notion of the nation as a home, as a domestic space, relies structurally on its intimate opposition to the notion of the foreign. "Domestic" has a double meaning that links the space of the familial household to that of the nation, by imagining both in opposition to everything outside the geographic and conceptual border of the home. The earliest meaning of "foreign," according to the *Oxford English Dictionary,* refers to the physical space "out of doors" or to concerns "at a distance from home." Contemporary English speakers refer to national concerns as domestic in explicit or implicit contrast with the foreign. The notion of domestic policy makes sense only in opposition to foreign policy; uncoupled from the foreign, national issues are never labeled domestic. The idea of foreign policy depends on the sense of the nation as a domestic space imbued with a sense of at-homeness, in contrast to an external world perceived as alien and threatening. Reciprocally, a sense of the foreign is necessary to erect the boundaries that enclose the nation as home. In reimagining America as "the homeland," what conceptions of the foreign are implicitly evoked? What is the opposite of "homeland"? Foreign lands? Exile? Diaspora? Terrorism?

The entry on "homeland" in the *OED* starts with a delightfully deadpan definition: "the land which is one's home or where one's home is." It shows that only in the late nineteenth century does it take on its nationalist meanings. Other dictionaries define "homeland" as "fatherland, motherland"; as "a state, region or territory that is closely identified with a particular people or ethnic group"; and as "a state or area set aside for a people of a particular national, cultural or racial origin."[9] Homeland thus conveys a sense of native origins, of birthplace and birthright. It appeals to common bloodlines, ancient ancestry, and notions of racial and ethnic homogeneity. Though American national identity has always been linked to geography, these meanings, which are bounded and self-enclosed, represent a departure from traditional images of American nationhood, as boundless and mobile. In fact, the exceptionalist notion of America as the New World pitted images of mobility against what might be seen as a distinctly Old World definition of "homeland." A nation of immigrants, a melting pot, the western frontier, manifest destiny, a class-less society, all involve metaphors of spatial mobility rather than the spa-tial fixedness and rootedness that "homeland" implies. "Homeland" also connotes a changed relation to history, a reliance on a shared mythic past engrained in the land itself. This implies a sense of time, as well as space, different from nineteenth-century notions of America as a "Nation of Futurity," throwing off the shackles of the past, or President Kennedy's rhetoric of the New Frontier.

The White House has called the creation of the Department of Home-land Security in January 2003 "the most significant transformation of the U.S. government since 1947," a paradigm shift reflected in language as well as institutional change.[10] When, in October 2001, President Bush swore in Secretary Tom Ridge as the director of what was then the Office of Homeland Security, Ridge's acceptance speech brought together the new image of the homeland with older images of national mobility:

> We will work to ensure that the essential liberty of the American people is protected, that terrorists will not take away our way of life. It's called Homeland Security. While the effort will begin here, it will require the involvement of America at every level. Everyone in the homeland must play a part. I ask the American people for their patience, their awareness and their resolve. This job calls for a national effort. We've seen it before, whether it was building the Trans-Continental Railroad, fighting World War II, or putting a man on the moon.[11]

All of his examples involve the mobilization and expansion of state power, across the continent, across the oceans, and across outer space in the Cold War. There is a relation between securing the homeland against the encroachment of foreign terrorists and enforcing national power abroad. The homeland may contract borders around a fixed space of nation and nativity, while it simultaneously expands the capacity of the United States to move unilaterally across the borders of other nations.

Although supporting the homeland, according to Ridge, calls for a unified nation, the meaning of "homeland" has an exclusionary effect that underwrites a resurgent nativism and anti-immigrant sentiment and policy. There is little room for immigrants in the space of the homeland as a site of native origins, ethnic homogeneity, and rootedness in common place and past. Many immigrants and their descendants may identify with America as their nation but locate their homeland elsewhere, as a spiritual, ethnic or historical point of origin. Many go back and forth between two homes—for instance, New York and the Dominican Republic. Many American citizens see Ireland or Africa or Israel or Palestine, all in very different ways, as their homeland, as a place to which they feel spiritual or political affiliation and belonging, whether literally a place of birth or not. The idea of America as the homeland makes such dual identifications suspect and threatening, something akin to terrorism. To paraphrase Bush, you are either a member of the homeland or with the terrorists. What a terrible irony the idea of the United States as a homeland must be to Native Americans.

At a time when the rights of so-called aliens and immigrants have been attacked and abrogated by the USA Patriot Act, when they can be detained indefinitely incommunicado and deported in the name of homeland security, the notion of homeland itself contributes to making the life of immigrants terribly insecure. It plays a role in policing and shoring up the boundaries between the domestic and the foreign. Yet it does this not simply by stopping foreigners at the borders, but by continually redrawing those boundaries everywhere throughout the nation, between Americans who can somehow claim the United States as their native land, their birthright, and immigrants and those who look to homelands elsewhere, who can be rendered inexorably foreign. This distinction takes on a decidedly racialized cast through the identification of the homeland with a sense of racial purity and ethnic homogeneity that even naturalization and citizenship cannot erase. These connotations have taken institutional form in the incorporation of the enforcement division of the Immigration and Naturalization Service, into the Department of Homeland Security, whose first priority is to protect Americans from terrorist attack.

The notion of homeland has historically been associated with ideas of racial purity. This can be seen in the cynical use of this term by the South Africa regime in 1969 in the Bantu Homelands Citizenship Bill, which codified an enforced racial segregation that relegated blacks to their supposed sites of tribal origins and kept them out of the cities and the white

South African nation. A related implication of homeland is its folksy rural quality that combines a German romantic notion of the folk with the heartland of America to resurrect the rural myth of American identity (perhaps reclaiming it from the domestic terrorism in Oklahoma). It is hard to imagine New Yorkers referring to their city as "the homeland." Home, yes, but homeland? Not likely. Even in the upwelling of support for New York in the wake of 9/11, most Americans are unlikely to claim the city as part of the homeland, which has a decidedly anti-urban and anticosmopolitan ring to it. As Tom Ridge put it in his homey way, "the only turf is the turf we stand on," which appropriates the language of the streets to preclude an urban vision of America as multiple turfs with contested points of view and conflicting grounds on which to stand.

Although the fascist connotations of "homeland" may seem far-fetched and overly alarmist, a revealing faux pas was made by the then newly appointed Texas Homeland Security chief David Dewhurst in October 2002, when he purchased a full-color, four-page advertisement in *Texas Monthly* magazine that depicted a military officer standing in front of an unfurled American flag, with the following caption: "As chairman of the Governor's Task Force on Homeland Security, David Dewhurst encourages you to support President Bush and the brave men and women of our Armed Forces as they fight to eliminate terrorism and work to restore confidence in our economy." Controversy erupted over the ad when people noticed that the officer in the photograph was not an American general but clearly a German Luftwaffe officer—complete with military decorations, insignias, and a name tag bearing the German flag. Dewhurst fired his ad agency.[12]

An especially dissonant meaning of "homeland" in the American context lies in its reference to a nation that does not yet fully exist but to which a people or ethnic group aspires, such as Palestine, Kurdistan, or the Sikh, Tamil, or Basque homeland. In this usage, a people, whom others may see as an ethnic group, consider themselves to be a nation not yet embodied in a territory and a sovereign state. Such groups are often viewed as the underdog whose legitimate claims to territory have been usurped by another state. This meaning has special resonance in the American depiction of the violent struggle between Palestinians and Israelis over their homelands, and it implicitly places the United States in an analogous position to Israel, which sees its homeland threatened by the national aspirations of the Palestinians to a homeland, aspirations often conflated with terrorism.

Related to the concept of homeland as national aspiration is its connection to the discourse of diaspora and exile, to a sense of loss, longing, and nostalgia. A place you came from—no matter how long ago—and long to go back to but cannot ever really return to, except perhaps in the form of what Salman Rushdie has called "imaginary homelands."[13] In this meaning, homeland evokes a sense not of stability and security, but uprootedness, deracination, and desire. The image of America aspiring to a lost homeland depends on the potential of terrorism to sever Americans from their own territory, from their legitimate aspirations. "Homeland" embodies this profound sense of nostalgia, in its Greek etymology, *nostos,* the return home. In this sense, homeland is created not out of unbroken connections to a deeply rooted past, but from the trauma of severance and threat of abandonment. Homeland is something a larger power threatens to occupy or take away, and you have to fight to regain. The word "homeland" has a kind of anxious redundancy, home and land, as though trying to pin down an uneasy connection between the two that threatens to fly apart.

Thus the idea of the homeland works by generating a profound sense of insecurity, not only because of the threat of terrorism, but also because homeland is a fundamentally uncanny place, haunted by prior and future losses, invasions, abandonments. The uncanny, after all, in Freud is a translation of *unheimlich,* the unhomelike. The homeland is haunted by all the unfamiliar yet strangely familiar foreign specters that threaten to turn it into its opposite.

Theorists of nationalism have reminded us that the nation-state is a modern phenomenon, even though nationalism represents itself as the opposite, the embodiment of an eternal mythical identity rooted in a premodern past. The current nostalgia for the homeland contributes to the development of new forms of imperial state power in the post-9/11 world order. A column in the *Guardian* commented that "home" is an easier word for patriotic Americans than it would be for "us" (read sophisticated British).[14] Yet in the British context, the terms "Home Secretary" and "Home Office" have meanings that demarcated the space of England as home as distinct from the colonial possessions of the British Empire. The idea of the American homeland has a similar meaning as the cordoned off center of the far-flung American empire, which many now see as the most extensive hegemon since Rome, not just a superpower, but what the French call a "hyper power." Contracting the borders around the territorial homeland is related to waging a highly mobile and deterritorialized war against terrorism, conducted by a nation that has announced its unilateral right to launch overt and covert attacks across any sovereign borders regardless of international law or whose homeland is involved. This imperial right to what has been called preemptive war is at the heart of President Bush's national security strategy and has been evoked as the justification for the war against Iraq.

The concept of homeland security did not emerge full-blown from ground zero. It has been propounded in government and military circles since the 1990s as part of the effort to redefine the role of the Department of Defense and the armed forces in the post–Cold War world (the Hart-Rudman Commission on National Security, for example, discussed this strategy and used this term).[15] The concept of homeland security goes hand in hand with a more flexible multifront mobile role for the armed forces abroad, as one department of a globalized police force. Advocates of homeland security argue for the need for more government, military, and intelligence coordination to enable the armed forces to be involved in this country as well, and for the government through surveillance and policing to intrude into more areas of civil life at home. In the words of a homeland security policy group, "Homeland security consists of those private and public actions at every level that ensure the ability of Americans to live their lives the way they wish, free from fear of organized attack."[16] Although homeland security may strive to cordon off the nation as a domestic space from external foreign threats, it actually entails breaking down the boundaries between inside and outside and seeing the homeland in a state of constant emergency from threats within and without. In these policy circles, "homeland defense" is a subcategory of "homeland security." The homeland is not like the home front for which war is a metaphor; homeland security depends on a radical insecurity where the home itself is the battleground. If every facet of civilian life is subject to terrorist attack, such that a commercial airliner can be turned into a deadly bomb, then every facet of domestic life—in the double sense of the word as private and national—must be both protected and mobilized against these threats. Homeland security calls for vast new intrusions of government, military, and intelligence forces not just to secure the homeland from external threats but also to become an integral part of the workings of home, which is in a continual state of emergency.

Policy makers did not conspiratorially choose the word "homeland" with these multiple meanings in mind. I do suggest, however, that the choice of the word puts into play a history of multiple meanings, connotations, and associations that work on the one hand to convey a sense of unity, security, and stability, but more profoundly, on the other hand, work to generate forms of radical insecurity by proliferating threats of the foreign lurking within and without national borders. The notion of "the homeland" draws on comforting images of a deeply rooted past to legitimate modern forms of imperial power.

Guantánamo

There is a space uncannily close to home that lacks the currency and visibility of ground zero and the homeland but that has become crucial to both: Guantánamo Bay, Cuba, the site of the U.S. naval station. The use of the name "Guantánamo" is itself confusing, as it refers interchangeably to the bay and the base, as though no distinction existed between geography and the political imposition of a military institution. At this location, the United States government has incarcerated over six hundred prisoners captured in Afghanistan since January 2002 without bringing charges against them. The justice department has classified them as "unlawful combatants" on the grounds that they were not nationals of any state, even though the prisoners come from forty different countries. The government refused to classify them as prisoners of war, a status that would afford them protection under the Geneva Conventions. Held in small, isolated cells, they have been denied access to family and the representation of lawyers, and they are subject to indefinite detention and the possibility of military tribunals. As this book goes to press, twenty-three prisoners have attempted suicide in response to the inhumane conditions and indefinite future in what Amnesty International has condemned as a "legal black hole" and "legal limbo."[17]

While the detainees at Guantánamo have no rights under the international agreements of the Geneva Conventions, they also have no legal recourse domestically to the U.S. Constitution. In March 2003, a federal appeals panel denied a petition for a writ of habeas corpus and ruled that the prisoners had no constitutional right to challenge their detention.[18] The court based this decision not on who the prisoners were, or on what they had done, but on *where* they were being held. The court did not rule on their status as unlawful combatants or on whether they engaged in international terrorism, nor did it uphold the legality of the detentions. Instead it determined that the United States has no sovereignty over the territory of Guantánamo and therefore that the prisoners "cannot seek release based on violations of the Constitution or treaties or federal law; the courts are not open to them."[19] Even though the U.S. Navy operates a self-sufficient enclave and exercises complete juridical control over the base, the court ruled that "control is surely not the test" of sovereignty.[20] Instead, it ruled that sovereignty meant "supreme dominion exercised by a nation. The United States has sovereignty over the geographic area of the States and . . . over insular possessions. . . . Guantánamo fits within neither category."[21] The only category it seems to fit is what Gerald L. Neuman has called an "anomalous zone, . . . a geographical area in which certain legal rules, otherwise regarded as embodying fundamental policies of a larger legal system, are locally suspended."[22] Guantánamo is doubly anomalous, a geographical area in which both national and international laws are suspended, leaving it hovering in a realm that is neither domestic nor foreign. The United States has total jurisdiction over this space that the court considers extraterritorial; Cuba has nominal sovereignty but no jurisdiction over the same territory it has leased in perpetuity to a foreign power with which it has no diplomatic relations.

Thus the limbo status of the space of Guantánamo underwrites the legal limbo of the detainees, who are not labeled prisoners of war nor charged with crimes, who are not subject to the national laws of the United States or Cuba nor to those of international conventions. The prisoners are alien but, in some sense, not fully foreign; they do not have the constitutional rights as aliens that they might have had if they were held on U.S. territory. As the *New York Times* commented, "The ruling confirms the wisdom of the decision of the United States authority to use Guantánamo as a place that would be out of reach of American constitutional law."[23] It is a ready-made site for the proposed military tribunals, which under executive command would have the power to hand down death sentences, unfettered by checks and balances or the right to appeal.

This absence of sovereignty over Guantánamo Bay does, however, stem from a long history that links the current American empire to the exercise of imperial power at the turn of the century. Although in its March 2003 decision the court drew on the language of the lease of 1903 to determine Cuban sovereignty over Guantánamo, it did not address the historical conditions under which this lease was negotiated. In 1898, the United States intervened in the Cuban War for Independence, ostensibly to liberate Cuba from Spanish dominion. During the subsequent U.S. occupation, Washington pressured Cuba to adopt provisions in its new constitution favorable to U.S. intervention, including a ninety-nine year lease of the naval base. When the lease was renewed in 1934, its term was made indefinite: it could be canceled only by the agreement of both parties or the navy's abandonment of the base. This open-ended arrangement makes Guantánamo a chillingly appropriate place for the indefinite detention of prisoners in what the administration has called a war without end against terrorism.

Guantánamo can be seen as an uncanny site for the return of America's repressed imperial history. In the aftermath of the war in 1898, the Supreme Court took up the question (which it might have to face again in relation to Guantánamo) of whether the Constitution followed the flag to the newly acquired possessions of Puerto Rico, Guam, and the Philippines—a question resolved ambiguously in each case at that time.[24] This imperial history, however, has been subject to amnesia in governmental as well as popular discourse. President Bush claimed in a May 2002 speech that the Cuban independence movement one hundred years ago was not usurped by U.S. intervention but hijacked by Fidel Castro, whom Bush accused of "turning this beautiful island into a prison," without acknowledging the U.S. prison on the same island.[25] The current role of the naval base at Guantánamo (like the presence of U.S. troops in the Philippines) shows that the routes of the American empire today follow well-worn tracks, not only throughout the Middle East but also to the locations around the globe where the United States first emerged as a world power in the early twentieth century.

The anomalous character of the U.S. naval base at Guantánamo Bay was created not only by the history of U.S. imperialism, but also, more recently, by its related history of immigration, specifically in reference to Haitian refugees trying to enter the United States in 1991. (Haiti also has a long history of U.S. imperial relations, of which the occupation of 1914–1940 is only one chapter.) The military's role on the naval base expanded to immigration control, as the navy interdicted Haitians on the high seas and brought them to Guantánamo to be processed and then detained in camps under horrendous living conditions. Camp X-Ray, in which the detainees from Afghanistan were first imprisoned, was originally built to house Haitian refugees. In response to suits brought on behalf of the detainees, the Eleventh Circuit Court of Appeals accepted the argument of the government that the Haitians had no constitutional rights at Guantánamo, and that to appeal on their behalf to the Bill of Rights was nonsensical.[26] Thus the denial of constitutional rights to immigrants perceived as "undesirable" laid the groundwork for the treatment of alleged illegal combatants, furthermore conflating the identification of immigrants as potential terrorists and terrorists as unwanted immigrants. In the case of the Haitian refugees, the functions of the military and Immigration and Naturalization Services merged, anticipating in a way the official incorporation of the INS into the Department of Homeland Security. This site of unchecked U.S. power over a nominally extraterritorial space is mirrored in the proliferation of sites within the territory of the homeland where immigrants have been detained incommunicado without the right of representation.

Guantánamo is an uncanny space; as Michael Ratner, President of the Center for Constitutional Rights, writes, "It is as if Guantánamo is on another planet, a permanent United States penal colony floating in another world."[27] A lawless arena, Guantánamo has been voided of legal rights and protections by the intersecting historical trajectories of U.S. imperialism and immigration. This lawlessness gives the United States inordinate power to impose a military/penal regime over every aspect of the prisoners' lives. We face the danger today that this floating colony will become the norm rather than the anomaly, that homeland security will increasingly depend not on drawing strict boundaries between home and abroad, but on proliferating these mobile, ambiguous spaces between the domestic and the foreign. It is not hard to imagine a new constitution for Iraq containing provisions for leasing extraterritorial U.S. bases, as Cuba's constitution did a century ago. The uncanny space of Guantánamo, the repository of repressed imperial history, may in fact become a new ground zero, a foundation on which both the American homeland and American empire are being rebuilt.

Notes

1. *Merriam-Webster's Collegiate Dictionary*, 10th ed., s.v., "ground zero," available at http://www.m-w.com/home.htm.
2. Marita Sturken, *Tangled Memories: The Vietnam War, the AIDS Epidemic, and the Politics of Remembering* (Berkeley: University of California Press, 1997), 29. See also Marita Sturken, "Memorializing Absence," Social Science Research Council, *After September 11 Archive*, http://www.ssrc.org/sept11/essays.
3. Thomas L. Friedman, "A Failure to Imagine," *New York Times*, May 19, 2002, sec. 4, p. 15.
4. Ariel Dorfman, "Americans Must Now Feel What the Rest of Us Have Known," *Independent*, October 3, 2001, http://argument.independent.co.uk/commentators/story.jsp?story=97282.
5. Sigmund Freud, "The Uncanny" (1919), in *The Complete Works of Sigmund Freud*, vol. 17, ed. James Strachey (London: Hogarth Press, 1955), 241.
6. W. E. B. Du Bois, *Dusk of Dawn: An Essay toward an Autobiography of a Race Concept* (1940; reprint, New Brunswick, N.J.: Transaction Publishers, 1994), 222.
7. James A. Bartlett, "Homeland: Behind the Buzzword," *Ethical Spectacle*, December 2001, www.spectacle.org; see also William Safire, "On Language: Homeland," *New York Times Magazine*, January 10, 2002, 12.
8. James Der Derian, "The War of Networks," *Theory and Event* 5, no. 4 (2002): 15.
9. *American Heritage College Dictionary*, 3d ed., s.v., "homeland"; *Merriam-Webster's Collegiate Dictionary*, 10th ed., s.v., "homeland."
10. Department of Homeland Security, http://www.dhs.gov/dhspublic/theme_home1.jsp.
11. White House Press Release, "Gov. Ridge Sworn-In [*sic*] to Lead Homeland Security," October 8, 2001, http://www.whitehouse.gov/news/releases/2001/10/20011008-3.html.
12. Hugh Aynesworth, "Political Ad Is Uniformly Embarrassing," *Washington Times*, October 29, 2001, sec. A, p. 9.
13. Salman Rushdie, *Imaginary Homelands: Essays and Criticism, 1981–1991* (New York: Viking, 1991).
14. John Mullian, "Protection Racket; Word of the Week: Homeland," *Guardian* (London), October 24, 2001, 23.

15. For government documents that use the concept of homeland security and homeland defense, see Jeff Greenspan, "What Is Homeland Security? Info from Government Websites," *Lew Rockwell.com,* September 27, 2001, http://www.lewrockwell.com/orig2/greenspan1.html.

16. David McIntyre, "What Is Homeland Security? A Short History," *Anser Institute for Homeland Security,* http://www.homelanddefense.org/bulletin/ActionPlan_WhatIsHLS.htm#_ednref1.

17. "One Year On: The Legal Limbo of the Guantánamo Detainees Continues," Amnesty International, January 10, 2003, http://www.amnestyusa.org/news/2003/usa01102003_2.html. During the first week of the war against Iraq in March 2003, commentators pointed out the hypocrisy of calling on Iraq to respect the Geneva Conventions regarding the treatment of prisoners of war, while the U.S. violated them in Guantánamo.

18. *Khaled A. F. Al Odah et al. v. United States,* 321 F.3d 1134 (D.C. Cir. 2003).

19. Ibid., 1144.

20. Ibid., 1143.

21. Ibid.

22. Gerald Neuman, "Anomalous Zones," *Stanford Law Review* 48 (1996): 1201.

23. Neil A. Lewis, "Bush Administration Wins Court Victory on Guantánamo Detentions," *New York Times,* March 12, 2003, sec. A. p. 14.

24. The clarity of the recent court decision about U.S. sovereignty over its "insular possessions" was murkier in the *Insular Cases* a century ago. For analyses of these cases and their ramifications, see Christina Duffy Burnett and Marshall Burke, eds., *Foreign in a Domestic Sense: Puerto Rico, American Expansion, and the Constitution* (Durham: Duke University Press, 2001).

25. "President Bush Announces Initiative for a New Cuba: Remarks by the President on Cuba Policy Review," May 20, 2002, http://www.whitehouse.gov/news/releases/2002/05/20020520-1.html.

26. Neuman, 1228–33.

27. Michael Ratner, "The War on Terrorism: The Guantánamo Prisoners, Military Commissions, and Torture," Center for Constitutional Rights, January 14, 2003, http://www.ccr-ny.org/v2/viewpoints/viewpoint.asp?ObjID=oCjCco5Q9n&Content=142.

9/11 and the Muslim Transformation

KHALED ABOU EL FADL

Several years ago, I remember seeing a picture of Osama bin Laden that ominously foretold the tragedy that would come in 9/11. The picture showed bin Laden, with his typical slothful and even indifferent look, sitting while gripping his Kalashnikov with neatly organized and impressive-looking books filling the background. What caught my attention in this picture were the titles of books. With the help of a magnifying glass, I was able to figure out the titles of the books appearing in the picture, and to my surprise, and dismay, these were the same titles that I have in my own personal library. I could have been looking at a section of my library where I keep books on classical Muslim jurisprudence. There they were—the texts that represent the cream and kernel of the intellectual tradition of the Islamic civilization. With very few exceptions, bin Laden's library contained no works by modern writers; nearly all the books were heavy-duty, profound works on premodern Islamic law and legal theory. Bin Laden is not a Muslim jurist, and he does not have the training that would enable him to read or understand these classical texts. I do not know if it is possible to describe the pain that a Muslim, like myself, feels when they see the heart of the Islamic tradition co-opted in this fashion by a terrorist like bin Laden. Much of what is actually in these books would condemn everything bin Laden represents, but bin Laden was making a symbolic point. The point was not simply to claim Islamic authenticity. In fact, considering bin Laden's neo-Wahhabi orientation, which tends to be anti-juristic and also tends to be dismissive of the dialectical hermeneutic methods of classical jurisprudence, his display of the books is quite paradoxical. But with his paltry and rustic furniture, Kalashnikov, and tradition-oriented library, bin Laden symbolized a rebellion against the prevailing paradigms of postcolonialism and the culture of modernity.

The Significance of 9/11 and Orphans of Modernity

None of the Muslim revolutionaries of the past concerned themselves with displaying a formidable Islamic classical library. Even activists, such as the founder of the Muslim Brotherhood, Hasan al-Banna, who, unlike bin Laden, actually wrote a few books in his lifetime, were not bookish people. Bin Laden has not shown much interest in systematic thought, not even of the revolutionary type, and does not exhibit much familiarity with the constructs or methodologies of Islamic jurisprudence. In addition, as discussed later, bin Laden considers the vast majority of the Islamic intellectual tradition to be a *bid'a,* a deviant and heretical innovation in the true and uncorrupted religion. Furthermore, unlike the national liberation movement leaders of the 1950s and1960s, bin Laden is not interested in publicly claiming responsibility or, in his view, taking credit for his attacks,[1] and unlike the Palestinian Hamas or Lebanese Hizbullah, for instance, he does not make a list of demands or articulate specific objectives, the fulfillment of which would bring an end to the attacks.[2] Bin Laden's violence has a global and apoplectic quality to it; it seeks to do nothing less than alter the power structures of the world.[3] The classical juristic texts displayed might generate the impression that bin Laden is the champion of a lost Islamic authenticity to which he seeks to return, but in reality there is a considerable degree of what might be described as modernistic nihilism in bin Laden's worldview.[4] Unlike Islamic revolutionaries of the past, bin Laden is not focused on overthrowing particular Muslim governments, the establishment of the caliphate, or even the implementation of the rule of Shari'ah in particular states. Rather, in many ways, bin Laden and his followers are the orphaned children of postcolonialism. He employs the technological instruments of modernity; for instance, in many of his pictures he appears smiling with a cell phone in hand. But bin Laden and his followers do not see themselves as partners in the culture of modernity. It is as if the modern world has imposed a fate upon them that is evil, and this fate must be resisted, even if the resistance is suicidal or utterly self-destructive. In one of his television appearances, bin Laden expressed this idea when he claimed that, in general, most nations of the world, and all the Muslim countries, in particular, do not have freedom of will or autonomy.[5] But this begs the question: in what way was the 9/11 attack on the United States supposed to empower these countries that have lost their autonomy, or otherwise shift the balance of power in the modern world? I think that it is not possible to provide a coherent response to this question, and this is why I describe bin Laden's thought as somewhat nihilistic. The point of the attacks is to protest against modernity by destroying its symbols, to deconstruct what exists without much thought for what can be constructed in its place, and to draw attention, in the most negative way, to the plight of Muslims in the postcolonial age.

Though the event occurred only a couple of years ago, one can safely assert that 9/11 has become a powerful symbolic moment in world history. Whether 9/11 can be considered a transformative point in history, and very few events can authentically claim this status, remains to be seen. But as a symbolic moment, the status of 9/11 is secure. This is not just the date in which thousands of people were tragically murdered, but 9/11 also represents the culmination of trends, many of them suicidal, set in motion in the nineteenth and twentieth centuries. The attacks of 9/11 are the incipient outgrowth of social and political frustrations that have steadily grown since the onset of modernity. In many ways, these attacks are extreme acts of deconstructionism, a suicidal rejectionism and obstructionism toward the hegemonic power structures that have come to dominate human history for the past two centuries. Whether or not the attacks of 9/11 will, in fact, lead to a transformation in the world, these attacks ought to serve as a powerful warning to Muslims and non-Muslims alike. At the most basic level, they are a clear signal that subaltern cultures continue to exist in the shadow of postcolonialism, and that many people who belong to these cultures feel that they do not have a vested interest in the life created by modernity.[6] I would argue that we ought to be enormously worried that modernity has lost credibility, or perhaps never had credibility in the first place, in the eyes of the subaltern cultures that have not played much of a role in the shaping of modernity. The makers of modernity are the same nations, and races, that perpetuated colonialism, and in the age of postcolonialism, subaltern cultures, for the most part, continued to be economically dependent, culturally marginalized, and politically dominated. Contributing to modernity's lack of credibility is the perceived rampant hypocrisy of its leaders. Countries that have been at the forefront of modernity have employed language that invokes uplifting values. One cannot exaggerate the impact that such concepts as self-determination, development, social justice, individual rights, and democracy have had on the social imagination of the Muslim world; nor can one exaggerate the enormous letdown felt after it became abundantly clear that the same nations and races who invented the concepts and espoused them are the only ones who continue to enjoy them.[7]

And, whether justifiably or not, it was believed, and continues to be believed, that the leaders of Muslim nations were placed and sustained in power through the support of the same countries that once colonized the Muslim world.[8]

Here, my primary concern is not to ascribe fault to certain civilizations or vindicate others. As I argue below, the notion of civilizational superiority, as opposed to supremacy, is a simplistic and unhelpful idea. A civilization can flourish and become supreme at a particular point in history, but the assessment of the influence and credibility of a civilization ought not become akin to a beauty pageant competition, in which we engage in the pretentious act of selecting superiors and inferiors. Contrary to the assertions of some students of Samuel Huntington, 9/11 is not a symptom of a clash of civilizations, and it does not exemplify the tensions between the moral values of the West and Islam.[9] These types of assertions ignore the fact that the Islamic experience in the modern age has been lived largely in the shadow of colonialism and postcolonialism. In the past two centuries, the Islamic experience has been largely reactive, and not proactive; it has struggled to come to terms with modernity, with its own marginality and loss of autonomy, and with the concentration of power in the hands of the non-Muslim "other." The attacks of 9/11 were not an expression of an Islamic authenticity, anymore than the impressive display of books transformed bin Laden into a scholar of Islamic thought. But to say this is not to say that bin Laden is not a Muslim or that his experience is not part of the Islamic experience. Whether one likes it or not, and for better or worse, what a Muslim does in the name of Islam is in fact a part of the Islamic experience. This is why Muslims should be concerned about what bin Laden represents. Although one can plausibly maintain that bin Laden's behavior was foremost an act of vengeance against a modern reality that has increasingly alienated and marginalized Muslims, and that the classical literary sources of Islam do not support his vengeful behavior, the fact remains that what bin Laden did does have normative value. If Muslims do not succeed in debunking, rejecting, and marginalizing bin Laden's behavior, his ideology, vengeful as it is, will set a normative precedent. In the absence of an effort to counteract it, bin Laden's behavior could acquire a legitimacy and authenticity that it may not possess at the current time. I will elaborate on this below, but perhaps a helpful way of understanding this problem is to assume that meaning in Islam is acquired through the formation of communities of interpretation. In effect, bin Laden, through his actions, has offered an interpretive community that is at odds with the main interpretive communities of classical Islam. If not dealt with appropriately, bin Laden's interpretive community could become larger, more convincing, more effective, and more mainstream. But the challenge, I believe, is that violent suppression will not effectively respond to the community of meaning that bin Laden offers. The only effective way of responding is to offer alternative communities of meaning that are more convincing to Muslims and that would act to challenge and negate the worldview of the bin Ladens of the world. The problem is, however, that any alternative communities of meaning offered by any Muslim will make sense, or not, only in light of the overall sociopolitical context in which Muslims live. For instance, attempts to disseminate an interpretation of Islam that is consistent with normative values that are considered Western in origin, such as democracy or individual rights, often falter because of the perceived hypocrisies of the West.

The Transformation of Islam after 9/11

Whether the dominant powers, especially the United States, will heed the warnings of 9/11 and act to empower and incorporate the orphans of modernity remains to be seen. Considering the policies, thus far, of the United States and England post-9/11, I am quite skeptical. American support of highly authoritarian regimes, such as the ones in Saudi Arabia, Kuwait, and Egypt, has not wavered. In what can be described as typical imperialistic fashion, the United States installed a puppet government in Afghanistan that, to say the least, is of questionable legitimacy and effectiveness. American support of Israel, despite its consistent and systematic brutalization of the Palestinians, has continued unabated.[10] In addition, the American and British administrations seem to act on the assumption that it is possible, and even desirable, to beat Muslim dissenters into submission. President Bush's colorful language about the axis of evil and the crusade against terrorists has emphasized the unreasonableness and absolutism of the American administration. The polarizing policies and statements of the wielders of power in modernity has led some commentators to characterize the events of 9/11 as symbolizing the clash of fundamentalisms, the fundamentalism of bin Laden against that of Bush.[11] Unfortunately, all indications seem to point to the conclusion that the problems that led to 9/11 are only being aggravated in the current political climate.[12]

Be that as it may, the question is: what about the Islamic side of things? Are the events of 9/11 a point of transformation for Islam, and if they are not, should they be? To begin with, let's consider an important symbolic point, which has been raised by several Muslim commentators.

There have been many shocking massacres in the world including the slaughter of Muslims in Srebrenica and Muslim-Palestinians in Sabra and Shatila. More recently, Israel has brutally murdered Palestinians in the refugee camp of Jenin. Several commentators writing in the Arab world have protested the significant amount of attention dedicated to the death of Americans when compared to the attention given to the slaughter of Arabs or other subalterns. Such commentators have noted, for instance, that every Muslim, and even the religion of Islam itself, is held vicariously responsible for any acts of violence. Often, it is demanded of Muslims to condemn terrorism and to clearly disassociate themselves from acts of violence committed by their coreligionists. Acts of violence by Christians and Jews are not met with the same expectations. Jews, for instance, are not regularly asked to condemn massacres of civilians, like the one in the Jenin camp; nor are they expected to disassociate themselves from any other acts of terror committed by their coreligionists. Recently, for example, a Pakistani commentator accused me of being an apologist for the West and a "sell-out" because, since 9/11, I have argued that Muslims ought to rethink certain aspects of their tradition. This commentator protested that I, and people like me, have not called on Jews to reexamine their tradition in light of the crimes Israelis have committed against the Palestinians. In addition, in light of Bush's declared Christian convictions, and his invocation of Christian symbolism in his so-called war against terrorism, I failed to call on Christians to examine critically their traditions regarding war.[13] The point he is making is that even Muslims like myself internalize and project the hypocrisies of postcolonialism. He, like many commentators in the Muslim world, contends that even the perception of trauma in the modern world has become relativized. The slaughter of Muslims is treated as an unfortunate fact of life, but it does not induce people to call for transformations or reconstructions. Meanwhile, any large-scale loss of Western lives does generate calls for transformations and reconstructions, and it also creates demands for a new world order in which villains and violence must be suppressed.

This criticism, although quite rhetorical and even dogmatic, cannot be dismissed as simple propaganda. I do think, however, that it does exaggerate and essentialize the discourses of non-Muslims about their own shortcomings. Compared to Muslims, one can argue that Jews and Christians do deal with their own traditions with critical insights that sometimes border on the malicious. Modernity, with its paradigms of secularism and critical scientism, is often unkind to all religious traditions, including the traditions of Christianity and Judaism. Moreover, I think that this criticism often ignores the fact that, unlike the major social movements of Christians and Jews, Muslim movements in the modern age often claim to act on behalf of Islam. Bush and Sharon do not explicitly pretend to carry out the will of God and do not explicitly cite canon or Rabbinic law as justifications of their policies.[14] Activists such as bin Laden, whether one likes it or not, do claim to act on behalf of Islam. He not only claims that God approves of what he does; he goes much further in claiming that Islam affirmatively commands him to adopt certain paradigms and then act on them. My point is not to justify what I have described as the hypocrisy of the world powers that are dominant today, and I do, in fact, agree that there is considerable bigotry and prejudice that acts to undervalue the worth of Muslim life. But it is important that we are able to assess the plight of modern Muslims and Islam from an honest and well-informed perspective.

The issue raised by many Muslims and some non-Muslims is that it is unfair to focus on Islam as a source of problems after 9/11. These commentators contend that 9/11 would have happened with or without religion, that there are sociopolitical reasons behind the attacks of 9/11, and that religion plays a marginal role at best. The likes of bin Laden abuse religion to justify their actions, but they are not led or influenced by religion to opt for a specific course of action in the first place. Recently, Tariq Ali went as far as arguing that theology is marginal to either understanding or reacting to the events of 9/11 and that, in fact, theological arguments are of no real consequence.[15] Perhaps Ali's point is that it is more useful to speak in terms of transforming the dynamics of power and exploitation than it is to think about the role of religion.

I agree that material conditions related to who possesses power and how power is used and exploited is very significant. Most certainly, Muslims such as the Taliban and bin Laden, despite the practice of waving the banner of Islamic authenticity and legitimacy, are far more anti-Western than they are pro-Islamic. Their primary concern is not to explore or investigate the parameters of Islamic values, but to oppose the West. As such, Islam is simply the symbolic universe in which they function. Their protest is framed in Islamic terms because they are Muslim, but it is not the case that they protest because they are Muslims. In many ways, they are not so much the outgrowth of a religious process as they are a reaction to external, secular forces, such as colonialism, corporate capitalism, or imperialism. Therefore, at the most basic level, one reason for thinking seriously about the Islamic tradition and engaging in religious discourse is to wrestle away from such groups their Islamic banner and to challenge their claim to authenticity. But aside from the largely apologetic goal of salvaging the image of Islam, there is also the more important and challenging issue of the identity of the Islamic message in the modern world. In light of the claims of the Taliban and bin Laden about the religion, the difficult issue that confronts Muslims today can be framed as follows: what normative role is Islam to play, and what ought to be the role of Muslim intellectuals in the world today?

The claim that Islamic normative doctrines played no role, or even a minor role, in bin Laden's and the Taliban's moral paradigms is, I think, both inaccurate and dishonest. Religion does not perform a merely cosmetic function in constructing the moral paradigms of a believer. For a believer, religion is the most authoritative and effective source of ideals.[16] Confronted by constraining material conditions, a believer will seek to modify these conditions or reconstruct and reinvent his system of belief so as to adapt to the constraints. But in reconstructing and reinventing his system of belief, the believer also creates normative doctrines for other followers of the faith. Put differently, believers such as bin Laden, when confronted with the power dynamics that exist in the world today have two options: either they can seek to alter those power dynamics or they can reinvent Islamic normativities so as to make them consistent with the material realities that confront them today. There is a third option, if one can call it an option, and that is to exist in a state of perpetual dissonance. This state of dissonance can appropriately be described as a condition of social schizophrenia in which believers survive with irresolvable conflicts between their lived reality and their convictions, between life as it is and life as it ought to be.[17] Of course, these three potential responses— modification of reality, reinvention of belief systems, and dissonance— are not mutually exclusive. For most believers, all three play a role at various times and to different extents. Importantly, these responses are issue specific; depending on a variety of factors, believers may reinvent their system of belief on some issues, while continuing in a state of dissonance vis-à-vis others. This depends on the extent to which particular material realities are pressing, the centrality of a particular religious doctrine to the faith of a believer, and the susceptibility of the culture of the believer to change in regard to certain issues. For example, a wealthy patriarchal society confronted with material conditions that necessitate the economic and social mobility of women will react very differently than a financially impoverished society. The former society might be tempted to alter the material conditions so that they become consistent with its religious convictions, while the latter might be tempted to reinterpret or reinvent its religious doctrines. But, in all cases, the response will be affected by the perceived centrality of the religious doctrine to the faith.[18]

Generally speaking, religion matters; it matters because it is an integral part of the frame of reference for a believer, which will guide how a believer chooses to respond to a given situation. Even a state of dissonance is not a condition of inertia or perpetual dormancy. It is a state of unrest that is bound to have consequences both for the lived reality and the religious consciousness of a believer. In many ways, bin Laden and the Taliban grew out of this state of dissonance. In all probability, they understood their faith to demand certain things of them and then proceeded to alter the reality of the world to make it consistent with what they believed are the precepts of Islam. In doing so, bin Laden and the Taliban acted on conviction and also set a precedent for future Muslims. In this sense, 9/11 could prove to be a point of transformation for Islam. Unless Muslims carefully analyze and understand bin Laden's and the Taliban's systems of belief, and also carefully assess the normative impact of the precedents set by them, Muslims will be running the risk of unwittingly acquiescing to a reconstructed religion that, in my view, is immoral and inhumane. While what bin Laden did in 9/11, by itself, will not transform or reinvent the Islamic tradition, Muslims are forced to deal with the reality that, considering its scale and impact, bin Laden's and the Taliban's actions are precedent setting. The role of Muslim intellectuals is to engage the various precedents set in the name of Islam and to negotiate the meaning of their religion. Far from being a "sell-out" position, quite simply, this is exactly what the Islamic duty of enjoining the good and rejecting what is wrong (*al-amr bi'l ma'ruf wa al-nahy 'an al-munkar*) is all about.[19] This is also why the Qur'an commands Muslims to bear witness, on God's behalf, for truth and justice even if the testimony is against themselves or against their loved ones.[20] In my view, the truthful testimony is rendered on God's behalf because silence in the face of a wrong committed in the name of Islam is a form of suborning the corruption of the religion.

Bearing Witness in the Shadow of Postcolonialism

When it comes to the issue of Islam and violence, Muslim discourses, for the most part, remain captive to the postcolonial experience. These discourses are sufficiently politicized and polarized to the extent that Muslim intellectuals who address the subject often feel that they are stepping into a highly volatile minefield. It is difficult for contemporary Muslim scholars to take a critical position on Islam and violence without becoming the subject of suspicion and even accusations as to their loyalties and commitments. For instance, if a contemporary Muslim scholar emphasizes the imperatives of tolerance and peaceful coexistence in Islam, or emphasizes the importance of moral commitments over political expedience, or perhaps condemns terrorism, this is often understood as a thoroughly political position. Such a scholar becomes susceptible to accusations of being a sell-out to the West, an apologist for Israel and the United States, or of being insufficiently sensitized to the suffering of the Palestinians, Kashmiris, Chechnyans, or any other oppressed Muslim population. In addition, it has become a rather powerful rhetorical device to contend that the West is perpetuating false universalisms and to accuse Muslim critics of being deluded into accepting these universalisms as a God-given truth. These Muslim critics, it is claimed, then project the West's truth onto the Islamic tradition, as if what the West sees as true and good must necessarily be so and therefore must be adopted by all Muslims.[21] Most often, this type of accusation is leveled against Muslim critics with feminist agendas, but it also has been utilized rather widely against Muslim intellectuals calling for self-critical reevaluations post-9/11. It is a powerful rhetorical device because the users of such a device are positioning themselves as the guardians of integrity and authenticity, while positioning their opponents as gullible and even simple-minded.[22]

The issue of what is now commonly described as cultural relativism versus universalism is very complex, and this is not the place to delve into it. I will only note that this whole discourse becomes rather incoherent unless one clearly identifies what specific value is being identified as relative or universal. In addition, Islam itself, like all religions, is founded on certain universals such as mercy, justice, compassion, and dignity.[23] Claims of ontological truth, which could be based on reason or revelation, are not an anathema to Islam.[24] From an Islamic perspective, Muslims are not forbidden, and in my opinion are even encouraged, to search for moral universals that could serve as shared and common goals with non-Muslims. However, aside from the philosophical point concerning the existence of universal and invariable human moral principles, I think that the silencing tactic, mentioned above, points to an unfortunate sociological fact, and that is the primacy of politics in contemporary Islam.

The Siege Mentality in Contemporary Islam

The real challenge that confronts Muslim intellectuals is that political interests have come to dominate public discourses to the point that moral investigations and thinking have become marginalized in modern Islam. In the age of postcolonialism, Muslims have become largely preoccupied with the attempt to remedy a collective feeling of powerlessness and a frustrating sense of political defeat, often by engaging in highly sensationalistic acts of power symbolism. The normative imperatives and intellectual subtleties of the Islamic moral tradition are not treated with the analytical and critical rigor that the Islamic tradition rightly deserves; they are rendered subservient to political expedience and symbolic displays of power. Elsewhere, I have described this contemporary doctrinal dynamic as the predominance of the theology of power in modern Islam, and this theology is a direct contributor to the emergence of highly radicalized Islamic groups, such as the Taliban or Al Qaeda.[25] Far from being authentic expressions of inherited Islamic paradigms, or a natural outgrowth of the classical tradition, these are thoroughly a byproduct of colonialism and modernity. Such groups ignore the Islamic civilizational experience with all its richness and diversity and reduce Islam to a single dynamic, the dynamic of power. They tend to define Islam as an ideology of nationalistic defiance to the other, a rather vulgar form of obstructionism to the hegemony of the Western world.[26] Therefore, instead of Islam being a moral vision given to humanity, it becomes constructed into the antithesis of the West. In the world constructed by these groups, there is no Islam; there is effectively only opposition to the West. This type of Islam that the radicalized groups offer is akin to a perpetual state of emergency where expedience trumps principle and illegitimate means are consistently justified by invoking higher ends. In essence, what prevails is an aggravated siege mentality that suspends the moral principles of the religion in pursuit of the vindications of political power.[27] In this siege mentality, there is no room for analytical or critical thought, and there is no room for seriously engaging the Islamic intellectual heritage. There is only room for bombastic dogma and for a stark functionalism that ultimately impoverishes the Islamic heritage.

It seems to me that certain commentators play into the hands of this siege mentality—those who responded to the events of 9/11 by engaging in a knee-jerk reaction of protesting false Western universals and by rejecting introspective self-critical approaches. If critical approaches to the tradition will be consistently dismissed as Western-influenced, or as a form of "Westoxification,"[28] it is difficult to imagine how Muslims will be able to emerge out of what I have called a state of dissonance and enter into a more constructive engagement with modernity. Even more, there is the very real risk that in our defensive effort to expunge the moral universals of the West, we will also end up dismissing the moral universals of Islam itself. For instance, when contemporary Muslim scholars rise to emphasize the numerous moral and humanistic aspects of the Islamic tradition, and they are accused by their fellow Muslims of seeking to appease the West, the real danger is that in this highly polarized and politicized climate, much of what is authentically Islamic and genuinely beautiful will be lost or forgotten for a long period to come. This, however, points to a more fundamental and serious fallacy, and that is the tendency, clearly emboldened and becoming more pronounced because of the events of 9/11, to presume that values can be precisely identified as Islamic or Western. Values, according to this view, can be identified as belonging to a particular culture, and often they are not transferable or susceptible to being transplanted into a different culture. Not surprisingly, the more dogmatic elements in this tendency ended up imagining a grand battle being waged by the bearers of civilizations. In one corner is the civilization of the West and in the other is Islam. Presumably, every terrorist organization from Al Qaeda to Hamas is the representative of the values of the Islamic civilization, which are clearly at odds with Western values.

9/11 and the Paradigm of Battling Civilizations

There is already a rather large body of literature on the myth of the clash of civilizations.[29] To an extent, this issue has passed from the realm of rational conversation based on historical and doctrinal evidence to the realm of dogma and ideology. I do not wish to deconstruct the notion that there are cultural values that become prevalent at a particular point in time. I also do not contest the idea that, as put by Samuel Huntington and Lawrence Harrison, culture matters.[30] But I think that there are several important points that ought to be kept in mind when thinking about cultural values, and the role that they are purported to play. The first point pertains to what I will call "claims of lineage," the second pertains to "claims about the other," the third relates to "the enterprise of meaning," and the fourth addresses what I call "competence."

Proponents of the notion of the clash of civilizations seem to rely on an unfounded claim about the specificity and purity of particular values. Accordingly, they are willing to classify particular values as squarely Judeo-Christian while others are Islamic. It is as if values have a genealogy that can be clearly and precisely ascertained, which then can be utilized in classifying what properly belongs to the West and what belongs to the Islamic "other." But the origin and lineage of values are as much of a sociohistorical construct as are claims about racial genealogical purity. Considering the numerous cultural interactions and cross-intellectual transmissions between the Muslim world and Europe, it is highly likely that every significant Western value has a measure of Muslim blood in it.[31] But this is not merely a matter of acknowledging the Muslim contribution to Western thought. Rather, by recognizing the mixed lineage of ideas, a simple and straightforward taxonomy of civilizations and what they are supposed to stand for becomes much more problematic. One ought to recognize that, like racial categories, civilizational categories are artificial political constructs that do not necessarily fit comfortably with sociohistorical realities.

Claims about the so-called pure lineage of values lead me to the second point. Often the attempt to identify one's own civilization and distinguish it from the "other" has much more to do with one's own aspirations than the reality of the "other." Put differently, descriptions of the "other," whoever the other may be, often tell us much more about the author of the description than the subject of the description.[32] For instance, when Westerners attempt to describe the Islamic civilization and what it represents, there is a real risk that the constructed image of the Islamic civilization will only reflect the aspirations and anxieties of those Westerners. Therefore, for example, if those Westerners aspire to achieve a greater degree of democracy, or are anxious about their own shortcomings vis-à-vis women's rights, it is likely that they will invent an image of the Muslim "other" as the exact antithesis of their own aspirations. By constructing the other as the exact antithesis, one is then able to feel more secure about one's own cultural achievements. The colonial images of the Orient—its exoticness, mystique, and harems, had much more to do with the anxieties and fantasies of the Western colonizer than it did with the sociological reality of the Orient.

There is a further problem with approaches that focus on civilizational paradigms and conflicts. Values, and their meaning in culture, are not constant or stable. They are constantly shifting, evolving, and mutating in response to a variety of influences and motivators. For instance, concepts such as *shura* (government by consultation), the caliphate, or enjoining the good and forbidding the evil have had very different meanings and connotations from one century to another and one culture to another in Islamic history. Even when one is considering divinely revealed values, such values acquire meaning only within evolving and shifting contexts. As noted earlier, interpretive communities coalesce around revealed injunctions and values, and then endow them with meaning. Put differently, there is a sociohistorical enterprise formed of various participants that partake in the generation of meaning. When one speaks of Islamic justice, for instance, one is really speaking of various interpretive enterprises that existed at different times in Islamic history, which gave the notion of justice in Islam a variety of imports and connotations.[33] When commentators speak of a civilizational conflict between the West and Islam, there is a further creative and inventive process engaged in by the commentators themselves. Since meaning is the product of cumulative enterprises that generate communities of meaning, a student of Huntington, for instance, cannot speak in terms of an Islamic notion of justice or an Islamic notion of human liberty. The most that this student can do is to speak of prevailing meanings within specific communities of interpretation. Therefore, a student of Huntington, for instance, would have to speak in terms of a Mu'tazali notion of justice, or an Ash'ari notion of justice. This argument about meaning being the product of interpretive enterprises generated by various communities has both vertical and horizontal implications. Vertically speaking, we are reminded of the point about the purity of lineage. There are a variety of historical contributors to the production of meaning, and it is quite difficult to find a value with a purely Western or Islamic pedigree. From a horizontal perspective, what is identified as a civilization is in reality a complex bundle of competing interpretations generated by a variety of communities of meaning, with some interpretations becoming more dominant than others at different times and places. This brings me to the final point, which I described as a problem of competence.

Put simply, who has the competence to describe which of the competing communities of meaning becomes the legitimate and credible representative of the values of a civilization? In this context, I am not interested in the problem of the dynamics of power and authority within a particular system of thought. Rather, my concern here takes us back to the problem of the invention and construction of the "other." It is imperative to keep in mind that when a student of Huntington, for example, claims that the Islamic civilization stands for a particular proposition, this student is in effect endowing a certain interpretive community with the power of representation. This student is engaging in choice making by selecting what, in his mind, is the community that best represents the Islamic civilization. For example, the interpretive community to which someone like Muhammad 'Abduh belongs may make an assertion, which we will designate as "y." Meanwhile, bin Laden, and his interpretive community, may make an assertion designated as "x." By claiming that the Islamic civilization stands for "x," but not "y," Huntington's student is making a choice about representation. Again, this choice might have much more to do with the choice maker, that is, Huntington's student, than with the actual dynamics of Islamic societies.

These various cautionary points are intended to emphasize that claims of civilizational conflict are fraught with conceptual pitfalls. From a pedagogical point of view, such claims are likely to degenerate into powerful vehicles for the expression of prejudice.[34] As such, they tend to further misunderstandings and promote conflict. It is no wonder that when one examines the arguments of the Western proponents of the clash of civilizations, one finds that these proponents invariably ascribe most of what they perceive to be good and desirable to the West, and most of what they find distasteful or objectionable to Islam. They then condescendingly contend that the values of the "other," as terrible as they might be for Westerners, ought to be respected. Despotism, oppression, and degradation, for example, might be terrible for Westerners, but they are acceptable for Muslims because, after all, Muslims themselves do not consider their social institutions as despotic, oppressive, or degrading.[35]

The effect of this doctrinal commitment to the paradigm of clashing civilizations only serves to obfuscate the real dynamics that are in fact taking place in Islam. There are significant tensions within contemporary Islam that are bound to materially impact on the world today. Bin Laden's terrorism is not simply the product of a system of thought that he single-handedly invented. Rather, his violence is an integral part of the struggle between interpretative communities over who gets to speak for Islam and how.

The Roots of 9/11

Islam is now living through a major paradigm shift the like of which it has not experienced in the past. There is a profound vacuum in religious authority, where it is not clear who speaks for the religion and how. Traditionally, the institutions of Islamic law have been decentralized, and Islamic epistemology has tolerated and even celebrated differences of opinions and a variety of schools of thought. Islamic law was not state-centered or state-generated; it was developed by judges and jurists through a slow creative, indeterminate, and dialectical process, somewhat similar to the Anglo-American common law system.[36] Classical Islam did develop semi-autonomous institutions of law and theology that trained and qualified jurists, who then provided a class of individuals who authoritatively spoke for, and most often disagreed about, the divine law. The institutions of religion and law were supported by a complex system of private endowments (*awqaf*), which enabled Muslim scholars to generate a remarkably rich intellectual tradition.[37] The guardians of this were the *fuqaha'*, whose legitimacy to a large extent rested on their semi-independence from the political system, which was already fairly decentralized, and on their dual function of representing the interests of the state to the laity and the interests of the laity to the state.[38] Importantly, however, much of this has changed in the modern age. The traditional institutions that once sustained the juristic discourse have all but vanished. Furthermore, the normative categories and moral foundations that once mapped out Islamic law and theology have disintegrated, leaving an unsettling epistemological vacuum. Colonialism formally dismantled the traditional institutions of civil society, and Muslims witnessed the emergence of highly centralized, despotic, and often corrupt governments that nationalized the institutions of religious learning and brought the *awqaf* under state control. This contributed to the undermining of the mediating role of jurists in Muslim societies.[39] The fact that nearly all charitable religious endowments became state-controlled entities and that Muslim jurists in most Muslim nations became salaried state employees delegitimated the traditional clergy and effectively transformed them into what may be called "court priests."[40] In addition, Western cultural symbols, modes of production, and normative social values aggressively penetrated the Muslim world, seriously challenging inherited normative categories and practices, and adding to a profound sense of sociocultural alienation.

Most Muslim nations experienced the wholesale borrowing of civil law concepts. Instead of the dialectical and indeterminate methodology of traditional Islamic jurisprudence, Muslim nations opted for more centralized, determinative, and often code-based systems of law.[41] These developments only contributed to the power of the state, which had become extremely meddlesome and which was now capable of a level of centralization that was inconceivable just two centuries ago. Even Muslim modernists, who attempted to reform Islamic jurisprudence, were heavily influenced by the civil law system, and thus they sought to resist the indeterminate fluidity of Islamic law and increase its unitary and centralized character. But not only were the concepts of law heavily influenced by the European legal tradition, but even the ideologies of resistance employed by Muslims were laden with Third World notions of national liberation and self-determination. For instance, modern nationalistic thought exercised a greater influence on the resistance ideologies of Muslim and Arab national liberation movements than anything in the Islamic tradition. The Islamic tradition was reconstructed to fit Third World nationalistic ideologies of anticolonialism and anti-imperialism, rather than the other way around.

While national liberation movements such as that of the Palestinian or Algerian resistance resorted to guerilla or nonconventional warfare, modern-day terrorism of the variety promoted by bin Laden is rooted in a different ideological paradigm. There is little doubt that organizations such as the Jihad, Tanzim al-Qaʻidah, and Hizb al-Tahrir were influenced by national liberation and anticolonialist ideologies, but they have anchored themselves in a theology that can be described as puritan, supremacist, and thoroughly opportunistic in nature. This theology is the by-product of the emergence and eventual primacy of a synchronistic orientation that unites Wahhabism and Salafism in modern Islam. Puritan orientations, such as the Wahhabis, imagine that God's perfection and immutability are fully attainable by human beings in this lifetime. It is as if God's perfection had been deposited in the divine law, and, by giving effect to this law, it is possible to create a social order that mirrors the Divine Truth. But by associating themselves with the Supreme Being in this fashion, puritan groups are able to claim a self-righteous perfectionism that easily slips into a pretense of supremacy.

Wahhabism, Salafism, and Salafabism

The foundations of Wahhabi theology were set into place by the eighteenth-century evangelist Muhammad b. ʻAbd al-Wahhab (d. 1792). With a puritanical zeal, ʻAbd al-Wahhab sought to rid Islam of all the corruptions that he believed had crept into the religion, corruptions that included mysticism and rationalism. Wahhabism resisted the indeterminacy of the modern age by escaping into a strict literalism in which the text became the sole source of legitimacy. Wahhabism exhibited extreme hostility to all forms of intellectualism, mysticism, and any sectarianism within Islam. The Wahhabi creed also considered any form of moral thought that was not entirely dependent on the text as a form of self-idolatry and treated humanistic fields of knowledge, especially philosophy, as the "sciences of the devil." According to the Wahhabi creed, it was imperative to return to a presumed pristine, simple, and straightforward Islam, which was believed to be entirely reclaimable by a literal implementation of the commands and precedents of the Prophet and by a strict adherence to correct ritual practice. Wahhabism also rejected any attempt to interpret the divine law from a historical, contextual perspective and in fact treated the vast majority of Islamic history as a corruption or aberration from the true and authentic Islam. The dialectical and indeterminate hermeneutics of the classical jurisprudential tradition were considered corruptions of the purity of the faith and law. Furthermore, Wahhabism became very intolerant of the long-established Islamic practice of considering a variety of schools of thought to be equally orthodox, and it attempted to narrow considerably the range of issues about which

Muslims may legitimately disagree. Orthodoxy was narrowly defined, and 'Abd al-Wahhab himself was fond of creating long lists of beliefs and acts that he considered hypocritical and the adoption or commission of which would immediately render a Muslim an unbeliever.

In the late eighteenth century, the Al Saud family united itself with the Wahhabi movement and rebelled against Ottoman rule in Arabia, at one point reaching as far as Damascus. Egyptian forces under the leadership of Muhammad 'Ali in 1818, however, after several failed expeditions, quashed the rebellion, and Wahhabism, like other extremist movements in Islamic history, seemed to be on its way to extinction. Nevertheless, Wahhabi ideology was resuscitated once again in the early twentieth century under the leadership of 'Abd al-'Aziz b. Sa'ud, who adopted the puritanical theology of the Wahhabis and allied himself with the tribes of Najd, thereby establishing the nascent beginnings of what would become Saudi Arabia. Importantly, the Wahhabi rebellions of the nineteenth and twentieth centuries were very bloody because the Wahhabis indiscriminately slaughtered Muslims, especially those belonging to the Shi'i sect. In 1802, for example, the Wahhabi forces massacred the Shi'i inhabitants of Karbala, and in 1803, 1804, and 1806 the Wahhabis executed a large number of Sunnis in Mecca and Medina, whom they considered heretical. This led several mainstream jurists writing during this time period, such as the Hanafi Ibn 'Abidin (d. 1837) and the Maliki al-Sawi (d. 1825), to describe the Wahhabis as a fanatic fringe group and labeled them the "modern day Khawarij of Islam."[42] Interestingly, the Wahhabis introduced practices into Islam that were quite unprecedented and which considerably expanded the intrusive powers of the state. For instance, the Wahhabis introduced the first reported precedent of taking roll call at prayers. They prepared lists of the inhabitants of a city and called off the names during the five daily prayers in the mosque. Anyone absent without a sufficient excuse was flogged. In 1926 the Wahhabi hostility to all forms of musical instruments led to a crisis between Egypt and Saudi Arabia, when Egyptian soldiers carrying the ceremonial palanquin to the sound of bugles during pilgrimage were attacked and beaten and had their musical instruments destroyed. The Wahhabis also criminalized all forms of Sufi chants and dances in Mecca and Medina and, eventually, in all of Saudi Arabia.[43] Perhaps the most extreme form of Wahhabi fanaticism took place recently, on March 11, 2002, when the *mutawwa'in* (religious police) prevented school girls from exiting a burning school in Mecca, or from being rescued by their parents or firemen, because they were not properly covered. At least fifteen girls are reported to have burned to death as a result.[44]

There were four main factors that contributed to the survival and, in fact, the thriving of Wahhabism in contemporary Islam. First, by rebelling against the Ottomans, Wahhabism appealed to the emerging ideologies of Arab nationalism in the eighteenth century. By treating Muslim Ottoman rule as a foreign occupying power, Wahhabism set a powerful precedent for notions of Arab self-determination and autonomy. Second, as noted above, Wahhabism advocated the return to the pristine and pure origins of Islam. Accordingly, Wahhabism rejected the cumulative weight of historical baggage and insisted on a return to the precedents of the rightly guided early generations (*al-salaf al-salih*). This idea was intuitively liberating for Muslim reformers since it meant the rebirth of *ijtihad,* or the return to de novo examination and determination of legal issues unencumbered by the accretions of precedents and inherited doctrines. Third, by controlling Mecca and Medina, Saudi Arabia became naturally positioned to exercise a considerable influence on Muslim culture and thinking. The holy cities of Mecca and Medina are the symbolic heart of Islam, and they are the sites where millions of Muslims perform pilgrimage each year. Therefore, by regulating what might be considered orthodox belief and practice while on pilgrimage, Saudi Arabia became uniquely positioned to influence greatly the belief systems of Islam itself. For instance, for purely symbolic purposes, the king of Saudi Arabia adopted the lowly title of the custodian and servant of the two Holy Sites. Fourth, and most importantly, the discovery and exploitation of oil provided Saudi Arabia with high liquidity. Especially post-1975, with the sharp rise in oil prices Saudi Arabia aggressively promoted Wahhabi thought around the Muslim world. Even a cursory examination of the predominant ideas and practices would reveal the widespread influence of Wahhabi thought on the Muslim world today. Part of the reason for Saudi Arabia's aggressive proselytizing of its creed is related to the third element mentioned above. It would have been politically awkward for Saudi Arabia to be the custodian of the two Holy Sites yet, at the same time, to adopt a system of belief at odds with the rest of the Muslim world. To say the least, custodianship of the Holy Sites is a sensitive position in the Muslim world, and the Saudi claim to exclusive sovereignty over these cities remained problematic from the 1920s through the 1960s, especially because of the Wahhabis' intolerant attitude toward ritualistic practices that they deem unorthodox. In the 1950s and 1960s, Saudi Arabia was coming under considerable pressure from republican and Arab nationalist regimes who tended to consider the Saudi system archaic and reactionary. In the 1970s, Saudi Arabia finally possessed the financial means to address its legitimacy concerns. Either the Wahhabis had to alter their own system of belief to make it more consistent with the convictions of other Muslims, or they had to aggressively spread their convictions to the rest of the Muslim world. The first choice would have required the Saudi regime to reinvent itself; but in many ways it was easier to attempt to reinvent the Muslim world, and that is the option they chose.

Wahhabism, however, did not spread in the modern Muslim world under its own banner. Considering the marginal origins of the Wahhabi creed, this would have been quite difficult to accomplish. Wahhabism spread in the Muslim world under the banner of Salafism. It is important to note that even the term "Wahhabism" is considered derogatory to the followers of Ibn 'Abd-al-Wahhab since Wahhabis prefer to see themselves as the representatives of Islamic orthodoxy. According to its adherents, Wahhabism is not a school of thought within Islam; it is Islam itself, and it is the only possible Islam. The fact that Wahhabism rejected the use of a school label gave it a rather diffuse quality and made many of its doctrines and methodologies eminently transferable. Salafism, unlike Wahhabism, was a far more credible paradigm in Islam, and in many ways it was an ideal vehicle for Wahhabism. Therefore, in their literature, Wahhabi clerics have consistently described themselves as Salafis (adherents of Salafism), and not Wahhabis.

Salafism is a creed founded in the late nineteenth century by Muslim reformers such as Muhammad 'Abduh, al-Afghani, al-Shawkani, al-San'ani, and Rashid Rida. Salafism appealed to a very basic and fundamental concept in Islam: that Muslims ought to follow the rightly guided precedent of the Prophet and his companions (al-salaf al-salih). Methodologically, Salafism was nearly identical to Wahhabism, except that the latter is far less tolerant of diversity and differences of opinions. In many ways, Salafism was intuitively undeniable, partly because of its epistemological promise. The founders of Salafism maintained that on all issues Muslims ought to return to the original textual sources of the Qur'an and the Sunnah (precedent) of the Prophet. In doing so, Muslims ought to reinterpret the original sources in light of modern needs and demands without being slavishly bound to the interpretive precedents of earlier Muslim generations. As originally conceived, Salafism was not necessarily anti-intellectual, but like Wahhabism it did tend to be uninterested in history. By emphasizing a presumed golden age in Islam, the adherents of Salafism idealized the time of the Prophet and his companions and ignored or demonized the balance of Islamic history. Furthermore, by rejecting juristic precedents and undervaluing tradition as a source of authoritativeness, Salafism adopted a form of egalitarianism that deconstructed traditional notions of established authority within Islam. According to Salafism, effectively, anyone was considered qualified to return to the original sources and speak for the Divine Will. By liberating Muslims from the burdens of the technocratic tradition of the jurists, Salafism contributed to a real vacuum of authority in contemporary Islam. However, unlike Wahhabism, Salafism was not hostile to the juristic tradition or to the practices of various competing schools of thought. In addition, Salafism was not hostile to mysticism or Sufism. The proponents of Salafism were eager to throw off the shackles of tradition and to engage in the rethinking of Islamic solutions in light of modern demands. As far as the juristic tradition was concerned, Salafi scholars were synchronizers; they tended to engage in a practice known as *talfiq*, in which various opinions from the past are mixed and matched in order to generate novel approaches to problems. Significantly, for the most part, Salafism was founded by Muslim nationalists who were eager to read the values of modernism into the original sources of Islam. Hence, Salafism was not necessarily anti-Western. In fact, its founders strove to project contemporary institutions such as democracy, constitutionalism, or socialism onto the foundational texts and to justify the paradigm of the modern nation-state within Islam. In this sense, Salafism, as originally conceived, betrayed a degree of opportunism. Its proponents tended to be more interested in the end results than in maintaining the integrity or coherence of the juristic method. Salafism was marked far more by an anxiety to reach results that would render Islam compatible with modernity than by a desire to critically understand either modernity or the Islamic tradition itself. For instance, the Salafis of the nineteenth and early twentieth centuries heavily emphasized the predominance of the concept of *maslaha* (public interest) in the formulation of Islamic law. Accordingly, it was consistently emphasized that whatever would fulfill the public interest ought to be deemed a part of Islamic law.[45]

By the mid-twentieth century, it had become clear that Salafism had drifted into a stifling apologetics. The incipient opportunism in early Salafi approaches had degenerated into an intellectual whimsicality and carelessness that had all but destroyed any efforts at systematic and rigorous analysis. Such apologetics consisted of an effort by a large number of commentators to defend and salvage the Islamic system of beliefs from the onslaught of Orientalism, Westernization, and modernity by simultaneously emphasizing both the compatibility and also the supremacy of Islam. Apologists responded to the intellectual challenges of modernity by adopting pietistic fictions about the Islamic traditions;

such fictions eschewed any critical evaluation of Islamic doctrines and celebrated the presumed perfection of Islam. A common heuristic device of apologetics was to argue that any meritorious or worthwhile modern institutions were first invented and realized by Muslims. Therefore, according to the apologists, Islam liberated women, created a democracy, endorsed pluralism, protected human rights, and guaranteed social security long before these institutions ever existed in the West. Nonetheless, these concepts were not asserted out of critical understanding or ideological commitment, but primarily as a means of resisting the deconstructive effects of modernity, affirming self-worth and facilitating emotional empowerment. The main effect of apologetics, however, was to contribute to a sense of intellectual self-sufficiency that often descended into moral arrogance. To the extent that apologetics were habit-forming, they produced a culture that eschewed self-critical and introspective insight and embraced the projection of blame and a fantasy-like level of confidence and arrogance. Effectively, apologists got into the habit of paying homage to the presumed superiority of the Islamic tradition while marginalizing the Islamic intellectual heritage in everyday life.[46]

By the 1960s the initial optimistic liberalism had dissipated, and what remained of this liberal bent had become largely apologetic. Through a complex sociopolitical process, Wahhabism was able to rid itself of some of its extreme forms of intolerance and proceeded to co-opt the language and symbolisms of Salafism in the 1970s until the two had become practically indistinguishable. Both theologies imagined a golden age within Islam; this entailed a belief in a historical utopia that is entirely retrievable and reproducible in contemporary Islam. Both remained uninterested in critical historical inquiry and responded to the challenge of modernity by escaping to the secure haven of the text. And both advocated a form of egalitarianism and anti-elitism to the point that they came to consider intellectualism and rational moral insight to be inaccessible and thus corruptions of the purity of the Islamic message. These similarities between the two facilitated the Wahhabi co-optation of Salafism. Wahhabism, from its very inception, and Salafism, especially after it entered into the apologetic phase, were infested with a kind of supremacist thinking that prevails to this day. To simplify matters, I will call this unity of Wahhabism with the worst that is in Salafism Salafabism.

Salafabism took things to their logical extreme. The bonding of the theologies of Wahhabism and Salafism produced a contemporary orientation that is anchored in profound feelings of defeatism, alienation, and frustration. The synchronistic product of these two theologies is one of profound alienation, not only from the institutions of power of the modern world, but also from the Islamic heritage and tradition. Neither Wahhabism nor Salafism, nor the synchronistic Salafabism, is represented by formal institutions; these are theological orientations and not structured schools of thought. Therefore, one finds a broad range of ideological variations and tendencies within each orientation. But the consistent characteristic of Salafabism is a supremacist puritanism that compensates for feelings of defeatism, disempowerment, and alienation with a distinct sense of self-righteous arrogance vis-à-vis the nondescript "other," whether the "other" is the West, nonbelievers in general, or even Muslim women. In this sense, it is accurate to describe this widespread modern trend as supremacist, for it sees the world from the perspective of stations of merit and extreme polarization. It is important to note, however, that this trend devalues not only the moral worth of non-Muslims, but also those that it considers inferior or of a lesser station, such as women or heretical Muslims. Instead of simple apologetics, Salafabism responds to the feelings of powerlessness and defeat with uncompromising and arrogant symbolic displays of power, not only against non-Muslims, but even more so against fellow Muslims.

Salafabism anchored itself in the confident security of texts. But, in my view, far from being respectful toward the integrity of the text, Salafabism is abusive. As a hermeneutic orientation, it empowers its adherents to project their sociopolitical frustrations and insecurities on the text. Elsewhere, I have described the dynamics of Salafabism vis-à-vis the text as thoroughly despotic and authoritarian. Consistently, religious texts became like whips to be exploited by a select class of readers in order to affirm the reactionary power dynamics in society.[47] The adherents of Salafabism, unlike the apologists, no longer concerned themselves with co-opting or claiming Western institutions as their own. Under the guise of reclaiming the true and real Islam, they proceeded to define Islam as the exact antithesis of the West. Apologetic attempts at proving Islam's compatibility with the West were dismissed as inherently defeatist. Salafabists argued that colonialism had ingrained into Muslims a lack of self-pride or dignity and convinced Muslims of the inferiority of their religion. This has trapped Muslims into an endless and futile race to appease the West by proving Islam's worthiness. According to this model, in reality, there are only two paths in life—the path of God, or the straight path, and the path of Satan, or the crooked path. By attempting to integrate and co-opt Western ideas such as feminism, democracy, and human rights, Muslims have fallen prey to the temptations of Satan by accepting ungodly innovations (*bida'*, sing. *bid'a*). They believe that Islam is the only straight path in life, and such a way must be pursued regardless of what others think and regardless of its impact on the rights and well-being of others. Importantly, the straight path (*al-sirat al-mustaqim*) is firmly anchored in a system of divine laws that trump any considerations of morality or ethical normative values. God is manifested through a set of determinable legal commands that cover nearly all aspects of life, and the sole purpose of human beings is to realize the divine manifestation by dutifully and faithfully implementing the divine law. Salafabists insist that only the mechanics and technicalities of Islamic law define morality—there are no moral considerations that can be found outside the technical law. This fairly technical and legalistic way of life is considered inherently superior to all others, and the followers of any other way are considered either infidels (*kuffar*), hypocrites (*munafiqun*), or iniquitous (*fasiqun*). Anchored in the security and assuredness of a determinable law, it becomes fairly easy to differentiate between the rightly guided and the misguided. The rightly guided obey the law; the misguided either deny, attempt to dilute, or argue about the law. Any method of thought or process that would lead to indeterminate results such as social theory, philosophy, or any form of speculative thinking is part of the crooked path of Satan. According to the Salafabists, lives that are lived outside the divine law are inherently unlawful and, therefore, an offense against God that must be actively fought or punished.

Bin Laden, along with most extremist Muslims, belongs to the orientation that I have called Salafabist. Although he was raised in a Wahhabi environment, bin Laden is not, strictly speaking, part of that creed. Wahhabism is distinctively introverted—though focused on power, it primarily asserts power over other Muslims. This is consistent with its obsession with orthodoxy and correct ritualistic practice. Militant puritan groups, however, are both introverted and extroverted—they attempt to assert power against both Muslims and non-Muslims. As populist movements, they are a reaction to the disempowerment most Muslims have suffered in the modern age at the hands of harshly despotic governments and at the hands of interventionist foreign powers. In many ways, these militant groups compensate for extreme feelings of disempowerment by extreme and vulgar claims to power. Fueled by the supremacist and puritan creed of Salafabism, these groups' symbolic acts of power become uncompromisingly fanatic and violent.

The existence of this puritan orientation in Islam is hardly surprising. All religious systems have suffered at one time or another from absolutist extremism, and Islam is no exception. Within the first century of Islam, religious extremists known as the Khawarij (literally, the secessionists) slaughtered a large number of Muslims and non-Muslims and were even responsible for the assassination of the Prophet's cousin and companion, the Caliph 'Ali b. Abi Talib. The descendants of the Khawarij exist today in Oman and Algeria, but, after centuries of bloodshed, they became moderates, if not pacifists. Besides the Khawarij, there were other extremists such as the Qaramites and Assassins whose terror became the reason for their very existence, and who earned unmitigated infamy in the writings of Muslim historians, theologians, and jurists. Again, after centuries of bloodshed, these two groups learned moderation, and they continue to exist in small numbers in North Africa and Iraq. The essential lesson taught by Islamic history is that extremist groups, such as those mentioned above, and others are ejected from the mainstream of Islam; they are marginalized, and they eventually come to be treated as a heretical aberration to the Islamic message. The problem, however, as discussed earlier, is that the traditional institutions of Islam that historically acted to marginalize extremist creeds no longer exist. This is what makes the events of 9/11 particularly significant for the future of Islam. 9/11 symbolizes the culmination of a process that has been in the making for the past two centuries, in the same way that Salafabism has become the culmination of Salafism, Wahhabism, apologetics, and Islamic nationalism. It would be inaccurate to contend that the fanatic supremacist groups fill the vacuum of authority in contemporary Islam. Fanatical groups such as Al Qaeda or the Taliban, despite their ability to commit highly visible acts of violence, are a sociological and intellectual marginality in Islam. However, these groups are in fact extreme manifestations of more prevalent intellectual and theological currents in modern Islam. In my view, they are extreme manifestations of the rather widespread theological orientation of Salafabism. After 9/11 and the bloodletting that followed, the following question presents itself: now that we have witnessed the sheer amount of senseless destruction that the children of this orientation are capable of producing and the type of world that they are capable of instigating, will Muslims be able to marginalize Salafabism and render it, like many of the arrogant movements that preceded it, a historical curiosity?

Is There an Alternative?

The last issue I want to deal with here is perhaps the most significant. I noted earlier that I believe that theology matters. In fact, if there is any hope for reversing and marginalizing the supremacist and puritan orientation in modern Islam, it must be engaged and rebutted on theological grounds. This is not merely a functional point; it is a matter of principle.

For a believer, there is simply no alternative to the process of persuasion. A believing Muslim must ultimately confront the questions of faith, such as: What does God want? What would God approve of? And, does God care? After the events of 9/11, the issue for a Muslim is not only one of understanding the sociopolitical circumstances or ideological orientations that contributed to the tragedy, but also the quintessential questions: Is this Islam? Can this be Islam? And, should this be Islam? It is simply too easy to shirk off responsibility for the problem to imperialism, colonialism, fanaticism, terrorism, oppression, false universals, and everything else except a confrontation with one's own conscience. In every major human tragedy, I think that it is imperative for every person to put aside, for a while, the various intellectual methods by which responsibility is projected, transferred, diluted, and distributed, and to engage in a conscientious pause. In this pause, individuals ought to examine their own system of beliefs and reflect on the ways that their own convictions might have contributed to, legitimated, or in any way facilitated the tragedy. When I say that every Muslim, and non-Muslim, ought to engage in this pause, it is not because I discreetly or surreptitiously believe that Islam is at fault. But as a way of honoring human life, and honoring God's creation, it is of the essence to evaluate one's relationship to the world in which one lives.

Of course, every honest self-critical evaluation is susceptible to abuse by unsavory characters who exploit the honesty of others in the service of their own prejudice and hate. There is always the possibility, for instance, that bigoted anti-Semites will exploit the discourse of an honest Israeli who engages in self-critical evaluations of Israel's policies toward Palestinians. And the self-critical discourses of a Muslim will be open to exploitation by the same type of bigotry.[48] This is a serious concern, and in many ways, it is exactly this dynamic that has played a pivotal role in the promotion of apologetic discourses in contemporary Islam. In response to the often-searing criticisms of Orientalists, Muslims have been motivated to close ranks and to engage in a type of unthinking cheerleading on behalf of the Islamic tradition.[49] The most common comment that a Muslim critic hears from fellow Muslims is "Yes, you're making good points, but you are also playing into the hands of the enemies of Islam." For me, these types of comments raise questions of loyalty, integrity, and autonomy. As was noted earlier, the Qur'an instructs a Muslim to bear witness to the truth even if it is against oneself or against loved ones.[50] As was also noted earlier, the testimony is rendered for God, Who is, symbolically, an objective detachment that motivates and empowers aspirations for justice. It is naive, in my view, to presume that human beings are capable of transcending the contingencies of their context and rendering objective testimony. But, in Islamic theology, this is what differentiates the divine from the mundane. God is capable of perfect objectivity while human beings necessarily function in the realm of subjectivities. This, however, does not preclude human beings from reaching out to divinity. While humbled by the realization of their unavoidable contingencies, they aspire to transcend the mundane in order to attain the sublime. The closer that human beings move toward the sublime—to a state of balanced justice (*qist*)—the closer they are to divinity.[51] The purpose of rendering honest testimony is to reach out to the sublime and seek out a condition of *qist* or balanced justice.

In my view, conceding the power of setting the agenda of discourse to the hate promoters is a diversion from the sublime. Put differently, if Muslims shape their discourses in such a fashion only so as to respond to hate-filled attacks, they have conceded their autonomy to the bigots of the world. Instead of pursuing and attempting to establish the sublime, they become preempted from thinking constructively about their contribution to an existence of greater equanimity. As discussed below, the Qur'an advises that one of the core moral objectives for human beings is to engage in *ta'mir* on this earth. *Ta'mir* is one of those Qur'anic concepts that are teasingly open to interpretation. At a minimum, it means to civilize, build, and construct. I would argue, however, that the Qur'an is not referring simply to the setting up of homes made of bricks and walls, but to establishing the conditions for a habitable earth. Considering the centrality of the concepts of testimony, balance, and justice in the Qur'anic discourse, it is reasonable to conclude that the conditions for a habitable earth must include the maintenance and promotion of a state of serenity and equanimity between human societies. Aside from mere tolerance of the other, I would argue that Muslims and non-Muslims ought to engage in a collective enterprise for goodness. This would mean the acceptance and internalization of a paradigm of intercourse through discourse in an active engagement in a search for the sublime. It might be a dialectical process in some cases, in which the participants in the enterprise disagree and become the alternative to the other, but never the negation of the other. By the sublime, I mean visions of the conditions of life that are necessary in order to avoid injury and destruction to oneself or others and to create equanimity between human beings.[52] In the Islamic tradition, there are five core values that are necessary for a moral life: the preservation of life, intellect, reputation, dignity, and property. Importantly, these are not collective rights and not exclusive Muslim rights, but moral rights that each individual is entitled to enjoy.[53] I propose that an Islamic contribution to the sublime in human existence ought to focus on investigating the ways to maximize the attainment of these values in human existence while also finding the proper balance between them.

In arguing for a human collective enterprise for goodness, I am painfully aware of the various challenges to this project. Other than the issue of false universals dealt with above, a major objection will be the charge that hegemonic powers will inevitably engage in hypocrisy and double standards. But it seems to me that this is an argument for achieving a more equitable balance of power between societies and individuals, and not an argument against such an enterprise. Perhaps it is obvious that in the face of stark inequities, there will be no discourse or enterprise, but only domination and exploitation. Unless one believes that the best way to create a discourse is by destroying the human beings that could possibly engage in it, one has no choice but to call for respecting the voice and integrity of the diverse matrix of human beings. Ultimately, as a sociopolitical matter, it might be that human beings are doomed to dominate and exploit each other—the state of current affairs definitely does not give one much cause for hope. Yet, as a matter of principle and as a normative strategy, one must decide whether one ought to encourage the conflict or oppose it.[54] It is an entirely legitimate means of resisting oppression to insist on the desirability of an alternative normative vision of existence.[55]

The second and, from my standpoint, the more formidable objection is the basis in Islamic tradition for this collective enterprise. Put bluntly, doctrinally speaking, can the Islamic tradition possibly support such an enterprise? Can believing Muslims possibly contribute to a nonexclusivist vision of life? To this I turn next.

The Collective Enterprise of Goodness and Islam

In my view, Islam, as expounded in the classical books of theology and law, does not bear a message of violence. In fact, *salam* (peace and tranquility) is a central tenet of Islamic belief, and *amn* and *aman* (safety, security, or repose) are considered profound divine blessings to be cherished and vigilantly pursued. The Qur'an persistently speaks of the condition or state of peace as an inherent moral good. The absence of peace is identified in the Qur'an as a largely negative condition; it is variously described as a trial and tribulation, as a curse or punishment, or, sometimes, as a necessary evil. But the absence of peace is never in and of itself a positive or desirable condition. The Qur'an asserts that if it had not been for divine benevolence and grace, many mosques, churches, synagogues, and homes would have been destroyed because of the ignorance and pettiness of human beings.[56] Often, God mercifully intervenes to put out the fires of war and to save human beings from their follies.[57] In the Qur'anic discourse, enmity, conflict, and hate are identified as conditions of evil. Satan inspires enmity and hate in the hearts of people to ignite senseless conflicts between them.[58] Therefore, the Qur'an, in instructing the Prophet on how to deal with his enemies, advises him to avoid seeking courses of action that would exacerbate enmities and increase hate. For instance, it states: "Good and evil are not the same. So repel evil with goodness; then you will find that your erstwhile enemy has become like a close and affectionate friend."[59]

The Islamic historical experience, itself, was primarily concerned not with war making, but with civilization building. Islamic theology instructs that an integral part of the Divine covenant given to human beings is to occupy themselves with *ta'mir* (to civilize, build, and create), and not to ruin or destroy life. The Qur'an teaches that the act of destroying or spreading ruin on this earth is one of the gravest sins possible. *Fasad fi al-ard,* which means to corrupt the earth by destroying the beauty of creation, is considered an ultimate act of blasphemy against God.[60] Those who corrupt the earth by destroying lives, property, and nature are designated *mufsidun*—evildoers who, in effect, wage war against God by dismantling the very fabric of existence.[61] The Qur'anic discourse on the corruptors of life inspired an extensive juristic debate on extremist groups in Islamic history, such as the Khawarij, who were infamous for their terror-inducing tactics and for waging indiscriminate attacks against noncombatants. Classical Muslim jurists reacted sharply to these groups by considering them to be corrupters on the earth and the enemies of humankind. They were designated *muharibs* (literally, those who fight society), and they argued that such groups should not to be given quarter or refuge by anyone or at any place. In fact, Muslim jurists argued that any Muslim or non-Muslim territory that sheltered such a group is to be considered hostile territory that may be attacked by the mainstream Islamic forces. A *muharib* was defined as someone who attacks defenseless victims by stealth and spreads terror in society. Although the classical jurists agreed on the definition of this crime, they disagreed as to what type of criminal acts would be considered crimes of terror. For instance, many jurists included rape, armed robbery, assassination, arson, and murder by poisoning as crimes of terror and argued that such crimes must be punished vigilantly regardless of the theological or ideological motivations of the criminal. Most importantly, these doctrines were deemed religious imperatives, so that, regardless of the desired goals or ideological justifications, the terrorizing of the defenseless was recognized as a moral wrong and an offense against society and God.[62]

Obviously, this juristic discourse is relevant to modern-day terrorism. According to this tradition, bin Laden would be considered a *muharib* and thus an enemy of humankind. But even beyond the problem of bin Laden and terrorism, this discourse indicates an aversion in the Islamic tradition to certain emotional states or conditions that might be forced on people. Forcing people to live in a state of fear or insecurity was considered reprehensible.[63] Certain types of conduct were deemed unworthy of a Muslim and offensive to God. Therefore, for instance, Muslim jurists argued that treachery or betrayal, even in war, is unacceptable. Muslims must observe their treaty obligations, and in all circumstances they cannot attack their enemies without issuing warnings and giving notice of their intentions.[64] Building on the proscriptions of the Prophet Muhammad, Muslim jurists insisted that there are moral prescriptions that must be observed in the conduct of warfare. In general, Muslim armies may not kill women, children, seniors, hermits, pacifists, peasants, or slaves unless they are combatants. Vegetation and property may not be destroyed; water holes may not be poisoned; and flamethrowers may not be used unless out of necessity, and even then only to a limited extent. The torture, mutilation, and murder of hostages were forbidden under all circumstances. Importantly, the classical jurists reached these determinations not simply as a matter of textual interpretation, but as moral or ethical assertions.[65]

These discourses enunciate ethical limitations on conflict. But beyond the problem of regulating conflicts, the larger issue is the attitude toward the "other." Are there doctrinal means to include the other in an ethical enterprise? On this subject, the Qur'anic text sets moral trajectories that, one must confess, have not been adequately developed by Muslims. In several particularly interesting passages, the Qur'an seems to recognize the moral worth of non-Muslims who are just or good human beings. For instance, it states: "Surely, the believers, the Jews, the followers of Christ, the Sabians—whoever believes in God and the Last Day, and whoever does good, shall have his or her reward from God and will neither have to fear or regret."[66] Significantly, the Qur'an recognizes diversity among human beings and goes so far as to endorse this diversity as part of the divine purpose. It states that God has made people different and diverse, and that they will remain so until the Final Day. Accordingly, human heterogeneity and diversity are part of the divine plan, and the challenge is for human beings to coexist and interact despite their differences.[67] This is bolstered by a Qur'anic instruction as to the method or style of engagement with the other. The Qur'an commands that, apart from those who attack Muslims, Muslims should not argue with the followers of other religions except in a fair and kind way.[68] At one point, the Qur'an asserts: "To each of you We have given a law and a way of life. If God had so willed, He surely could have made you one people, professing a single faith. But God wished to try you by which He had given each of you. So try to excel in good deeds, and when you return to God in the Final Day, He will surely tell you about that upon which you disagreed."[69] In a rather unequivocal fashion, the Qur'an then proclaims: "God has made you into many nations and tribes so that you will come to know one another. Those most honored in the eyes of God are those who are most pious."[70] From this, classical Muslim scholars reached the reasonable conclusion that war is not the most conducive means of getting "to know one another" (known in Islamic discourses as ta'aruf). Thus, they argued that the exchange of technology and merchandise is, in most cases, a superior course of action to warfare. In the opinion of most classical jurists, war, unless it is purely defensive, is not to be preferred, and it must be treated as a last resort because war is not a superior moral virtue. Perhaps because of these moral imperatives, the Islamic civilization excelled in the sciences, arts, philosophy, law, architecture, and trade, and Islam entered into areas such as China, Indonesia, Malaysia, the Philippines, and sub-Saharan Africa primarily through traveling merchants and scholars, and not through warfare.

A Muslim ethic of a collective enterprise of goodness can be premised on the dual prongs of ta'aruf and ta'awun. The first, the obligation to know one another, is not achievable without a serious and involved engagement between human beings. One can reasonably conclude that if ta'aruf is a divine charge, there is value in the difference of the "other," or, put differently, that the other is worth knowing. In fact, it is highly doubtful that the duty to bear witness for God is possible without an involved knowledge of oneself and the other. As noted earlier, the risk is that instead of achieving a genuine knowledge of the other, people would simply project their anxieties and weaknesses on the other. In order to mitigate this risk, it is necessary to engage in critical self-knowledge and in a nondefensive discourse with others.

I already alluded to the obligation of ta'awun (cooperation) in the Qur'an. The Qur'an, addressing Muslims, advises them to cooperate in achieving goodness and piety and in the avoidance of evil and transgression.[71] Elsewhere, the Qur'an instructs Muslims to adhere to justice and not to be tempted by the injustice and enmity of others to commit injustice themselves.[72] Importantly, justice is to be expected from Muslims and non-Muslims alike, in the same way that transgression is wrongful whether committed by Muslims or non-Muslims. This appears to me to create a commonality of moral interests. This does not mean that Muslims are to be expected to dilute the distinctiveness of their laws or moral thinking. But it does support the idea of a cooperative venture to fend off transgressive behavior and to promote as much justice as possible.[73]

Having made an argument for a collective enterprise of goodness, one must somberly ask, but how about the bin Ladens of the world? Where and how do they get their doctrinal support? Admittedly, one can make a case for a tolerant and humanitarian Islam, but it does exist in tension with other doctrines in the Islamic tradition that are less tolerant or humanitarian. Many classical Muslim scholars, for instance, insisted on a conception of the world that is bifurcated and dichotomous. Those scholars argued that the world is divided into the abode of Islam (*dar al-Islam*) and the abode of war (*dar al-harb*); the two can stop fighting for a while, but one must inevitably prevail over the other. According to these scholars, Muslims must give non-Muslims one of three options: either become Muslim, pay the poll tax, or fight. These classical scholars were willing to tolerate differences as long as the existence of these differences did not challenge Muslim political supremacy and dominance. It is important to note, however, that this dichotomous and even imperialist view of the world did not go unchallenged. So, for instance, many classical scholars argued that, instead of a two-part division of the world, one ought to recognize a third category, and that is the abode of nonbelligerence or neutrality (*dar al-sulh* or *al-'ahd*)—an abode that is not Muslim, but that has a peaceful relationship with the Muslim world. In addition, many classical jurists argued that, regardless of the political affiliation of a particular territory, the real or true abode of Islam is wherever justice exists (*dar al-'adl*), or wherever Muslims may freely and openly practice their religion. Therefore, it is possible for a territory with a Muslim minority that is ruled by non-Muslims to be considered part of the abode of true Islam.[74]

The fact that the Islamic scholastic tradition is not unitary, and that it is often diverse and multifaceted, is hardly surprising. The same tensions exist when considering the concept of jihad, which has gained much notoriety especially since 9/11. Jihad is a core principle in Islamic theology; it means to strive, to apply oneself, to struggle, and to persevere. Jihad, in the most straightforward sense, connotes a strong spiritual and material work ethic in Islam. Piety, knowledge, health, beauty, truth, and justice are not possible without jihad—without sustained and diligent hard work. Therefore, cleansing oneself from vanity and pettiness, pursuing knowledge, curing the ill, feeding the poor, and standing up for truth and justice even at great personal risk are all forms of jihad. The Qur'an uses the term "jihad" to refer to the act of striving to serve the purposes of God on this earth, which includes all the acts mentioned above. Importantly, the Qur'an does not use the word "jihad" to refer to warfare or fighting; such acts are referred to as *qital*. While the Qur'an's call to jihad is unconditional and unrestricted, such is not the case for *qital*. Jihad is a good in and of itself, while *qital* is not. Therefore, every reference in the Qur'an to *qital* is restricted and limited by particular conditions, but exhortations to jihad, like the references to justice or truth, are absolute and unconditional. Consequently, the early Muslims were not allowed to engage in *qital* until God gave them specific permission to do so. The Qur'an is careful to note that Muslims were given permission to fight only after they had become the victims of aggression.[75] Furthermore, the Qur'an instructs Muslims to fight only those who fight them and not to transgress, for God does not approve of aggression.[76] In addition, the Qur'an goes on to specify that if the enemy ceases hostilities and seeks peace, Muslims should seek peace as well. Failure to seek peace without just cause is considered arrogant and sinful. In fact, the Qur'an reminds Muslims not to pick fights and not to create enemies because the fact that a particular party does not wish to fight Muslims and seeks to make peace is a divine blessing. God has the power to inspire in the hearts of non-Muslims a desire for peace, and Muslims must treat such a blessing with gratitude and appreciation, not defiance and arrogance.[77]

In light of this Qur'anic discourse, classical Muslim jurists debated what would constitute a sufficient and just cause for fighting non-Muslims. Are non-Muslims to be fought because of their acts of disbelief or only because they pose a physical threat to Muslims? Most classical jurists concluded that the justification for fighting non-Muslims is directly proportional to the physical threat they pose to Muslims. In other words, if they do not threaten or seek to harm Muslims, then there is no justification for acts of belligerence or warfare. In my estimation, while the Islamic tradition does not convey a unitary message and does not speak in a single voice, the case for a humanistic Islam is a particularly strong one.

Conclusion

Religious doctrine matters—as diverse and contested as it may be, doctrine has a direct impact on what people choose to believe and how they choose to act. The terrorist attacks of 9/11 came as a gruesome reminder that religion, which can inspire great beauty, can also inspire much ugliness. In the case of all strongly held systems of conviction, this is a lesson that history keeps teaching. It is also a lesson not limited to religion; one cannot forget that millions of people have died in the name of irreligious, or even antireligious, ideologies as well. But 9/11 ought to be a stark reminder to Muslims, specifically. It should remind them that what I called Salafabism has vulgarized their religion and emptied it of its humanistic spirit. It should also be a reminder about the role of human agency vis-à-vis religious doctrine. The impact of the doctrines of Islam entirely depends on how modern Muslims choose to understand, develop, and assert them. Perhaps it is painfully obvious that Muslims, as the interpreters of their tradition, shoulder the primary responsibility for deciding on the role that their religion will have in the world today. Perhaps it is also painfully obvious that, regardless of how rich, humanistic, and moral the Islamic tradition is, this tradition will be of very limited usefulness if it is not believed and acted on by Muslims. But here lies the true travesty of modern Islam—and the agony of every honest Muslim intellectual. Many non-Muslims suffer from much ignorance and prejudice about Islam and Muslims. But living in the shadow of the postcolonial experience, and suffering from the movements that arose in that period, contemporary Muslims have yet to seriously engage their own tradition. Not only are Muslims woefully ignorant about their own tradition, but also much of what they do know has been framed purely as a defensive reaction to the postcolonial experience. Bin Laden is the quintessential example of a Muslim who was created, shaped, and motivated by postcolonialism. In the past decades, when contemporary Muslim intellectuals have attempted a critical engagement with their tradition and a search for the moral and humanistic aspects of the intellectual heritage, invariably they have been confronted by the specter of postcolonialism. Their efforts have been evaluated purely in terms of whether it appeases or displeases the West. Post-9/11, it is clear that it is not Islam that should be transformed. Rather, Muslims must seek to emerge from the shadow of postcolonialism and take their own tradition seriously.

Notes

I offer sincere gratitude to my wife, Grace, for reading and commenting on this paper.

1. In fact, bin Laden has consistently refused to acknowledge his responsibility for the 9/11 attack. He has praised the attack and praised those who carried it out, but he has never clearly confessed the responsibility of his group.

2. At different times, bin Laden has cited a whole host of grievances, which include, among others, the American military presence in the Gulf, Israel's treatment of the Palestini-

ans, the embargo imposed against Iraq, the spread of Western culture and consumerism in Muslim countries, American support of autocratic and non-Islamic governments in the Middle East, the Shi'ite and Jewish conspiracy to destroy Islam, and the Western exploitation of Muslim wealth and natural resources. On bin Laden and his thought, see Peter L. Bergen, *Holy War Inc.: Inside the Secret World of Osama bin Laden* (New York: Free Press, 2001); Roland Jacquard, *In the Name of Osama Bin Laden: Global Terrorism and the Bin Laden Brotherhood,* trans. George Holoch (Durham, N.C.: Duke University Press, 2002); Rohan Gunaratana, *Inside Al Qaeda: Global Network of Terror* (New York: Columbia University Press, 2002). For a seemingly authentic and rather sad personal account of Al Qaeda by a disillusioned insider, see Aukai Collins, *My Jihad* (Guilford, Conn.: Lyons Press, 2002). For a thorough overview of the modern history of Islamic fundamentalism, the Taliban, and bin Laden, see Gilles Kepel, *Jihad: The Trail of Political Islam,* trans. Anthony F. Roberts (London: I. B. Tauris, 2002).

3. In statements broadcast on the al-Jazeerah satellite channel, bin Laden claimed that a few more strikes like the one that took place in 9/11 would cause the economic power of the United States to collapse.

4. This nihilistic bent was also noted by Niall Ferguson, "Clashing Civilizations or Mad Mullahs: The United States between Informal and Formal Empire," in *The Age of Terror: America and the World after September 11,* ed. Strobe Talbott and Nayan Chanda (New York: Basic Books, 2001), 115–41.

5. In this context, bin Laden used the expression "*maslubat al-iradah*," which literally means "of a robbed or stolen will."

6. On subaltern and postcolonial studies and the impact of colonialism on modern history, see Vinayak Chaturvedi, ed., *Mapping Subaltern Studies and the Postcolonial* (London: Verso Press, 2000); Dipesh Chakrabarty, *Habitations of Modernity: Essays in the Wake of Subaltern Studies* (Chicago: University of Chicago Press, 2002); Robert J. Young, *Postcolonialism: An Historical Introduction* (Oxford: Blackwell Publishers, 2001); Francis Barker, Peter Hulme, and Margaret Iversen, eds., *Colonial Discourse, Postcolonial Theory* (Manchester: Manchester University Press, 1996); Ania Loomba, *Colonialism and Postcolonialism* (London: Routledge Press, 1998); Gyan Prakash, ed., *After Colonialism: Imperial Histories and Postcolonial Displacements* (Princeton: Princeton University Press, 1995).

7. In the Muslim world, the most problematic and controversial promise of modernity is secularism. This is partly because, unlike values such as democracy, individual rights, and social justice, secularism is not an end in and of itself. It is seen as a possible means to an end—as a preceding condition that facilitates the fulfillment of ultimate values. This has led many Islamic thinkers to contend that moral values such as democracy and individual rights can be achieved without secularism. In addition, secularism has been associated often with moral hedonism or a lack of religiosity, which is seen as destructive and undesirable. Some Muslim activists claimed that secularism was advocated to Muslims by colonizing powers as a means of destroying Islam or countering the Islamic influence. For a reader-friendly introduction to historical misunderstandings, and the apprehensions of Muslims, see Rollin Armour Sr., *Islam, Christianity, and the West: A Troubled History* (Maryknoll, N.Y.: Orbis Books, 2002), esp. 167–82.

8. In nearly every recorded speech I have encountered by bin Laden, Ayman al-Zawahiri, and 'Umar 'Abd al-Rahman, they have emphasized the theme of the hypocrisy of the West in dealing with the Muslim world, especially as to the deference shown to Israel. They also emphasized the dependent status of Muslim leaders and described them as mere stooges of the West. These allegations are usually couched in highly conspiratorial lan-

guage. For instance, 'Umar 'Abd al-Rahman claimed that Saddam Hussein is engaged in a conspiracy with the United States to destroy Iraq and Iran.

9. For the argument that the American government is, in fact, dealing with this crisis as a civilizational conflict, see As'ad AbuKhalil, *Bin Laden, Islam, and America's New "War on Terrorism"* (New York: Seven Stories Press, 2002). Some writers are shameless in accusing Islam of inherent inferiority. For example, see Paul L. Williams, *Al-Qaeda: Brotherhood of Terror* (New York: Alpha Books, 2002). The publishers sent me this book before publication, and I advised them that it is rabidly Islamophobic; they decided to publish it anyway. The FBI purportedly hired the author as a consultant on Muslim terrorism. To my dismay, in order to bolster its credibility, they listed me as the coauthor of the book on Amazon.uk. Of course, I authored no part of this book.

10. One of the sensitive points that is consistently mentioned in the Arabic- and Persian-language press is the apparent callousness with which the United States and England treat Muslim casualties in Afghanistan, Palestine, and Iraq. No one knows the number of Afghans killed during the American bombardment of suspected Qaeda and Taliban sites. In addition, the American and British response to the suffering and killing of Iraqi and Palestinian civilians is quite mild, rarely exceeding the expression of general regret.

11. Tariq Ali, *The Clash of Fundamentalisms: Crusades, Jihads, and Modernity* (London: Verso Press, 2002). Ali argues that American and European imperialism has created the fundamentalism of bin Laden. Ali also characterizes American and European attitudes toward Muslims as no less fundamentalist than bin Laden.

12. See Roger Burbach and Ben Clarke, eds., *September 11 and the U.S. War: Beyond the Curtain of Smoke* (San Francisco: City Lights Books, 2002).

13. For this debate between me and several other commentators, including the Pakistani critic, see Khaled Abou El Fadl, ed., *The Place of Tolerance in Islam* (Boston: Beacon Press, 2002).

14. I am not claiming, however, that religious convictions do not play a role in American foreign policy. For a collection of articles examining the role of religion in U.S. foreign policy, see Elliott Abrams, ed., *The Influence of Faith: Religious Groups and U.S. Foreign Policy* (Lanham, Md.: Rowman and Littlefield, 2001). In fact, this book contains an article by Habib Malik titled "Political Islam and the Roots of Violence," 113–48, and a comment by Daniel Pipes, 149–51, that are rabid in their hostility to Islam and Muslims. These articles demonstrate the extent to which religious hate can motivate commentators seeking to influence the foreign policy of the United States. My point, however, is that in secular Western countries, religious motivations behind foreign policies normally function in a discreet and subtle fashion. Secular Western countries usually claim religious neutrality and do not openly herald the cause of God in the conduct of international relations.

15. For a discussion on the role that religion does play in terrorist attacks, see Bernard Lewis, *What Went Wrong?* (Oxford: Oxford University Press, 2002); John Esposito, *Unholy War* (Oxford: Oxford University Press, 2002). For Tariq Ali's views on this matter, see his article, "Theological Distractions," in Abou El Fadl, ed., *The Place of Tolerance in Islam*, 37–41.

16. There is a fairly huge corpus of literature on the sociology of religion and the effect of religious convictions on the behavior of human beings. Eric Hoffer's *The True Believer: Thoughts on the Nature of Mass Movements* (1951; reprint, New York: HarperCollins, 1989) remains among the best books published on the subject.

17. Some scholars have argued that most of Muslim society in the modern age is characterized by a cultural schizophrenia in which there are profound distortions in the self-

consciousness of Muslims. See Daryush Shayegan, *Cultural Schizophrenia: Islamic Societies Confronting the West,* trans. John Howe (London: Saqi Books, 1989).

18. For example, Saudi Arabia responded to the increasing social and economic mobility of women by banning women from driving cars. Egypt, however, responded very differently. Some Islamic doctrines, however, such as the man's exclusive power to initiate divorce, have proven extremely resilient against change. In large part, this is due to the perceived importance of a given matter to the Islamic faith.

19. For a valuable study on the duty to enjoin the good and forbid the evil in the Islamic tradition, see Michael Cook, *Commanding Right and Forbidding Wrong in Islamic Thought* (Cambridge: Cambridge University Press, 2000).

20. Qur'an 4:135, 5:8.

21. Interestingly, the expression "false universalisms" was used by Samuel Huntington in arguing that Westerners' belief in the universality of their values is both immoral and dangerous. Samuel Huntington, *The Clash of Civilizations and the Remaking of World Order* (New York: Simon and Schuster, 1996), 310.

22. Sometimes, this accusation descends into vulgarity. For instance, because of my critical writings post-9/11, recently a Muslim professor in Texas accused me of prostituting myself and of "pimping" my students.

23. On this subject, see Khaled Abou El Fadl, *And God Knows the Soldiers: The Authoritative and Authoritarian in Islamic Discourses* (Lanham, Md.: University Press of America, 2001), 138–56.

24. On this subject, see Khaled Abou El Fadl, *Reasoning with God: Rationality and Thought in Islam* (Oxford: Oneworld, forthcoming). Also see George F. Hourani, *Reason and Tradition in Islamic Ethics* (Cambridge: Cambridge University Press, 1985).

25. Khaled Abou El Fadl, "Islam and the Theology of Power Islam," *Middle East Report,* no. 221 (winter 2001): 28–33.

26. On the hegemony of the United States and the West and Muslim reaction, see Simon W. Murden, *Islam, the Middle East, and the New Global Hegemony* (Boulder, Colo.: Lynne Rienner Publishers, 2002), esp. 43–128.

27. For a study on Muslims, the West, and the prevalence of siege mentalities, see Graham E. Fuller and Ian O. Lesser, *A Sense of Siege: The Geopolitics of Islam and the West* (Boulder, Colo.: Westview Press, 1995).

28. "Westoxification" is a derogatory expression used to describe self-hating Muslims who are in awe of everything Western to the point that they seem to be intoxicated on the West.

29. On this issue, see Huntington, *The Clash of Civilizations;* John Esposito, *The Islamic Threat: Myth or Reality?* rev. ed. (Oxford: Oxford University Press, 1995); Fred Halliday, *Islam and the Myth of Confrontation* (London: I. B. Tauris, 1995); Colin Chapman, *Islam and the West: Conflict, Co-existence or Conversion?* (Carlisle, U.K.: Paternoster Press, 1998); Karim H. Karim, *The Islamic Peril: Media and Global Violence* (Montreal: Black Rose Books, 2000); Dieter Senghaas, *The Clash within Civilizations: Coming to Terms with Cultural Conflicts* (London: Routledge, 1998). For excellent studies on the historical misconceptions about Islam prevalent in Europe, see Franco Cardini, *Europe and Islam* (Oxford: Blackwell Press, 2001); Albert Hourani, *Islam in European Thought* (Cambridge: Cambridge University Press, 1991). The best work on the subject remains Norman Daniel, *Islam and the West: The Making of an Image* (1960, reprint Oxford: Oneworld, 2000). A particularly useful and sophisticated collection of studies is John Victor Tolan, *Medieval Christian Perceptions of Islam* (London: Routledge, 2000). For the impact of the Huntington thesis and misconceptions about Islam on American foreign policy, see

Maria do Ceu Pinto, *Political Islam and the United States: A Study of U.S. Policy towards Islamist Movements in the Middle East* (Reading, U.K.: Ithaca Press, 1999).

30. Lawrence E. Harrison and Samuel R. Huntington, eds., *Culture Matters: How Values Shape Human Progress* (New York: Basic Books, 2000).

31. There are many works that document the influence of Islamic culture and thought on Europe. The following two are impressive: George Makdisi, *The Rise of Humanism in Classical Islam and the Christian West* (Edinburgh: Edinburgh University Press, 1990); Mourad Wahba and Mona Abousenna, eds., *Averroës and the Enlightenment* (New York: Prometheus Books, 1996). Even when preserving the Greek philosophical tradition, Muslim scholars did not act as mere transmitters; they substantially developed and built on Greek philosophy. In a fascinating text that demonstrates the level of penetration that Islamic thought achieved in Europe, Thomas Aquinas, in an attempt to refute Ibn Rushd (Averroës)—whom he labels a "perverter of Peripatetic philosophy"—and Ibn Sina (Avicenna), ends up quoting Abu Hamid al-Ghazali in support of his arguments against Ibn Rushd's. Both al-Ghazali and Ibn Rushd were medieval Muslim philosophers and jurists. Thomas Aquinas, *On the Unity of the Intellect against the Averroists,* trans. Beatrice Zedler (Milwaukee: Marquette University Press, 1968), 46–47. For a collection of articles that demonstrate cross-intellectual influences, see John Inglis, *Medieval Philosophy and the Classical Tradition: In Islam, Judaism, and Christianity* (Richmond, U.K.: Curzon Press, 2002). For an awe-inspiring example of the contributions of medieval Muslim scholars to Greek philosophy, see Kwame Gyekye, *Arabic Logic: Ibn al-Tayyib's Commentary on Porphyry's Eisagoge* (Albany: State University of New York Press, 1979).

32. For an analysis of this process of projection and construction of an image of Islamic law, see Khaled Abou El Fadl, "Islamic Law and Ambivalent Scholarship," *Michigan Law Review* 100 (2002): 1421–43.

33. For a detailed study on the role of authorial enterprise, communities of interpretation, and Islamic law, see Khaled Abou El Fadl, *Speaking in God's Name: Authority, Islamic Law, and Women* (Oxford: Oneworld, 2001).

34. Not surprisingly, writers who clearly do not like Muslims very much have exploited Huntington's thesis. For an example of paranoid Islamophobia, a work that was unfortunately highly praised by various American politicians, see Anthony J. Dennis, *The Rise of the Islamic Empire and the Threat to the West* (Bristol, Ind.: Wyndham Hall Press, 1996). For another example of a work, written from the perspective of a Christian fundamentalist, that exploits Huntington's argument and that is hostile to Islam, see George Grant, *The Blood of the Moon: Understanding the Historic Struggle between Islam and Western Civilization,* rev. ed. (New York: Thomas Nelson, 2001). Typically, in this genre of literature, Christianity, Judaism, and Western culture are, rather jovially, all bundled up in a single unitary mass, placed in a corner, and then pitted against the fantasized concept of *Islam.*

35. This is the gist of Huntington's argument about the wrongfulness of believing in universal Western values; Huntington, *The Clash of Civilizations,* 308–12. This is also Lawrence Rosen's argument in his *The Justice of Islam: Comparative Perspectives on Islamic Law and Society* (Oxford: Oxford University Press, 2000), 153–75. See my critique of this book in Abou El Fadl, "Islamic Law and Ambivalent Scholarship." Also, see Ann Mayer, *Islam and Human Rights: Tradition and Politics,* 3d ed. (Boulder, Colo.: Westview Press, 1999), 6–9; Khaled Abou El Fadl, "Soul Searching and the Spirit of Shari'a," *Washington University Global Studies Law Review* 22, vol. 1, nos. 1 and 2 (2002): 553–77.

36. On the epistemology of Islamic law, see Wael Hallaq, *Authority, Continuity, and Change*

in Islamic Law (Cambridge: Cambridge University Press, 2001); Wael Hallaq, *A History of Islamic Legal Theories* (Cambridge: Cambridge University Press, 1997).

37. On this subject, see George Makdisi, *The Rise of Colleges in Islam* (Edinburgh: Edinburgh University Press, 1981).

38. Afaf Lutfi al-Sayyid Marsot, "The Ulama of Cairo in the Eighteenth and Nineteenth Century," in *Scholars, Saints, and Sufis,* ed. Nikki Keddie (Berkeley: University of California Press, 1972), 149–65.

39. Allan Christelow, *Muslim Law Courts and the French Colonial State in Algeria* (Princeton: Princeton University Press, 1985); J. N. D. Anderson, "Modern Trends in Islam: Legal Reform and Modernisation in the Middle East," *International and Comparative Law Quarterly* 20 (1971): 1–21, reprinted in *Islamic Law and Legal Theory,* ed. Ian Edge (New York: New York University Press, 1996), 547–67; William L. Cleveland, *A History of the Modern Middle East,* 2d ed. (Boulder, Colo.: Westview Press, 2000); Jasper Yeates Brinton, *The Mixed Courts of Egypt,* rev. ed. (New Haven: Yale University Press, 1968); Ruth Mitchell, "Family Law in Algeria before and after the 1404/1984 Family Code," in *Islamic Law: Theory and Practice,* ed. R. Gleave and E. Kermeli (London: I. B. Tauris, 1997), 194–204. Of course, at times, colonial powers took over the implementation of Islamic law, as in the case of the Anglo-Muhammadan law experience in India. Syed Ameer Ali, *Muhammadan Law* (New Delhi: Kitab Bhavan, 1986), 1–4; Joseph Schacht, *An Introduction to Islamic Law* (1964, reprint, Oxford: Clarendon Press, 1993), 94–97; N. J. Coulson, *A History of Islamic Law* (Edinburgh: Edinburgh University Press, 1964), 164–72. On the impact of colonialism on the institutions of Islamic law in India, see Radhika Singha, *A Despotism of Law: Crime and Justice in Early Colonial India* (Delhi: Oxford University Press, 1998), 52–53, 60–70, 294–96, 300.

40. For an example of this in Muhammad Ali's (r. 1805–48) Egypt, see Afaf Lutfi al-Sayyid Marsot, *Women and Men in Late-Eighteenth-Century Egypt* (Austin: University of Texas Press, 1995), 136, 141–42.

41. See J. N. D. Anderson, *Islamic Law in the Modern World* (New York: New York University Press, 1959); J. N. D. Anderson, *Law Reform in the Muslim World* (London: Athlone Press, 1976); Wael Hallaq, *A History of Islamic Legal Theories,* 207–11.

42. Muhammad Amin Ibn 'Abidin, *Hashiyat Radd al-Muhtar* (Cairo: Mustafa al-Babi, 1966), 6:413; Ahmad al-Sawi, *Hashiyat al-'Allamah al-Sawi 'ala Tafsir al-Jalalayn* (Beirut: Dar Ihya' al-Turath al-'Arabi, n.d.), 3:307–8. See also Ahmad Dallal, "The Origins and Objectives of Islamic Revivalist Thought, 1750–1850," *Journal of the American Oriental Society* 113, no. 3 (1993): 341–59.

43. On these events and others, see Cook, *Commanding Right and Forbidding Wrong,* 180–91.

44. Eleanor Doumato, "Saudi Sex-Segregation Can Be Fatal," *Providence Journal,* March 31, 2002, http://www.projo.com/opinion/contributors/content/projo. I confirmed this incident in a conversation with the father of one of the girls who was killed. Saudi Arabia initially said it would investigate, but a day later it denied that the incident had occurred.

45. On this process and on the use of *talfiq* and *maslaha* in modern Islam, see Coulson, *A History of Islamic Law,* 197–217.

46. For a critical, and similarly grim, assessment by a Muslim of the state of intellectual thought in the Islamic world, see Tariq Ramadan, *Islam, the West, and the Challenges of Modernity,* trans. Said Amghar (Markfield, U.K.: Islamic Foundation, 2001), 286–90. For an insightful analysis of the role of apologetics in modern Islam, see Wilfred Cantwell Smith, *Islam in Modern History* (Princeton: Princeton University Press, 1977).

47. Two of my books, *And God Knows the Soldiers* and *Speaking in God's Name,* are primarily concerned with this phenomenon.

48. Examples of this are not hard to find. Unfortunately, in his *Al Qaeda: Brotherhood of Terror* (New York: Alpha Books, 2002), 184, Paul Williams approvingly misquotes me; this book aims to convince the reader that Islam is inferior to Christianity and that it is an inherently violent and hate-filled religion. Another example of an author who unscrupulously quotes and misquotes the internal self-critical discourses of Muslims to promote a rabid type of Islamophobia is Steven Emerson, *American Jihad: The Terrorists among Us* (New York: Free Press, 2002), 159–75. In his chapter on "unsung heroes," Emerson primarily relies on the statements of Shaykh Kabbani and Hasan Ashmawi in support of his argument that most Muslim organizations in the United States are nothing but fronts for terrorist organizations. Effectively, this book incites non-Muslim Americans to be suspicious and even hate American Muslims. Unfortunately, I have seen this book in every bookstore I have visited in the United States.

49. On the searing criticisms of Islam by Orientalists, see Edward Said's *Orientalism* (New York: Random House, 1979) and *Culture and Imperialism* (New York: Vintage Books, 1994).

50. Qur'an 4:135, 5:8.

51. The Qur'an identifies balance (*mizan*) with godliness. See Qur'an 6:152, 7:85, 11:84–85, 42:17, 55:7–9, 57:25. God's perfection is manifested in the fact that God can maintain the balance—a state of perfect equanimity between all things. The maintenance of the balance is crucial for the achievement of justice, which among human beings means that no one is made to suffer because of the transgression of the other. This idea is exemplified in the Islamic expressions *la darar wa la dirar* and *la tazir wazira wizra ukhra* (no one should suffer for the faults of the other); see Qur'an 6:164, 17:15, 35:18, 39:7, 53:38.

52. There is a large body of Western literature on the notion of the sublime and its relationship to aesthetics, morality, and culture. See, for instance, Paul Crowther, *The Kantian Sublime: From Morality to Art* (Oxford: Oxford University Press, 1991); Stanford Budick, *The Western Theory of Tradition: Terms and Paradigms of the Cultural Sublime* (New Haven: Yale University Press, 2000); Clayton Crockett, *A Theology of the Sublime* (London: Routledge, 2001); Peter De Bolla, *The Discourse of the Sublime: Readings in History, Aesthetics, and the Subject* (Oxford: Blackwell Publishers, 1989); Frances Ferguson, *Solitude and the Sublime: Romanticism and the Aesthetics of Individuation* (London: Routledge, 1992); Jean-François Lyotard, *Lessons on the Analytic of the Sublime,* trans. Elizabeth Rottenberg (Stanford: Stanford University Press, 1994); Immanuel Kant, *Observations on the Feeling of the Beautiful and Sublime,* trans. John T. Goldthwait (Berkeley: University of California Press, 1991); Bjorn K. Myskja, *The Sublime in Kant and Beckett: Literature, Aesthetic Judgment, and Ethics* (London: Walter de Gruyter, 2001); Martin Ryle, *To Relish the Sublime: Culture and Self-Realization in Postmodern Times* (London: Verso, 2002); Lap-Chuen Tsang, *The Sublime: Groundwork towards a Theory* (Rochester: University of Rochester Press, 1998); Slavoj Žižek, *The Sublime Object of Ideology* (New York: Verso, 1997). This is not the place to engage these theoretical debates, but I do note that I tend to lean toward the Kantian tendency to connect aesthetics to morality. The vast classical debate on *husn* (beauty) and *qubh* (ugliness) was, in essence, a discourse on the aesthetics and morality of the sublime, but the subject has been thoroughly ignored by contemporary Muslims. For an intriguing premodern work, which is one of the very few works related to the subject that have been translated to English, see Shaykh 'Abd

al-Qadir al-Jilani, *The Sublime Revelation,* trans. Mukhtar Holland (London: al-Bazz Publications, 1993).

53. Muslim jurists would typically list life, intellect, religion, lineage, and property. I would argue that religion is subsumed under intellect and that the issue of lineage is better guarded by dignity and reputation. For a discussion on this, see Khaled Abou El Fadl, "Constitutionalism and the Islamic Sunni Legacy," *UCLA Journal of Islamic and Near Eastern Law* 1 (2001): 67–101.

54. Confronted by the same type of moral dilemma, Dieter Senghaas "pleads" for a major reorientation in intercultural dialogue; Senghaas, *The Clash within Civilizations,* 105–17.

55. The idea of a collective enterprise of goodness does not mean that acts of self-defense are illegitimate. It only means that responses to aggression must be measured, proportional, and necessary. This means that resistance might be necessary, but it must avoid injury to the innocent and must aspire to ending the hostilities and returning once again to the collective enterprise.

56. Qur'an 22:40.

57. Qur'an 5:64.

58. Qur'an 5:91.

59. Qur'an 41:34.

60. For instance, see Qur'an 2:27, 2:205, 5:32, 13:25.

61. Qur'an 2:27, 13:25.

62. For a detailed study on this subject, see Khaled Abou El Fadl, *Rebellion and Violence in Islamic Law* (Cambridge: Cambridge University Press, 2001).

63. Qur'an 8:60 advises Muslims to maintain their military strength so that their enemy will fear them. Various Islamophobes gleefully jumped on this verse to prove that the Qur'an supports terrorism. This verse emphasizes the importance of deterrence, in the hope of avoiding war. It does not endorse terrorizing people. However, the fact that bin Laden has cited this verse in support of the morality of terrorism has definitely contributed to the misunderstanding.

64. The Qur'an repeatedly emphasizes the importance of observing one's treaty obligations and all other contracts; see 2:177, 6:152, 9:4, 17:34.

65. It is reported that the Prophet used to instruct his armies not to hurt a noncombatant or needlessly destroy property or vegetation. It is also reported that, on finding the corpse of a woman after a battle, the Prophet became very upset and reproached his army for killing a noncombatant. On this subject, see Khaled Abou El Fadl, "The Rules of Killing at War: An Inquiry into Classical Sources," *Muslim World* 89, no. 2 (1999): 144–57; Khaled Abou El Fadl, "Holy War versus Jihad: A Review of James Johnson's *The Holy War Idea in the Western and Islamic Traditions,*" *Ethics and International Affairs* 14 (2000): 133–40.

66. Qur'an 2:62, 5:69.

67. Qur'an 11:118.

68. Qur'an 29:46.

69. Qur'an 5:48.

70. Qur'an 49:13.

71. Qur'an 5:2.

72. Qur'an 5:2, 5:8.

73. Tariq Ramadan contends that with the onslaught of secularism the West lost the moral meaning in life. He argues that Muslims should assist the West in returning to an ethical and purposeful modernity. Ramadan, *Islam, the West, and the Challenges,* 296.

74. On this subject, see Khaled Abou El Fadl, "Islamic Law and Muslim Minorities: The Juris-

tic Discourse on Muslim Minorities from the Second/Eighth to the Eleventh/Seventeenth Centuries," *Islamic Law and Society* 1, no. 2 (1994): 141–87.

75. Qur'an 22:39, 60:8, 2:246.

76. Qur'an 2:190, 2:194, 5:87.

77. Qur'an 4:90.

Islam(s) East and West: Pluralism between No-Frills and Designer Fundamentalism

SHERMAN A. JACKSON

It was William Edward Burghardt Du Bois who made the prescient prediction that the problem of the twentieth century would be the problem of the color line. The twentieth century has come and gone, and, while the color line remains with us,[1] I predict that the problem of the twenty-first century will be the problem of the false universal. In my use of "false universal," I am referring to that convenient confusion between abstract and concrete universals on the basis of which only those who share one's concretions of "justice," "beauty," or "civilization" are justified in laying claims to these values. The false universal conceals itself in the habit and or privilege of speaking as if the shape that one's values and preferences assume in concrete social, political, or interpersonal contexts is not grounded in cultural, historical, or even ideological perspectives but, instead, is reflective of a transcendent, "natural" order whose validity is obvious to everyone, save the stupid, the primitive, or the morally depraved. In a word, the false universal is a manifestation of history internalized, normalized, and then forgotten as history—at least for those on the inside looking out.

The horrific events of September 11, 2001, are likely to accelerate the pace with which American Muslims are forced to confront the problem of the false universal. To begin with, the international dimensions of the tragedy (though the perpetrators were substate actors) have prompted appeals to laws and institutions whose very legitimacy lay in their claim to universal validity and jurisdiction. At the same time, American Muslims' need to confirm Islam's participation in the global consensus condemning the carnage has added credence and momentum to the efforts of Muslim reformists who were declaring even before 9/11 that the sacred law of Islam is out of step with modern sensibilities and needs to be brought into conformity with "universally recognized" rights and obligations.

All of this must be seen against the backdrop of the racial and ethnic makeup of America's Muslim community. Among the major Western democracies (Britain, France, Germany) America is unique in that indigenous people who did not emigrate from the Muslim world form the second largest (and according to some the largest) single group of its Muslims. In fact, prior to the Johnson administration's repeal of the national origins quota system in 1965, American Islam had been dominated by a black presence. Black American Islam had been largely grounded, however, not in the religious and scholarly tradition of historical Islam but in the thoroughly American phenomenon of "black religion," essentially a God-centered holy protest against white supremacy and antiblack racism.[2] Since black religion had virtually no authority outside the black community and since immigrants, via the *imprimatur* of both provenance and precedence, could assume the authority to speak for Muslims everywhere, the steady influx of immigrant Muslims effected a major shift in the basis of religious authority in American Islam. Possessed of this newly established monopoly over Islamic religious authority, immigrant Muslims moved quickly to establish their ascendancy as *the* definers of a properly constituted religious life for American Muslims.

In the aftermath of September 11, reform has emerged as *the* preoccupation of American Muslims, especially those whose ethnic identity with the hijackers has rendered them particularly vulnerable. Given the aforementioned redistribution of Islamic religious authority, it comes as no surprise that immigrant Muslims are leading the way in this regard. Herein, however, lie the seeds for potential conflict. For to the extent that the aim of this enterprise is to disabuse non-Muslims of their negative assessments of Islam, reform will invariably entail an attempt to reconcile Islam with the dominant culture. And to the extent that this attempt conflates "dominant" with "universal" (the better to substantiate the propriety of specific reforms) black American Muslims are likely to remain skeptical if not hostile toward reform. This is because their historical legacy has endowed them with a deep suspicion of all claims to universal norms, white supremacy, their perennial nemesis, being itself little more than a false universal. Speaking in this regard, Richard Dyer notes in his provocative book, *White:*

> There is no more powerful position than that of being "just" human. The claim to power is the claim to speak for the commonality of humanity. Raced people can't do that—they can only speak for their

race. But non-raced people [i.e., whites] can, for they do not represent the interests of a race.[3]

. . . The position of speaking as a white person is one that white people now almost never acknowledge, and this is part of the condition and power of whiteness; white people claim and achieve authority for what they say by not admitting, indeed not realizing, that for much of the time they speak only for whiteness.[4]

If, from the perspective of those within the Muslim community who enjoy the greatest margin of religious authority, September 11 has heightened the urgency of obviating Islam's compatibility with "universal" or even "Western"[5] values, such an effort, if it is to avoid the treachery of the false universal, will have to satisfy the requirement that black American Muslims be included among those who contribute to the conferring of universal or Western status. So far, however, this has rarely proved to be the case. Rather, more often than not, the "universal" appears to remain suspiciously close if not limited to the sensibilities and predilections of the dominant group.

To take just one example, the Sudanese immigrant reformist 'Abdullahi An-Na'im declared Islamic law to be in violation of universal human rights because of its allowance of polygyny. This, notes An-Na'im, goes against Article 1 of the 1979 International Convention on the Elimination of All Forms of Discrimination against Women, to which Muslim countries (he focuses on Egypt) are a party.[6] Lest he be mistaken for a legal positivist (who takes the right or power to issue law rather than law's substance as the source of its legitimacy) An-Na'im is careful to point out that a woman's right to equal consideration in this regard derives its authority not from treaties or agreements but from its status as a universally recognized value: "It is not suggested that the given rights are accepted as universal simply because they are recognized as such by the documents. Rather, the rights are recognized by the documents because they are universal human rights, that is, rights to which every human being is entitled by virtue of being human."[7]

We shall ignore for the moment that, although this statement appeared in 1990 (which means that An-Na'im actually wrote it a year or so earlier), the *Multilateral Treaties Deposited with the* [UN] *Secretary General* in 1989 indicated that only ninety-four of the 165 UN members had signed the treaty in question.[8] We shall also ignore An-Na'im's explicit admission of Egypt's reservations regarding the potential impingement of this agreement on its right to conduct its affairs in accordance with Islam.[9] More to the point, if *inequality* between men and women is both the source of the violation and An-Na'im's real concern, this should be remedied not by banning polygyny, since Islam only allows and does not require it, but by *allowing* polyandry, which on An-Na'im's approach should be no more difficult than the former option.[10] The latter option, however, is never even contemplated, which suggests that the universal value of equality is not at all an end but rather a *means* to an end, which is to bring Muslim life into conformity not simply with universal values but with very specific concretions of these values by the dominant civilization.[11]

An-Na'im is representative, however, of a class of modern Muslim reformists who are adamant and unabashed in their insistence that Muslim tradition, specifically its legal and jurisprudential dimensions, is the cause of rather than solution to the problem of Islam's maladjustment to the modern world. In this capacity, he is likely to exercise little influence among black American Muslims or even the masses of non-black American Muslims whose thinking he purportedly seeks to reform. September 11 has brought into sharper focus, however, another school of Muslim reform, namely the American Muslim romantics. In contradistinction to the modernist reformists of the An-Na'im variety, American Muslim romantics begin with Muslim tradition as the repository of all that is beautiful, civilized, and responsible. Tradition, in their thinking, is not the antithesis of modernity but rather of Muslim nontradition, which, as the product of postcolonial decadence and brutality, is the source of all that is wrong and stifling in modern Islam.[12] It is nontradition, for example, that lay behind the tortured interpretations and murderous deeds of Usāmah b. Lādin and his ilk. In the view of American Muslim romantics, not only is tradition inherently superior to nontradition, it is only tradition that can provide the antidote to the kind of stultifying interpretive madness that abounds in modern Islam.

In a forthcoming book, *Islam and the Black American,* I too, as a neo-traditionalist and not a romantic, argue that Muslim tradition holds the greatest promise for the future of Islam in America. The great promise of tradition resides, however, precisely in its ability to accommodate and, indeed, authenticate multiple, even mutually contradictory interpretations and expressions of Islam. From this perspective, tradition is emphatically opposed to any effort at artificially fordizing Muslim doctrine or practice or reducing these to any single expression. Under the pressure of post-9/11 anti-Muslim mania, however, American Muslim romantics have turned to tradition as a means of "compressing" Islam into a single-minded commitment to one or another moral or aesthetic vision, categorically denying or affirming this or that contemporary "vision of the truly Islamic." This enterprise often entails both an appeal to the dominant culture and the invocation of a false universal. More importantly, it exposes tradition itself to being converted into a tool for "domesticating" Islam,[13] whereby the religion forfeits any ability to challenge the dominant culture and finds itself in a position where it can only support the latter.[14] To the extent, again, that this process equates "dominant" with "universal," those who are or perceive themselves to be disadvantaged by the dominant culture will be called on to acquiesce, this time in the name of Muslim tradition, and accept such disadvantage as both normal and normative—indeed, Islamic. This is the great liability posed by American Muslim romanticism. And it is essentially this liability that the remainder of this essay will seek to address.

On the Ubiquity of the False Universal

Among the charges levied against Muslims who complain about false universals is that their real aim is to insulate and place beyond critique the kind of wrong-mindedness that denied Afghan women the opportunity for an education or that prompted the vicious attacks of 9/11. The insinuation here is that these Muslims view any effort to reassess or critique Muslim thought or practice as an unjustified attempt to appease if not "sell out" to the West, equating virtually all such critical activity with buying into the West's false universals. Contrary to this insinuation, however, the charge of invoking the false universal is not at all limited to those who seek to "project the West's truth onto the Islamic tradition."[15] For there is also an "East's truth" that is habitually "projected onto the Islamic tradition." At bottom, the inclination to resort to false universals is not exclusively a manifestation of pro-Western bias. It is born, rather, of a fundamental fear and recognition that *no* system of open intellectual exchange can guarantee the emergence or suppression of any particular view. Given the need to provide ironclad assurances to non-Muslim Americans in the aftermath of 9/11, the indeterminacy of the sources of Islam and the unreliability of its processes for negotiating doctrine have translated into significant liabilities for American Muslim romantics. In this context, the appeal to supposedly universal values is ultimately an attempt to circumvent the unpredictability of open debate. Ironically, it is precisely this tendency that Muslim romantics (rightly) condemn in their "extremist" and "fundamentalist" coreligionists.

Even before 9/11, Middle Eastern Muslims of all stripes had taken to the habit of presenting the part as the whole in order to be able to preempt views that lay outside the boundaries of their imagination or experience.

The American flag quickly became a symbol for remembering September 11,
as in this display of toy cars and trucks in a Park Avenue store window in New York.
September 2001. Photo by Simin Farkhondeh.

American flags were featured prominently in September 11 memorial displays, such as this one at a New York City fire station. September 2001. Photo by Stacy L. Howell.

In November 2001, a building in Manhattan was covered with a gigantic American flag.
Photo by Barbie Leung.

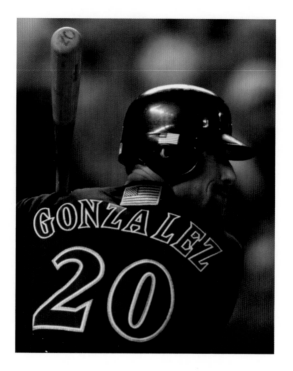

People wore and displayed American flags to remember September 11.
Major league baseball players wore the flag on their uniforms and helmets
during the first game to be played after the professional baseball season was
halted for one week following September 11. September 17, 2001.
Copyright Reuters NewMedia Inc./CORBIS.

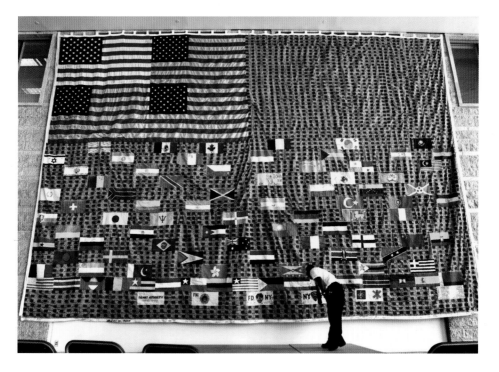

A flag displayed in Ottawa, Canada, composed of 3,000 small American flags,
featured flags of all nations that lost citizens in the September 11 attacks. September 4, 2002.
Copyright Reuters NewMedia Inc./CORBIS.

More than 3,000 people formed a human American flag on
Queensland's Surfer's Paradise Beach in Australia. September 11, 2002.
Copyright Reuters NewMedia Inc./CORBIS.

The flag took on new and contested meanings as the United States advocated a war against Iraq. A veteran waved an American flag in support of troops as the USS *Boxer* departed from San Diego for the Middle East. January 17, 2003. Copyright Reuters NewMedia Inc./CORBIS.

As war broke out, the American flag was a prominent symbol in antiwar protests
around the world. Some protesters changed the stars into a peace symbol,
while others burned the flag, as in this antiwar protest at the
Polytechnic University of the Philippines in Manila. February 27, 2003.
Copyright Reuters NewMedia Inc./CORBIS.

While the negative consequences of this practice fell almost exclusively on non–Middle Eastern Muslims, this did not render the practice itself any less an exercise in invoking a false universal. Nor did it render it any less of an effort, to quote one Muslim romantic, to position oneself as the guardian "of integrity and authenticity, while positioning [one's] opponents as gullible and even simple-minded."[16] Yet, while this was clearly not an effort to impose the West's truth onto the Islamic tradition, it does not follow that it owed nothing to the hegemonic impact of the West.

The early encounter between the modern West[17] and the Muslim world bequeathed to the latter both a new ideological tool and a new disease. This was the habit, ultimately defensive, of thinking and speaking in universals, according to which only that which is universally true is true at all, and all that is true (or useful) must also be "Islamic." In fact, the very neologism "Islamic" (itself virtually unknown in premodern times) emerged in part out of the early modern Muslim desire to parallel the European commitment to a specifically Western identity. In other words, if the achievements of Darwin, Descartes, and Hegel now reflected an ideological *and* an ethnic/geographical provenance, so would those of Ibn Sina (Avicenna), Ibn Rushd (Averroës), and Sinān. The resulting "*Islamic* medicine," "*Islamic* philosophy," and "*Islamic* architecture" reflected thus not simply the genius of persons presumably inspired by Islam but also of persons who hailed from a particular part of the world. As scholars such as Janet Abu-Lughod pointed out, there was nothing particularly "Islamic" about philosophical principles or architectural motifs taken over from the Greeks or Byzantines.[18] Nor, as Marshall Hodgson observed, was there much logic in applying the term "Islamic" to ideas and activities that were patently banned by the religion.[19] But its ability to elevate the achievements of Muslims to the level of a civilization rivaling that of Europe, alongside its utility as a mechanism for converting Middle Eastern ways and preferences into normative institutions for Muslims everywhere, rendered the neologism "Islamic" irresistible and secured for it a permanent place in the lexicon of modern Islam.

Throughout the twentieth century, however, the right to define the "Islamic" remained almost the exclusive prerogative of Muslims in the "Muslim world," or, more precisely, the Middle East. September 11, however, brought Muslim émigrés to the West into the act. Today, often acting on their own "Islamic" version of the "white man's burden," "liberal" Middle Eastern Muslim immigrants routinely affirm that "true" Islam is fundamentally tolerant, committed to gender equality and opposed to violence. Their "extremist" counterparts will challenge all of this and insist that "the Islamic" and "the Western" are mutually incompatible. Ultimately, however, what lurks beneath the surface of both of these approaches is a commitment to the view that Islam is an immutable, ahistorical abstraction that can only be represented, in all its aspects, by categorical, universally applicable declarations.

To be sure, there is nothing unique about religious newcomers arguing in this fashion over the proper relationship between their religion and America's dominant culture. Writing of German and Irish Catholics in the nineteenth century, for example, Sydney Ahlstrom notes: "Inevitably, the largest [group] was a traditional party that assumed Catholicism and the American way of life to be fundamentally at odds. Pope Pius IX with his detailed Syllabus of Errors (1864) had provided support for such a stand, and Leo XIII, surprisingly, would bolster this support in the 1890s. All that conservative Catholics hoped for, therefore, was a kind of mutually advantageous truce between two hostile cultures. Most militant in this regard were the Germans."[20]

At the other end of the spectrum was a group of Irish-American Catholics, including men like Archbishop John Ireland, who, at the Plenary Council of 1884, loudly proclaimed, "There is no conflict between the Catholic Church and America. I could not utter one syllable that would belie, however remotely, either the Church or the Republic, and when I assert, as I now solemnly do, that the principles of the Church are in thorough harmony with the interests of the Republic, I know in the depths of my soul that I speak the truth."[21]

What is noteworthy in the case of Muslim immigrants, however, is their attempt to subsume Old *and* New World realities simultaneously under a single articulation of Islam. These articulations are far less dependent, moreover, on a set of texts or a particular hermeneutic tradition than they are on a "vision of the truly Islamic," which is both prior and exterior to revelation. Ultimately, it is the conflation of these historically informed visions with ahistorical revelation[22] that metamorphoses into a false universal, converting time- and space-bound expressions of Islam into binding and normative models for Muslims everywhere. The universally normative status imputed to these "derivations" both embodies and perpetuates the new hegemony: history internalized, normalized, and then forgotten as history.

Let me share here a concrete example of how this hegemony works. In response to certain misgivings born of their interactions with a group of American converts, a group of Middle Eastern Muslims who had settled in the United States decided to seek clarity from a Muslim cleric "back home." They introduce their question in the following terms:

We are among the Arab Muslims who have lived in North America for a number of years. God the Exalted has blessed us to be involved in Islamic work dealing with Muslims of all nationalities, colors and classes. Among us are Arabs; and among us are Indians and Pakistanis; among us are Malaysians and Africans; and among us are Americans, both black and white. From time to time, we are confronted with questions for which there are no precedents in our Arab and Muslim lands. Many of these questions are posed by our American brothers and sisters. And some of them are connected with the issue of sexual relations between men and women, including things that are common to this environment and have become a part of this people's lives and are deeply ingrained in their customs. Among these are such questions as [the permissibility of] stripping naked when having sex, or [the permissibility of] a man looking at his wife's private parts or a woman looking at her husband's. There are other questions of this nature, which we are too embarrassed to mention publicly, including questions about various means of arousing a man or woman sexually, it apparently being the case that widespread explicitness, nudity and promiscuity has brought a certain frigidity upon this people who now need arousers and aphrodisiacs for which we have no need in our Arab and Muslim lands. Now, it has been our habit to respond to these questions by flatly proscribing and forbidding [all of these things], based on what had settled in our minds in the way of statements and traditions that we heard from popular preachers, not religious scholars [back in our Arab and Muslim lands].[23]

Clearly, the presumption here is that the precedent in "Arab and Muslim lands" is not only dispositive but *universally* so. Muslim realities outside this religious "homeland" are to be dealt with not directly but analogously based on this universally valid "Islamic" norm. On this understanding, the reference point for all that is "Islamic" is neither a particular set of verses nor a particular set of legal texts, nor even a particular interpretive method. It is rather the history and experience of a particular people in a particular time and in a particular part of the world. This is rendered no less so by the fact that these understandings are able to conceal their provenance in the inscrutable neologism "Islamic."

There is, of course, a bitter irony at work in all of this. In the name of preserving Islam and protecting it from the corrosive effects of a zeitgeist that seems to have fallen out of sympathy with the religion, the claim that the Prophet Muhammad was sent for all peoples, at all times and in all places, is utterly compromised. For, on this nativist construction, Muslims are rendered more authentic, indeed, more "Islamic," not by the deeds wrought or the doctrines taught but by the time, place, or authorship of the deeds and doctrines themselves. One can only imagine how the Muslim world would have responded had the recent Crown Prince Abd Allah Peace Initiative been proffered by a Senegalese, Indonesian, or white American Muslim. And, whereas no one would speak today of a "Christian diaspora," not even Catholics looking to the Holy See from the deepest jungles of the Amazon, Muslims who hail from or belong to communities outside the Middle East are routinely considered diasporic. These "diasporic Muslims" are seen, and often see themselves, as followers of, rather than bona fide adherents to, a religion whose true understanding and manifestation are located in another time and place. Ultimately, it is not revelation but the experience of this time and place with which diasporic Muslims must reconcile their expressions of Islam if these are to be considered truly "Islamic."

For their part, American Muslim romantics are quite familiar with the manner in which "fundamentalists" and "Muslim nativists" in the Muslim world pass off their "postcolonial" vision and experience for objective readings of scripture and/or tradition.[24] This, indeed, is the mechanism via which the latter often deny both the modern and the Western any presumption of legitimacy and dismiss those suspected of being in sympathy with the latter as being either insufficiently "Islamic" or guilty of "selling out." It appears, however, that it is often only the *substance* of the fundamentalists' "Islamic" that is problematic for the romantics, not the fact of their abstracting a historically informed vision to the level of a universally valid (or invalid) norm. For, in the end, romantics also appear to be driven by a historically informed "vision of the truly Islamic," which they seek to raise to a universal standard for all Muslims.

The False Universal and "Designer Fundamentalism"

If, through the apotheosis of its historical experience and the resulting invocation of a false universal, the Muslim world is able to exercise a certain power of validation over its coreligionists in the West, the latter's attempt to validate their articulations through an identical process is no less hegemonic in its implications. While Western Muslim advocates of reform, and more specifically Muslim romantics, passionately aver their commitment to an Islam that is tolerant, nonviolent, and egalitarian, their effort to validate such an Islam routinely includes a combination of fictions and false universals that ultimately makes it impossible either to establish or sustain such a tolerant, pluralistic religion. For, at bottom, Muslim romantics tend to grant the time, place, and experience of modernity and the dominant culture of the West the same universal validity that their opponents tend to attribute to premodernity and the East.[25] In the end, their approach includes a subtle civilizing mission that aims at obliterating one historical consciousness, without altering the history that produced it, in favor of another historical consciousness, without recognizing and critically analyzing the history behind it.

Let me be clear about something here. I share with the romantics their commitment to any number of concrete views and general principles: I condemn(ed) the attacks of September 11, whether they were committed in the name of jihad or on any other justification;[26] I deplore the "intellectual terrorism" visited on those Muslims who have had the courage to hazard novel or dissenting views; I have been critical of uncritical appropriations of tradition; I agree that the interests of Muslim women are often ignored and that women are often denied rights that are recognized as God-given on even the most traditional readings of Islam; and I too have my issues with Wahhābīs and Salafīs, among others.[27] But I disagree—strongly—with my romantic coreligionists on at least two counts: (1) the manner in which they use history or tradition to substantiate their claims and characterizations; and (2) their lack of attention and commitment to an independent *methodology* on the basis of which those who do not share their interests, experiences, or cultural presuppositions could verify and authenticate those interpretations whose validity and "Islamicity" are presumably so painfully clear. These shortcomings reflect the fact that the romantics' approach is grounded in and seeks to promote a false universal. It is a chic, prestigious, and powerful universal; but it remains nonetheless, *qua* universal, patently false. Steeped in this false universal, romantics often end up engaging in a highly sophisticated form of "designer fundamentalism," which, however seductive, can neither promote nor accommodate true pluralism or tolerance.

History or his story? Romantics habitually contrast their approach to that of the "fundamentalists" by grounding their critique of the latter in the pluralistic, egalitarian, aesthetically vibrant tradition of classical Islam. While this is generally the beginning of the romantic project, it is rarely maintained with consistency. On the contrary, the classical tradition serves more often than not as a means of enlisting an initial presumption of legitimacy and credibility. Once this is achieved, the excesses (and even failures)[28] of the classical tradition are glossed over, and its commitment to true pluralism and tolerance is abandoned in favor of a false universal.

While romantics are quick to intimate the strengths and advantages of the classical tradition, that is, as an alternative to modern "fundamentalism," they are rarely so forthcoming regarding its limitations. By "limitations," I am referring in this context to one thing: the classical tradition's commitment to procedure over substance and its resulting willingness to countenance all manner of substantively repugnant views as long as these were derived (or authenticated) through proper and recognized procedures. This impeded both the speed and the degree to which repugnant views could be banished and denied the opportunity to "infect" the community. At the same time, it ensured, *ceteris paribus,* that the only views that could be imposed on the community as a normative code of behavior were those that had been substantiated and ratified by mutually recognized methods of interpretation. Fear of authoritarianism was offset by a basic acceptance and understanding that while the purpose of adducing any argument was precisely to reduce adversaries to silence, silence could only be *imposed* through the agency of what constituted for Muslims a "true universal," namely the unanimous consensus of the recognized community of interpreters. Fear of authoritarianism was also diminished by the fact that premodern Muslim society was not home to a culture that equated freedom or liberty with the ability to go about one's business "unmolested" by opposing views.

Early in its theological development, Sunni Islam embraced a doctrine of Prophetic infallibility (*iṣmat al-anbiyā'*).[29] According to this doctrine, the Prophet Muhammad, like all prophets, was divinely protected from committing errors of interpretation. In the context of the competition among the various interpretations of the religion, the most operative feature of this doctrine was actually its corollary, namely that *only* the Prophet was immune to interpretive error. On this understanding, from the time of the Prophet's death up to the Coming of the Hour, no *individual,* not even the Caliph, would be able to claim interpretive infallibility. Rather, this status passed to the interpretive *community* as a whole, that is, the jurists, and was manifested in its so-called *ijmā'* or unanimous consensus. On this principle, only those interpretations on which there was unanimous consensus among the community of recognized jurists were binding on the entire community. Where unanimous consensus could not be reached and there was disagreement, the various disputed views simply had to be left standing. For, again, in the absence of the infallible Prophet (or any other infallible individual), there was no legitimate, and certainly no objective, basis on which to make the claim that one view was correct to the exclusion of all others.[30]

This synergy between Sunnism's doctrine of Prophetic infallibility and the juridical principle of unanimous consensus (*ijmā'*) constituted in effect classical Islam's "free speech" provision. As long as an advocate's view was grounded in authentic and authoritative sources and based on recognized interpretive methods, no one could deny him the right to express it—regardless of its substance—as long as it did not violate a preexisting unanimous consensus. Concomitantly, while there might be many views that could justifiably claim to represent *an* "Islamic" position, the only views that could claim to represent *the* "Islamic" position were those that were backed by unanimous consensus.

This was the ideological template that sustained the hyperpluralism and "constructive chaos" of classical Islam's golden age. Depending on the perspective and presuppositions of the individual interpreter, the agreed-on sources and methodologies could sustain an embarrassingly broad range of lamentable, dangerous, or even downright repulsive views. Thus, for example, al-Shāfi'ī, eponymous leader (often referred to as founder) of one of the four Sunni schools of law, held that if a man sired a female through an act of fornication or adultery, he could marry her because she was legally not his daughter![31] Abū Ḥanīfa (eponymous leader of another orthodox school) held that if a man (or woman) presented false evidence affirming marriage to a woman (or man) and a judge accepted this, this man could cohabitate with this woman despite his (and/or her) knowledge that no marriage had taken place![32] Mālik (eponym of a third orthodox school) is reported to have held that while under normal circumstances a valid marriage required the agency of a male relative to represent the bride, this could be relaxed under certain conditions, such as when the woman was of lowly origins, was "unattractive," or was black![33]

The romantic implication, thus, that "extreme" or substantively repugnant views are the exclusive preserve of modern "fundamentalist" interlopers who are insufficiently trained in or committed to the classical tradition cannot sustain scrutiny. Nor can such claims as those to the effect that the classical jurists unanimously supported aesthetically vibrant expressions of Islam. In point of fact, the overwhelming majority of them categorically proscribed music, most of the plastic arts (drawing, painting, sculpture), and even the artistic embellishment of mosques (*zakhrafat al-masājid*). Nor, as we have seen, can it be claimed that premodern Muslim jurists were universally committed to gender or racial equality. In fact, the only major claim of the romantics regarding the classical tradition that can be sustained on the historical record is the claim that premodern Islam was emphatically pluralistic and tolerant. Here, however, it must be recognized that the values of pluralism and tolerance could only be concretized by a parallel willingness to pay the price that such an enterprise inevitably incurred. Insincere, wrong-minded, and even repugnant views could not be simply stamped out or interdicted; nor could they be "shamed" away through loud and categorical denials of their "Islamicity"; nor, indeed, could they even be condemned through appeals to vague and malleable notions such as "beauty" or "morality."[34] Infelicitous views could only be displaced through the production of other views that showed integrity to agreed-on sources and methods and were broader and deeper in their appeal within the interpretive community. In this context, the entire system turned on both a willingness to throw one's views into competition with those of others *and* to accept the results of this unpredictable enterprise.

This is the manner by which entire orthodox schools of law were literally ushered out of existence. The Ẓāhirite school, for example, refused to accept analogy (*qiyās*) as a method of extending scripture to cover unprecedented circumstances. After an initial success of a few centuries, social evolution reached the point where this approach could no longer respond effectively to change. The Ẓāhirites went the way of the dinosaur. In a similar fashion, the aforementioned view of Mālik regarding black women fell into oblivion among the followers of his school in sub-Saharan Africa. In fact, the Mauritanian jurist al-Shinqīṭī cites Arabic poetry in praise of the beauty of *les dames noires*.[35] Meanwhile, later Shāfi'ī jurists would jettison the view of their eponym by arguing that it was based on a presumption of uncertainty about the child's paternity (given the implied moral laxity of the mother). Where there was certainty, these jurists argued (in agreement with all the other schools) that it was flatly forbidden for a man to marry his daughter.[36]

In sum, all was neither beautiful nor egalitarian nor even what many would consider "civilized" in premodern Islam. Romantic appeals to this legacy (for a description of which Western audiences are at their revisionist mercy) are often thoroughly misleading. While Muslims like to think of classical Muslim civilization as inherently good and only accidentally evil, like all human constructions, it included its share of both qualities, certainly by modern standards. As such, contrary to the insinuation of the romantics, we will search in vain in the manuals of the ancients for answers that satisfy our every sensibility. For theirs was simply another time. And it was *their* time, not ours, out of which they sought to carve a meaningful and dignified existence.

If the Muslim ancients are to be credited with anything (in this context) it should be that they were patient and willing to allow the mechanisms for tolerance and pluralism to run their course. The great liability in their system, of course, was that bad and dangerous ideas and interpretations could be picked up and spread like a virus throughout society. But in the absence of a church and given the synergy between the doctrine of Prophetic infallibility and unanimous consensus, this was simply a liability that would have to be absorbed. In the second century (eighth CE), the great Meccan scholar Ṭāwūs was noted for refusing to attend weddings between a black and a white, considering this to be "unnatural," an act of "changing God's creation," on his rendering of Qur'ān 4:119.[37] In the year 659/1261, however, the Egyptian historian Shafi' b. 'Alī reports that a black man appeared in Cairo claiming to be a member of the 'Abbasid house. Amid great fanfare, his genealogy was confirmed and, taking the name "al-Mustanṣir," this black man joined the ranks of the Prophet's most prominent companions, Abū Bakr, 'Umar, 'Uthmān, and 'Alī, and was inaugurated caliph, *amīr al-mu'minīn!*[38] The opinion of Ṭāwūs remained on the books, could have caught on, and can still be accessed today. But, in its best tradition, premodern Islam's open competition summarily banished the attitude of Ṭāwūs to the ideological margin.

9/11 and the need to appease the West. It is perhaps the greatest of all tragedies to befall modern Muslim societies that the kind of confidence that classical Islam exhibited in the process of open debate has faded among Muslims everywhere—including romantics. Instead, substance has become everything, and without the guarantee that this or that particular substance will emerge, none of the competing parties are willing to gamble on process. This has been compounded by the events of September 11, which have engendered a heightened sense of urgency and a feeling among Muslims in the West that they simply cannot afford to allow certain views to be associated with Islam. For, at the very least, they fear, the Islamophobes will seize on these views as proof that "real" Islam, that is, before the age of apology, is woefully out of step with modern sensibilities and a threat to world peace.

Given the present climate, such fears are understandable. Indeed, for many Muslim Americans, not only has Big Brother arrived, he has arrived invoking a double standard frightfully close to that of the "fundamentalists." President George W. Bush can proclaim Islam to be a "great religion," and nobody reminds him that the New Testament proclaims Christ to be *the* way. Paul Wolfowitz can say that the war in Afghanistan is not a war against Islam, and neither Bill Maher, Bill O'Reilly, nor anyone else will blindside him with Deuteronomy 12:2–3: "You shall certainly destroy all the places where the nations whom you shall dispossess served their gods . . . you shall tear down their alters and dash in pieces their pillars."[39] But if a handful of Muslims blow up innocent people in New York or Tel Aviv, this is a direct and inevitable result of the Qur'ānic injunction to "slay them wherever you find them." And any attempt by Muslims to claim otherwise is dismissed as a duplicitous, on-the-spot rerendering of Islam. America can accept that the Jewish and Christian traditions have evolved beyond the point where every literal or medieval interpretation represents binding orthodoxy. But the American collective psyche is unprepared to grant the same recognition to Islam. The result is that Muslim Americans end up in the unenviable position of being damned if they do and damned if they don't. If they speak out, they are guilty of duplicity. If they remain silent, they are assumed to be in sympathy with terrorists.

At bottom, however, there is more behind the sense of desperation detected among Muslim Americans—particularly romantics—than the simple desire to assuage the fears of the American public or avoid the punitive arm of Attorney General John Ashcroft. The simple truth is that Western civilization is today the ascending one, and, as every Westerner knows instinctively, the "Phantom of the West" peers over the shoulder of every "non-Westerner" as s/he attempts to write his or her way out of the company of the primitive and into the ranks of the civilized. In this capacity, the West sits in judgment over everyone who seeks to make a claim to civilization. While the charge by Muslim extremists that all Muslim reformists are "sell-outs" is often a shorthand exercise in "intellectual terrorism," for Muslim reformists, including romantics, who live in the West and write largely to a *Western* audience to deny that they are trying to appease or appeal to the West is, to borrow the depiction of a medieval Muslim jurist, "like a blind man urinating on a roof, facing the people with his pudendum, and supposing that no one sees him, since he himself is incapable of seeing his own person."[40]

The problem with the Muslim romantics is not their attempt to appease the West. I, for one, cannot imagine what else one would expect Muslims in the West to do. Do not Muslims in China, Russia, or Arabia all seek to appeal to the sensibilities of their respective societies? Why should this be denied to Muslim romantics in the West? The problem, however, is that in many instances romantics attempt to appeal to the West through categorical arguments that are grounded in a false universal. Why should a black American Muslim whose parents, grandparents, and great-grandparents were systematically (even legally) denied access to a quality education be bound by categorical constructions of Islam's commitment to equality that preempt affirmative action? Why should a Palestinian mother who has watched her home crushed by bulldozers and lost three or four or five sons be bound by the claim by Muslims living comfortably in America that Islam renounces violence? Why should an African Muslim whose family structure will not accommodate illegitimate children and whose society is too poor to afford social welfare services be embarrassed by Western reactions to the Islamic punishment for adultery? Indeed, why should a poor Muslim widow and mother of four living in South-Central Los Angeles or North Philadelphia listen to a Muslim feminist in the top 3 percent income bracket condemning and belittling polygyny as both a personal *and* an Islamic option?

The fact of the matter is that in every one of these cases (with the exception of affirmative action)[41] there is strong scriptural evidence, massive juridical precedent, and agreed-on interpretive methodology to support the "traditional" view. And once deconstructed, even the interpretive methods of the romantics, if applied consistently, will show themselves to be capable of yielding these conclusions. But if this is true, then this must certainly jeopardize the romantic project. And it is here that we come to the very crux of the matter. If the indeterminacy of the sources and the free-speech provision of tradition make it impossible for "conservatives" and "fundamentalists" to sustain their absolutist claims, we can hardly expect these sources or tradition to evince qualities that would render the veracity of romantic interpretations any more incontrovertibly obvious. At bottom, the issue, strictly speaking, is not at all about "interpretation." The issue is rather about extrascriptural "visions" and presuppositions that are grounded in individual histories and experiences, and whose vindication, normativeness, or abnegation we seek to achieve via appeals to scripture.[42] In the end, *all* claims of categorical correctness are nothing less than attempts to privilege one history over all others.[43] And it is ultimately here that we are brought full circle back to the problem of the false universal.

Whose history? I could not agree more that it is just as often (if not more often) the "fundamentalists" who are unwilling to pay homage to process and throw their views into competition with those of their adversaries, choosing instead to resort to all manners of scholastic calumny and intellectual terrorism. As romantics themselves have intimated, it is an unfortunate but undeniable fact that the religious consciousness of large segments of modern Muslim society has suffered massive atrophy. In fact, I would go so far as to say that the truth that many "fundamentalists" seek today is not at all the truth of Muhammad. It is, rather, another truth, one that "hurries on the break-up of the [post-]colonialist regime; it is that which promotes the emergence of the nation; it is all that protects the natives, and ruins the foreigners. In this . . . context there is no truthful behavior: and good is quite simply that which is evil for 'them.' "[44]

In "this context," the modern "fundamentalist" Muslim functions as a replica of Franz Fanon's "oppressed person whose persistent and permanent dream is to become the persecutor."[45] At bottom, it is "this context" that informs the "fundamentalist" "vision of the truly Islamic." And it is ultimately this context, far more than any particular set of texts or systematic method of interpolation, that renders acceptable to him only those articulations of Islam that conform to this vision.

It is precisely here, however, that we come to the Faustian divide. For if this is really "the context" that defines the modern Muslim world and explains the mentality and vision of the "fundamentalists," then we must admit that their social, political, and historical context is patently different from our own. But if this is true, we must ask by what authority, other than our own interests, we call on them to enter into a "virtual reality" in which they seek to interpret and draw meaning from religion through an existential prism other than the one that informs their lives. Is not the entire romantic project itself an attempt to privilege our modern, Western historical context over that of the ancient Easterners? If so, why should this effort have a vertical application but not a horizontal one? Why should this be a privilege that only Muslim reformists in the West enjoy?

To be sure, the answers to these questions are as plain as they are lamentable. Muslim reformists deny the "fundamentalists" the right to indulge their own context because they believe the latter to be "wrong," passé, or irrelevant, while theirs is "right," relevant, and esteemed: the state should enjoy and exercise a monopoly over the use of violence and the promulgation of law (even if the state is lawless—or racially biased—and will only use violence to its own advantage). Women should not be forced to wear a *burqa,* a *chador,* or a *hijāb* (but they may be forced to remove them). Polygyny is demeaning and unfair to women (though loneliness and poverty are none of our business). Patriarchy is bad and the source of untold evil (but we will examine neither matriarchy nor androgyny as alternatives).[46] Scriptural literalism reflects weak-mindedness (even if literalist interpretations of the Qur'ān prove to be more liberating and empowering). All of this is obvious, of course, to everyone, save "the stupid, the primitive, and the morally depraved."

Alas, it seems that designer fundamentalists are no less committed to their false universal than are their no-frills fundamentalist counterparts.

Legal Discourse over Philosophical Discourse

Where, then, does all of this leave us? Are Muslim reformists in a post–September 11 West to remain silent in the face of extremist views and acts of violence emanating from the Muslim world? Are they not to disassociate themselves and their religion from such views and actions, even as these jeopardize their livelihoods and safety and perhaps the dignity of Islam? Even if the foregoing criticism aimed at false universals is accepted as valid, are there not *true universals* that would empower Muslims everywhere to speak on certain views and actions of Muslims anywhere?

Two points: First, from the perspective of Muslim tradition, there are indeed true universals—true *concrete* universals—to which all Muslims may be said to be bound. Traditionally, these were captured in the unanimous consensus (*ijmā'*) of the recognized community of interpretive specialists. From Spain to China, no Muslim could deny the obligation to offer the five daily prayers, to pay the poor-due, to eschew murder, consumption of pork, or illicit sexual relations. Unlike the modern universal, however, these universals were, in theory at least, the result of an attempt to *canvas* the opinions of the entire community of jurists rather than *abstract* the views of any one of them. In fact, it was precisely the difficulty of meeting this canvassing requirement that bolstered the argument of those—like the Spanish Zāhirite, Ibn Ḥazm (d. 456/1063)—who rejected unanimous consensus.[47] So central, however, was unanimous consensus to the religious order of premodern Islam that the Zāhirites' rejection of it contributed to their ultimate demise.

Second, unanimous consensus, like the entire religious order of classical Islam, was the product of a *legal* rather than a *philosophical* discourse. Legal discourses deal in concretes and are guided by the question, "What should be *done,* given a specific context and a specific set of facts?" By contrast, philosophical discourses deal in abstract universals and are guided by the question, "What is the universal and permanent truth of the matter?" Legal discourses can accommodate change and diversity across space and time, which is why jurists in Timbuktu could openly recognize that what they sanctioned might be legitimately proscribed in Spain or Nishapur. Philosophical discourses, on the other hand, can only accommodate change and difference by asserting the categorical incorrectness of the previous or competing view. Either the philosophy of Der-rida or that of Foucault, either the creed of the Mu'tazilites or that of the Ash'arites, is correct. Both cannot be simultaneously correct.

If the basic aim of the romantics is to disassociate themselves from views and actions of extremists in the Muslim world, this can be done by simply declaring that Muslims *in the West* reject and disagree with these views and actions. There is no need to make *categorical* statements about the status of these actions from the perspective of Islamic law, unless of course Islamic law itself speaks in categorical terms or there exists a unanimous consensus. Where the religious law admits of disagreement, Muslims in the West, especially those who claim allegiance to tradition, must simply acknowledge the right of their coreligionists to follow the dictates of their own interpretive efforts. Where these result in views that are harmful to the interests of Muslims in the West, the latter might simply inform their Eastern coreligionists that their *acting* on these views is likely to jeopardize the interests of their brothers and sisters in the West; or they might warn them that their acting on these views is likely to result in severe penalties in the way of retaliation by Western powers; or they might advise them that there are other, more effective means of addressing their concerns. By choosing, however, to ground their arguments in a legal rather than a philosophical framework, American Muslim romantics will be far less prone to making categorical claims that smack of false universals.

Let me try to give a brief example of this approach in action. As mentioned earlier, I condemned the terrorist attacks of September 11. This was based, however, on a unanimous consensus, dating all the way back to classical times, to the effect that targeting innocent civilians, Muslim or non-Muslim, is flatly forbidden under a law called *hirābah,* as I discussed in lectures delivered in 1999 and 2000.[48] This condemnation was grounded, in other words, not in a false universal but in a true one (at least for Muslims). On the other hand, in a later article, "Jihad and the Modern World,"[49] I argue that with the institutionalization of the new world order expressed in Article 1 of the UN Charter, there is no religious obligation on Muslims to engage in aggressive jihad. This I based on the fact that the premodern world was characterized by a "general state of war," in which the assumed relationship between neighboring communities was one of aggression. The UN Charter established, however, a "general state of peace," in which the territorial boundaries of all nations on earth were rendered inviolable. I pointed out, however, that this was all theoretical and that a factual assessment of the situation on the ground might yield mutually divergent conclusions. Some Muslims might agree that we now live in a peaceful world; others might insist on the continued presence of a "general state of war." On these two assessments, one party might argue that there is a duty to prosecute jihad, while the other party might argue that there is not. Both of these views, however, would have an equal prima facie claim to be "Islamic." Indeed, to deny either view this status would be to deny one of the parties the right to believe in their own minds and their own experiences.

To be sure, many will find this approach to be either too dangerous, too pragmatic, or both. But if the danger represented by this approach resides in its apparent willingness to countenance the violence that is likely to result from "fundamentalist" or "extremist" thought, we must certainly note that the approach of the romantics is no less preemptive of violence. For they can hardly hope, through their dismissive approach, to bring the "fundamentalists" over to their view of things. And to the extent that they are truly committed to nonviolence, Muslim romantics should take perhaps a little less solace than they do in the fact that the violence visited on the "fundamentalists" will not come from them but from armies of crisply uniformed men backed by rich and powerful governments.

As for the charge of crass pragmatism, we should be reminded that we are dealing here not simply with a moral issue but with a political-legal one as well. The above approach is consistent with the practice of every political-legal order in history, including the Islamic one. What a litigant believes he has a right to, even if that belief is backed by the authority of an orthodox school of law, is one thing; what a judge in a case *decides* he or she has a right to may be altogether different. This difference is recognized and maintained in order to be able to uphold both the political-legal order and the moral one, the latter suffering necessarily by the collapse or even damage of the former. Moreover, the value of freedom of conscience and preserving the right to *believe* as one sees fit must be given its due and be appreciated in the light of the Qur'ānic declaration that domination (literally from the Latin *dominari,* "to be lord of") "is worse than murder" (*al-fitnah ashaddu min al-qatl*).[50] In other words, avoiding the false universal, via which opponents are called on to recognize and give assent to beliefs that they neither feel nor value, is a higher value than guaranteeing them the right to act on every belief that they might come to possess.

Conclusion

Never before in the history of Islam have Muslims operated on a notion of a homeland versus a diaspora. Even the oft-cited *Dār al-Harb* (abode of war) became, according to many jurists, a *Dār al-Islām* (abode of Islam) by the mere fact that Muslims were able to live there without being forcibly detached from their religion.[51] Historically speaking, wherever Muslims were able to settle, that was considered their home. Even the Prophet himself, after settling the affairs of Mecca, following his triumphant return to his place of birth, went back to his adopted home in Medina, where he died and was laid to rest. Perhaps when Muslims who have migrated to the West are able to give up the idea of a homeland other than the one in which they live, they will be less susceptible to the seductive power of the false universal. For neither will they feel the need to speak for Muslims everywhere nor will they accept that Muslims who do not share (and hardly understand) their reality should speak for them. But even here it will have to be recognized that America itself is no more a monolith than is the global community. America's Muslims do not all hail from the same histories or experiences. And if American Islam is to be truly pluralistic, it will have to be bold and vigilant in its refusal to ignore or jettison any of these histories and experiences in favor of appeals to a false universal, no matter how chic, powerful, or expedient the latter may be. Meanwhile, the concept of "collective enterprises of good" can only inspire us all. But even this, if it is to avoid yet another, though no less treacherous, manifestation of the false universal, must show itself to have as much application to inner-city Chicago and Detroit as it does to the prestigious capitals and upscale suburbs of "the West" in general.

Notes

1. Indeed, I would argue, it has transcended its domestic domain and assumed international proportions. See W. E. B. Du Bois, *The Souls of Black Folk* (New York: Fawcett, 1961), 23.
2. On black religion see, e.g., Gayraud S. Wilmore, *Black Religion and Black Radicalism: An Interpretation of the Religious History of African Americans*, 3d ed. (New York: Orbis Press, 1999), 1–50; Joseph R. Washington, *Black Religion: The Negro and Christianity in the United States* (Lanham, Md.: University Press of America, 1984); C. Eric Lincoln, *Race, Religion, and the Continuing American Dilemma*, rev. ed. (New York: Hill and Wang, 1999), xviii–xxv, 52–59, and passim.
3. Richard Dyer, *White* (London: Routledge, 1997), 2. Dyer, incidentally, is emphatic in insisting on disclosing his identity as white.
4. Ibid., xiv.
5. I use quotation marks around Western here to highlight my belief that in most instances it is only the *dominant* culture in the West that is being referred to by the designation "Western," which excludes, for example, Native American, Hispanic, and black American cultures, even though they are every bit as Western as the dominant culture. This is a habit, incidentally, engaged in by Muslims and non-Muslims alike. Throughout this essay, this point should be observed wherever the term "Western" is used, though I will eliminate the quotation marks from here on.
6. 'Abdullahi An-Na'im, "Shari'a and Basic Human Rights Concerns," in *Liberal Islam*, ed. Charles Kurzman (New York: Oxford University Press, 1998), 232–33. Interestingly, An-

Na'im, a scholar trained in law, ignores the principle of unconscionability, according to which formally consensual agreements between parties divided by gross disparities in power are rendered invalid.

7. Ibid., 232.

8. See Theodor Meron, *Human Rights and Humanitarian Norms as Customary Law* (New York: Oxford University Press, 1989), 79 n. 1.

9. An-Na'im, "Shari'a," 233.

10. An-Na'im argues, following the lead of his teacher, the late Mahmoud Mohamed Taha, that the Medinan phase of the Qur'ānic revelation constituted a transitional stage that should be ignored in extracting directives for modern Muslim life. Muslims should rely only on the "fundamental and eternal message of Islam, as revealed in the Qur'ān of the Mecca period." See "Shari'a," 234–35.

11. I should make it clear that I do not believe that opposition to the principle or practice of polygyny, in any particular manifestation, is necessarily an act of privileging the dominant civilization. In her book, *Qur'an and Woman: Rereading the Sacred Text from a Woman's Perspective* (New York: Oxford University Press, 1999), Amina Wadud, a black American Muslim scholar, comes out strongly against the practice. This is based, however, at least as far as her arguments reveal, on a particular reading of the Qur'an and not on any appeal to purportedly universal values. For an interesting alternative view by a black American non-Muslim scholar, see Adrien Katherine Wing, "Polygamy from South Africa to Black Britannia to Black America: Global Critical Race Feminism as Legal Reform for the Twenty-first Century," *Journal of Contemporary Legal Issues* 11, no. 2 (2001): 811–80.

12. There are, to be sure, American Muslim romantics who vehemently hold modernity in contempt. They, however, shall not be the focus of this essay.

13. On the domestication of religion, Yale law professor Stephen L. Carter writes: "The domestication of religion is the process through which the state tries to move religion from a position in which it threatens the state to a position in which it supports the state." See Stephen L. Carter, *God's Name in Vain: The Wrongs and Rights of Religion in Politics* (New York: Basic Books, 2000), 30.

14. Lamenting American Christianity's forfeiture of its ability and duty to challenge the dominant culture, Stephen Carter writes: "So much of American religion today has become so culturally comfortable that one can scarcely find differences between the vision of the good that is preached from the pulpit and the vision of the good that is believed by the culture." Ibid., 185. Moreover, Carter adds, "If a religion wants to be just like everything else, it needs no guarantee of religious liberty." Ibid.

15. See Khaled Abou El Fadl, "9/11 and the Muslim Transformation," in this volume.

16. Ibid.

17. See note 5 above.

18. See Janet Abu-Lughod, "The Islamic City: Historic Myth, Islamic Essence, and Contemporary Relevance," *International Journal of Middle East Studies* 19 (1987): 155–76.

19. See Marshall Hodgson, *The Venture of Islam* (Chicago: University of Chicago Press, 1974), 1:56–60.

20. See Sydney Ahlstrom, *A Religious History of the American People* (New Haven: Yale University Press, 1972), 828.

21. Ibid., 835. Incidentally, the Germans were also convinced that Christianity could only be properly understood and conveyed by those who were versed in their native language and culture. Ibid., 830.

22. That is, ahistorical in the sense that Muslims believe it to originate with a transcendent God who is beyond history.

23. Y. al-Qaraḍāwī, *Fatāwā mu'āṣirah* (Beirut: al-Maktab al-Islāmī, 1421/2000), 2:383–84.

24. This is not the place to enter into a detailed discussion over the meaning of objectivity. For the moment, I shall go along with the definition suggested by Richard Rorty, according to

whom objectivity resides in "unforced agreement." See Richard Rorty, "Exploring Diversity and Postmodernity," in *The American Intellectual Tradition,* ed. David A. Hollinger and Charles Capper (New York: Oxford University Press), 2:390–400.

25. I should add in this context that significant aspects of black American culture might be considered "premodern," and thus Western in a way quite different from that of the dominant culture in the West. As Cornel West once observed, "The great paradox of Afro-American history is that Afro-Americans fully enter the modern world precisely when the postmodern period commences." See Cornel West, *Prophesy Deliverance! An Afro-American Revolutionary Christianity* (Philadelphia: Westminster Press, 1982), 44.

26. See the section of this essay headed "9/11 and the Need to Appease the West."

27. On some of these differences, see Sherman A. Jackson, *On the Boundaries of Theological Tolerance in Islam: Abū Ḥāmid al-Ghazālī's Fayṣal al-Tafriqa Bayna al-Islām wa al-Zandaqa* (New York: Oxford University Press, 2002).

28. For example, Professor Abou El Fadl criticizes the Wahhābīs and Salafabists as being "uninterested in history" and "uninterested in critical historical inquiry" (see Abou El Fadl, "9/11"). Yet the lack of historical consciousness, on the basis of which contemporary jurists would hold their societies to the outdated contents of centuries-old law manuals, despite the massive change and evolution that had befallen these societies, was an *endemic* problem in *premodern* Islam. See, e.g., Sherman A. Jackson, *Islamic Law and the State: The Constitutional Jurisprudence of Shihāb al-Dīn al-Qarāfī* (Leiden: E. J. Brill, 1996), 123–41.

29. For an informative introduction to this topic, see Shahab Ahmed, "Ibn Taymiyya and the Satanic Verses," *Studia Islamica* 87, no. 2 (1988): 67–124.

30. On unanimous consensus, see Muhammad Hashim Kamali, *Principles of Islamic Jurisprudence* (Cambridge: Islamic Texts Society, 1991), 168–97; Bernard G. Weiss, *The Search for God's Law* (Salt Lake City: University of Utah Press, 1992), 181–258; Jackson, *Islamic Law and the State,* xxvi–xxv.

31. See Abū Zakarīyah Muḥyī al-Dīn b. Sharaf al-Dīn al-Nawawī, *Kitāb al-majmū',* ed. M. N. al-Muṭī'ī (Cairo: Dār Iḥyā' al-Turāth al-'Arabī, 1415/1995), 17:324.

32. See Burhān al-Dīn Abū al-Ḥasan 'Alī b. Abū Bakr b. 'Abd al-Jalīl al-Rushdānī al-Marghīnānī, *al-Hidāya sharḥ bidāyat al-mubtadi'* (Cairo: Muṣṭafā al-Bābī al-Ḥalabī and Sons, n.d.), 1:195–96.

33. See Muḥammad al-Amīn al-Shinqīṭī, *Aḍwā' al-bayān fī īḍāḥ al-qur'ān bi al-qur'ān* (Beirut: Dār al-Kutub al-'Ilmīya, 1421/2000), 1:330.

34. See Sherman A. Jackson, "The Alchemy of Domination? Some Ash'arite Responses to Mu'tazilite Ethics," *International Journal of Middle East Studies* 31 (1999): 187–94. The appeal to morality is a common tactic among both reformists (e.g., of the An-Na'im persuasion) and Muslim romantics. For example, in his essay in this volume, Professor Abou El Fadl repeatedly refers to morality without ever defining it. This is a glaring omission, given his vast knowledge of Muslim history and his explicit mention of such intellectual movements as Mu'tazilism and Ash'arism, whose very call to arms included the classical debate over the sources and bases of morality. Mu'tazilites insisted that good and evil were ontologically objective realities that could be apprehended by reason independent of revelation. The Ash'arites retorted that there was no such thing as objective good and evil, that divine fiat was the only basis for moral judgments, and that one was wholly dependent, therefore, on revelation for knowledge of good and evil. Historically, the Ash'arites defeated the Mu'tazilites (following the latter's attempt to impose their creed via inquisition in the third/ninth century). As a result, "ethics," as a formal exercise in speculative rationalism, never took root in Islam. Professor Abou El Fadl gives the impression that scripturalism (the view that good and evil are simply what God says they are) is a modern invention of Salafabists and other extremists. In point of fact, however, scripturalism was the *dominant* order among Muslim jurists and theologians throughout the premodern period. If the claim is now that it is time to revert to a Mu'tazilite approach

to ethics, that is well and good. But this should at least be joined by a refutation of classical Ash'arism (and perhaps traditionalism). Otherwise, given the incumbency of scripturalism in Muslim tradition, it is difficult to know how Professor Abou El Fadl intends for those who remain committed to tradition to go about the business of thinking morally. For more on the Mu'tazilite/Ash'arite debate, see Jackson, "The Alchemy of Domination?" 185–201.

35. Al-Shinqītī, Aḍwā', 1:330.
36. See al-Nawawī, al-Majmū', 17:327.
37. See al-Shinqītī, Aḍwā', 1:330.
38. See Shafi' b. 'Alī, Ḥusn al-manāqib al-sirrīyah al-muntaza'ah min al-sīrah al-ẓāhirīyah, 2d ed., ed. 'A. Khowaytar (Riyadh: 1410/1989), 79.
39. In the days and weeks following September 11, 2001, it was a common occurrence for one or another Muslim spokesperson to appear on television and denounce both the attacks and the unwarranted targeting of non-Muslims, only to be gleefully blindsided by Qur'ānic verses splashed across the screen, "And slay them wherever you find them"! For a historically contextualized understanding of such verses, see Sherman A. Jackson, "Jihad and the Modern World," Journal of Islamic Law and Culture 7, no. 1 (2002): 1–26.
40. See G. Makdisi, ed. and trans., Ibn Qudāma's Censure of Speculative Theology (Kitāb taḥrīm al-nazar fī kutub ahl al-kalām) (London: Luzac, 1962), 33.
41. It is not that scripture and tradition do not support affirmative action but that the issue has not been dealt with by enough jurists to establish a precedent. For an exception in this regard, however, see Sherman A. Jackson, "Islam and Affirmative Action," Journal of Law and Religion 14, no. 2 (1999/2000): 405–31.
42. For more on the vindicating, as opposed to strictly interpretive, activity of interpreters, see Sherman A. Jackson, "Fiction and Formalism: Towards a Functional Analysis of Uṣūl al-Fiqh," in Studies in Islamic Legal Theory, ed. Bernard G. Weiss (Leiden: E. J. Brill, 2001), 177–201.
43. The exception being, of course, a substantiated claim of unanimous consensus.
44. Franz Fanon, The Wretched of the Earth, trans. Constance Farrington (New York: Grove Press, 1963), 50.
45. Ibid., 53.
46. For an ultimately failed but intellectually honest attempt to vindicate androgyny, see John Stoltenberg, The End of Manhood: Parables on Sex and Selfhood, rev. ed. (London: UCL Press, 1999) and Refusing to be a Man, rev. ed. (New York: Routledge, 2000).
47. See Ibn Ḥazm, al-Iḥkām fī uṣūl al-aḥkām, ed. A. M. Shākir (Beirut: Dār al-Āfāq al-Jadīda, 1403/1983), 3:147–51.
48. See Sherman A. Jackson, "Domestic Terrorism in the Islamic Legal Tradition," Muslim World 91, nos. 3/4 (2001): 293–310. This article was the published proceedings of two lectures delivered in 1999 and 2000, at the University of Michigan law school, and Georgetown University law school, respectively.
49. Jackson, "Jihad and the Modern World."
50. For more on this understanding of "fitna," see Jackson, "Islam and Affirmative Action," 411–19.
51. For example, the great Shāfi'ī jurist, Abū al-Ḥasan al-Māwardī (d. 450/1058), defined the abode of Islam as any land in which Muslims enjoyed security and were able to isolate and protect themselves, even if they were unable to promote the religion. See Abū al-Ḥasan al-Māwardī, al-Ḥāwī al-kabīr, ed. A. M. Mu'awwaḍ and A. A. 'Abd al-Mawjūd (Beirut: Dār al-Kutub al-'Ilmīya, 1414/1994), 14:104.

Smoke rose above Manhattan after two hijacked airplanes flew into the World Trade Center, causing the two towers to collapse. September 11, 2001. Photo by Stacy L. Howell.

The impact of a hijacked airliner collapsed a portion of the Pentagon.
September 12, 2001. Copyright Reuters NewMedia Inc./CORBIS

Mourners visited the empty field outside Shanksville, Pennsylvania,
where United flight 93 crashed, leaving messages, flags, crosses, and other objects
in a "temporary" memorial that remained standing a year later.
March 10, 2002. Copyright AFP/CORBIS.

Photographs and messages covered a memorial wall near ground
zero in New York, visited by thousands daily. May 29, 2002.
Copyright Reuters NewMedia Inc./CORBIS.

In New York, people expressed their grief by writing messages in
chalk at Union Square. September 13, 2001.
Photo by Simin Farkhondeh.

American flags were displayed to memorialize September 11.
Soon after the attacks, a mannequin in a window on New York's Fifth Avenue
held American flag. September 2001. Photo by Andrea Ades Vásquez.

Around the world, people grieved with Americans by leaving flowers and candles
at American embassies. In this display at the American embassy in Warsaw, the words
"We shall overcome evil" were written across the American and Polish flags.
September 14, 2001. Copyright Mosur Jakub/CORBIS SYGMA.

At ground zero, attention turned quickly to both the recovery of human remains and the removal of the rubble. September 19, 2001. Photo by James Lightfoot.

Thought by many to be sacred ground, ground zero became a round-the-clock worksite. December 27, 2001. Photo by Harry E. Pherson Jr.

By June 2002, the ground zero cleanup had been completed,
but the controversy over what to do with the site had barely begun.
June 16, 2002. Photo by Charles Vitale.

The Citizen and the Terrorist

LETI VOLPP

In the year following the terrorist attacks of September 11, 2001, there were more than 1,000 incidents of hate violence reported in the United States.[1] How do we understand this violence and in particular, its emergence in a context of national tragedy? What were the seeds of this violence, and how did the political climate following September 11 allow them to grow? Of course, there are no easy answers to these questions. I would suggest that September 11 facilitated the consolidation of a new identity category that grouped together persons who appear to be "Middle Eastern, Arab, or Muslim." The category of those who appear to be "Middle Eastern, Arab, or Muslim" has been socially constructed, like all racial categories, and is heterogeneous—persons of many different races and religions were attacked as presumably appearing "Middle Eastern, Arab, or Muslim."[2] What has solidified this identity category is a particular racialization, wherein members of this group have been identified as terrorists, and disidentified as citizens.

The stereotype of the "Arab terrorist" is not an unfamiliar one. But the ferocity with which multiple communities were interpellated as responsible for the events of September 11 suggests there have been particular dimensions converging in this racialization. I offer three: the fact and legitimacy of racial profiling; the redeployment of old Orientalist tropes; and our conception of the relationship between citizenship, nation, and identity.

On Racial Profiling

Before September 11, national polls showed such overwhelming public opposition to racial profiling that both U.S. Attorney General John Ashcroft and President George W. Bush felt compelled to condemn the practice. There was a strong belief that racial profiling was inefficient, ineffective, and unfair. Following the attacks of September 11, polls indicated a strong public consensus that racial profiling was not only a good thing, but necessary for survival.

In the months after September 11, there were at least six ways in which racial profiling was practiced against persons who appeared to be "Middle Eastern, Arab, or Muslim." First, over 1,100 noncitizens were swept up into detention within two months of the attacks. We do not know the cumulative total to date because the government stopped releasing this figure after November 8, 2001; estimates range up to as many as 2,000 persons in detention. The purported basis for this sweep was to investigate and prevent terrorist attacks, yet, one year after the attacks, only a tiny fraction of the persons arrested and detained have been charged with engaging in conspiracy or support of terrorism. An Immigration and Naturalization Service (INS) official admitted that more than half of those detained were picked up on immigration offenses so minor that the charges were similar to "spitting on the sidewalk." Most of those detained have been secretly deported. While the government refused to release the most basic information about these individuals—their names, where they were held, and the immigration or criminal charges filed against them—the public did know that the vast majority of those detained appeared to be Middle Eastern, Muslim, or South Asian. We knew, too, that the majority were identified to the government through suspicions and tips based solely on perceptions of their racial, religious, or ethnic identity.[3]

The U.S. Department of Justice also engaged in racial profiling in what was described as a dragnet—the conducting of more than 5,000 investigatory interviews of male noncitizens between the ages of eighteen and thirty-three from "Middle Eastern" or "Islamic" countries or from countries with some suspected tie to Al Qaeda, who sought entry into the country since January 1, 2000, on tourist, student, and business visas. These were called voluntary interviews, yet they were not free of coercion or consequences. The Department of Justice directed the U.S. Attorneys to have investigators report all immigration status violations to the INS, which included minor visa violations. Many noncitizens were detained or removed through the use of laws that were previously largely unenforced. As a result, for example, one student in Cleveland, Ohio, was criminally charged and indefinitely detained for telling the Federal Bureau of Investigation that he worked twenty hours per week, when he actually worked twenty-seven.

U.S. officials also announced the "Absconder Apprehension Initiative," whereby the Department of Justice targeted for removal those noncitizens who had already received final orders of deportation but had not yet left the country and who came "from countries in which there has been Al Qaeda terrorist presence or activity."[4] Thus, the government moved to the head of the list of an estimated 320,000 individuals with final orders of deportation those noncitizens of Middle Eastern or Muslim background. Here, selective enforcement constituted a form of racial profiling.

More recently, the Justice Department has required some 82,000 students, employees, and other men over sixteen years of age on temporary visas from twenty-five countries—with the exception of North Korea, all with predominantly Muslim populations—to report to the INS to be fingerprinted and photographed. Failure to comply renders one deportable; of those who did register, over 13,000 face deportation for being out of status. The program, called "Special Registration," applies to those with dual citizenship or nationality, which led the government of Canada to express grave concern about this treatment of its citizens. Nearly 1,200 people were detained in the first two months of the program's implementation. Among those detained were many who had properly applied for permanent residency whose papers were delayed because of INS backlogs. Critics charged that the requirements of the program would increase distrust within Arab and Muslim communities, and pointed out that putative terrorists were in any case unlikely to comply with reporting to the INS.

Airport officials, airlines, and passengers have also practiced racial profiling against those appearing to be "Middle Eastern, Arab, or Muslim." Many men have been kicked off airplanes because airline staff and fellow passengers have refused to fly with them on board, despite U.S. Department of Transportation (DOT) directives aimed at protecting the civil rights of passengers. Within one year after September 11, the DOT was investigating thirty-one complaints of passengers not allowed to board their flights. And President Bush has said that he would be "madder than heck" if investigators find American Airlines racially profiled his Arab American Secret Service agent in removing him from a flight to the Crawford ranch.

Lastly, since September 11, the general public has engaged in extralegal racial profiling in the form of over 1,000 incidents of violence: homes, businesses, mosques, temples, and gurdwaras firebombed; individuals attacked with guns, knives, fists, and words; women with headscarves beaten, pushed off buses, spat on; children in school harassed by parents of other children, by classmates, and by teachers.[5] We know of at least five people who have been killed since September 11 in incidents of hate violence: a Sikh Indian, killed in Mesa, Arizona; a Pakistani Muslim killed in Dallas, Texas; an Egyptian Coptic Christian, killed in Los Angeles, California; a Sikh Indian killed in Ceres, California; and an Indian Hindu killed near Dallas, Texas.[6]

These myriad attacks have occurred, despite President Bush meeting with Muslim leaders, taking his shoes off before he visited the Islamic Center in Washington, D.C., and stating that we must not target people because they belong to specific groups. His statements did little to disabuse people of their "common sense" understanding as to who is the terrorist and who is the citizen, fueled by the fact that the government has explicitly engaged in racial profiling in terms of its targets of our "war on terrorism." At issue as well is the government's rhetoric: President Bush and other top officials characterized the war against terrorism as a battle for "civilization"—indeed, a "crusade." While these officials occasionally acknowledged the heterogeneity of Muslim practices, the ideological effect of this rhetoric was the legitimation of the religious and modern imperative to eradicate either from without or within the forces of despotism, terror, primitivism, and fundamentalism, each of which were coded as Middle Eastern, Arab, and Muslim. Through these actions and these statements, the American public was instructed that looking "Middle Eastern, Arab, or Muslim" equals "potential terrorist."

Despite conventional legal understandings of public versus private and our doctrine of state action that restricts what we define as governmental conduct, we can conceptualize the actions of the U.S. populace, in the form of hate violence, as bearing a relationship to the explicit racial profiling by the government. As we know from the writings of Michel Foucault, we should understand power not as limited to the system of "Law-and-Sovereign" and located exclusively in the state, but as far more broadly dispersed, in a triangle of sovereignty, discipline, and government.[7] Power is "exercised from innumerable points, in the interplay of nonegalitarian and mobile relations."[8] Legal realism, a school of legal thought ascendant in the 1920s and 1930s, also taught us that the state is implicated in all purportedly private transactions. Simply because the state does not officially sponsor an activity does not mean that the state bears no relationship to that activity. In simultaneously advocating policies of color blindness for citizenry while engaging in racial profiling for noncitizens, and publicly embracing all religions, while particularly privileging Christianity, the administration has, in the name of democratic inclusion, disingenuously excluded. That an epidemic of hate violence has occurred within the context of "private" relations thus does not mean that such violence is without "public" origins or consequences.[9]

While the Oklahoma City bombing certainly led to enormous concern about the militia movement in the United States, there was little coalescence of a national identity in opposition to Timothy McVeigh's terrorist attack. In contrast, post–September 11, a national identity that was both strongly patriotic and multiracial became consolidated. The multiracial consolidation of what it means to be American was represented in a cartoon in which various persons marked on their T-shirts as African American, Irish American, and Asian American dropped their hyphenated identities, so that all by the second frame had become "American." This expansion of who is welcomed as American has occurred through its opposition to the new construction, the putative terrorist who "looks Middle Eastern." Other people of color have become "American" through the process of endorsing racial profiling.[10] While we should note that racial policing continues apace in all communities of color, and we can anticipate that this new multiculturalist national identity is a momentary phenomenon, whites, African Americans, East Asian Americans, and Latinas and Latinos are in a certain sense now deemed safe and not required to prove their allegiance. In contrast, those who inhabit the vulnerable category of looking "Middle Eastern, Arab, or Muslim," and who are thus subject to potential profiling, have had to, as a matter of personal safety, drape their dwellings, workplaces, and bodies with flags in an often futile attempt at demonstrating their loyalty.

Racial profiling only occurs when we understand certain groups of people to have indistinguishable members who are fungible as potential terrorists. The Timothy McVeigh analogy helps clarify the strangeness of the post–September 11 moment. Under the logic of profiling all people who look like terrorists under the "Middle Eastern" stereotype, all whites should have been subjected to stops, detentions, and searches after the Oklahoma City bombing and the identification of McVeigh as the prime suspect.[11] This did not happen because Timothy McVeigh failed to produce a discourse about good whites and bad whites, because the public conceptualized McVeigh as an individual deviant, a bad actor. His actions were not considered representative of an entire racial group. This is part and parcel of how racial subordination functions: to understand nonwhites as directed by group-based determinism but to see whites as individuals.[12] Racial profiling also did not happen because, as a white man, Timothy McVeigh was seen by many as one of "us"—as the *New York Times* suggested at that time, there was "sickening evidence that the enemy was not some foreign power, but one within ourselves."[13]

The ill-advised nature of racial profiling is highlighted by the case of Richard Reid, a British citizen with a white English mother and a black Jamaican father, who attempted to light an explosive in his shoes on a flight from Paris to Miami. He appears to have been recruited to the cause of Al Qaeda in a British prison. Or we could consider Jose Padilla, a U.S. citizen from Chicago, who converted to Islam in a Florida prison and who has been held without charges as an "enemy combatant" these many months. Reports of a French citizen killed in Afghanistan, who had been recruited while he was in the French army, indicated that an estimated 100–150 French citizens were fighting with Al Qaeda, in the form of a nouveau French foreign legion.[14] The recruitment in prison and the recruitment in the army, reminiscent of Timothy McVeigh, raise sharp questions about the military and prison industrial complex as sites of a particular identity formation. Moreover, these cases—along with the case of John Walker Lindh, a U.S. citizen variously dubbed the "American Taliban" or the "Marin Taliban"—belie the purported effectiveness of racial profiling: not all of those the U.S. government would charge as terrorists are persons who appear to be "Middle Eastern, Arab, or Muslim."

And these cases in addition belie what sadly does not also seem to be apparent: very few persons who appear to be "Middle Eastern, Arab, or Muslim" are terrorists. Many men who fall into this category have been subjected to questioning. One friend, a law professor, was profiled for reading too slowly in Newark Airport. He was working his way through Heidegger and was questioned because someone had apparently reported a "Middle Eastern–looking man" engaging in the suspicious activity of reading a book for an hour without turning the page. As Arundhati Roy has written, the world post–September 11 has seemed to follow the logic of "War is Peace, Pigs are Horses."[15] And reading Heidegger is considered a potential terrorist activity.

On Orientalist Tropes

Post–September 11, we have witnessed the redeployment of old Orientalist tropes. Historically, Asia and the Middle East have functioned as phantasmic sites on which the U.S. nation projects a series of anxieties regarding internal and external threats to the coherence of the national body.[16] The national identity of the United States continues to be constructed in opposition to those categorized as "foreigners," "aliens," and "others."

The postcolonial theorist Edward Said describes Orientalism as a master discourse of European civilization that constructs and polarizes the East and the West. Western representations of the East serve not only to define those who are the objects of the Orientalizing gaze, but also the West, which is defined through its opposition to the East. Thus, for example, the West is defined as modern, democratic, and progressive through the East being defined as primitive, barbaric, and despotic.[17] Similar discourses sustain American national identity. American Orientalism historically referenced North Africa, the Middle East, and Turkey, as well as East Asia. Collectively, and often indistinguishably, these regions have functioned as the "East" to America's democratic and progressive "West." September 11 gave this discourse new currency in relation to what are depicted as the barbaric regions of the world that spawn terror.

Rather than understand Orientalism as solely a creature of purported racial difference, it is important to point out that American Orientalism, like European Orientalism, is gendered. Historically, the status of women in need of uplift was a source of justification for Western colonization of regions of the world—in the words of critical theorist Gayatri Spivak, "white men saving brown women from brown men."[18] This idea was resuscitated during the aftermath of September 11. One of the stated justifications for American intervention in Afghanistan—made by both President George W. Bush and First Lady Laura Bush—was that Afghan women needed to be saved from the Taliban and Islamic barbarism. But long before the Feminist Majority Fund began campaigning on the issue of Afghan women, many women in Afghanistan had been starving and faced with violence not only because of the Taliban regime but also because of a long history of conflict in the region in which the Unites States had been deeply implicated.[19] We must remember where the Taliban came from, that U.S. administrations thought that religious fundamentalists made better anti-Communist fighters, and so supported the mujahideen who became the Taliban. There has been a complete elision of the U.S. role in creating conditions in Afghanistan in the closed circular link made between women's oppression, Taliban evil, and Islamic fundamentalism.[20] Saving women from purdah was propounded as a reason for bombardment, even while, ironically, the epidemic of hate violence in the United States led to the seclusion of many women identified as "Middle Eastern, Arab, or Muslim" who otherwise faced harassment and violence when they ventured outside their homes.[21] Furthermore, the long-term impact of the war on the "liberation" of the women of Afghanistan remains an open question—both with regard to Feminist Majority Fund concerns as to women wearing the burka and with regard to concerns about the impact of the war on consolidating fundamentalisms.

In part, the gendering of colonial and Orientalist discourses was achieved by collapsing non-Europeans and women into an undifferentiated field in which passion reigned, not reason. The East was understood as the site of passivity and irrationality, awaiting the conquest by the masculine and rational West. While this bifurcation simplifies the heterogeneity of the process of Orientalism, the sexualization and gendering of sites of U.S. intervention do shape the relationship of U.S. national identity to race, gender, and sex. We should understand nationalism to be constituted through the simultaneous interworkings of racism, sexism, and homophobia. Fliers circulated in New York City depicting Osama bin Laden being sodomized by the World Trade Center, with the caption "You like skyscrapers, bitch?"[22] Post–September 11 nationalist discourses reinscribe both compulsory heterosexuality and the dichotomized gender roles on which it is based: the masculine citizen-soldier, the patriotic wife and mother, and the properly reproductive family.[23]

In 1997 critical theorist Lauren Berlant presciently suggested that there was a coupling of the ideas of suffering and American citizenship.[24] National civic identity, post–September 11, was experienced as a trauma that conflated patriotism, suffering, and abhorrence for what was constructed as oppositional to "America." As legal scholar Muneer Ahmad has written, cases of hate violence before September 11—such as the murders of Matthew Shepard, a gay man tied to a wooden fence, and James Byrd, a black man chained to and dragged by a pickup truck— were deemed incomprehensible. In contrast, hate attacks after September 11 were understood as the result of displaced anger, the underlying sentiment with which most Americans, bound together through national suffering, agreed. Thus, Ahmad argues, the former were understood as crimes of moral depravity, but the post–September 11 attacks were understood as crimes of passion, whereby the passion was love of nation. Perpetrators of post–September 11 hate violence, then, were guilty not of malicious intent but of only misdirecting their anger, so that there was something of an understanding of these acts. This helps explain why many thought it their patriotic duty to engage in racial profiling in the form of hate violence. For example, the man arrested for the murder of Balbir Singh Sodhi, the Sikh Indian killed in Mesa, Arizona, reportedly shouted as he was arrested, "I stand for America all the way!" Mark Stroman, who was convicted of the murder of Vasudev Patel, and confessed to also killing Waquar Hassan near Dallas, Texas, held a small American flag during his sentencing, and stated, "I'm not a serial killer. We're at war. I did what I had to do. I did it to retaliate against those who retaliated against us."[25]

At the same time that the category of "loyal American" became, post–September 11, a broad and encompassing one, there was also great heterogeneity in terms of who was singled out as a potential terrorist. In particular, Sikh men, who are religiously mandated to wear turbans, were conflated with Osama bin Laden and have suffered significant violence. South Asian Americans were suddenly both subjected to racist attack and galvanized as a political community. As a response to such a heterogeneous racial interpellation, the claim of racial or religious misrecognition ("I'm not Muslim") rather than condemnation of violence regardless of its target, was both troubling and reminiscent of the actions of Chinese Americans who wore buttons during World War II that read "I'm Chinese, not Japanese," so they would not be targeted. Others importantly argued that this was a moment for constructing coalitions.

We can recognize enormous resonances in what happened to the treatment of Japanese Americans during World War II, whereby the fungibility of members of a racially defined community was considered to make it impossible to screen individually loyal citizens from enemy aliens. A few months after the terrorist attacks, the publisher of the *Sacramento Bee* attempted to deliver a graduation speech at Cal State Sacramento. Booed and heckled, she was unable to finish her speech about the need for the protection of civil liberties; when she wondered what would happen if racial profiling became routine, the audience cheered. Witnesses described the event as terrifying; the president of the faculty senate was quoted in the *New York Times* as stating, "For the first time in my life, I can see how something like the Japanese internment camps could happen in our country."[26]

And, in fact, a Gallup poll found that one-third of the American public surveyed thought that we should intern Arab Americans.[27] Viewed historically, the motivation for the internment of more than 120,000 Japanese Americans was fear of what we today might call sleeper cells. The fact that the Japanese Americans did not attack after Pearl Harbor was understood to mean that they were patiently waiting to strike and therefore must be interned. Japanese American internment constituted a pivotal moment in American Orientalism; the treatment of persons who appear to be "Middle Eastern, Arab, or Muslim" following September 11 constitutes another.

On Citizenship and Identity

The shift in perceptions of racial profiling has been grounded in the fact that those individuals profiled were not considered to be part of "us." Many of those racially profiled in the sense of being the targets of hate violence or being thrown off airplanes were formally citizens of the United States, through birth or naturalization. But they were not considered citizens as a matter of identity, in that they in no way represent the nation.

We can understand citizenship as made up of four distinct discourses: citizenship as formal legal status, citizenship as rights, citizenship as political activity, and citizenship as identity/solidarity, as identified by legal scholar Linda Bosniak.[28] Citizenship as formal legal status means who can possess national citizenship—in the United States, as differentiated from the noncitizen, or "alien," and granted through birth or naturalization. Citizenship as rights signifies the rights necessary to achieve full and equal membership in society. This approach tracks efforts to gain the enjoyment of civil, political, and social rights in Western capitalist societies. In the context of the United States, citizenship as rights is premised on a liberal notion of rights, and the failure to be fully enfranchised through the enjoyment of rights guaranteed under the Constitution is often described as exclusion or as "second-class citizenship." Citizenship as political activity posits political engagement in the community as the basis for citizenship, as exemplified both by republican theories that played a key role in the founding of American democracy and by a recent renaissance of civic republicanism. Lastly, citizenship as identity is usually conceptualized as the connection between the citizen and those others with whom one feels kinship and solidarity. But in focusing on the question of citizenship as identity, it is imperative to isolate two very different conceptualizations of this idea.

The prevalent idea of citizenship as identity focuses on the notion of what I consider citizenship as a form of inclusion. Citizenship as a form of inclusion starts from the perspective of the citizen who proceeds to imagine fellow members who are to be included in a network of kinship or membership—those with whom the citizen feels affective ties of identification and solidarity. I want also to suggest that we must think about a very different idea of citizenship as identity, which we could call citizenship as a process of interpellation. Citizenship as a process of interpellation starts from the perspective that power both subordinates and constitutes one as a subject. As critical theorist Judith Butler suggests, power not only presses on the subject from the outside but also forms the subject.[29] The focus, then, is not initially from the perspective of the citizen who decides who to include; it foregrounds, instead, the role of ideology in either including one as a citizen or excluding one from membership and then shifts to the standpoint of the subject.

For the idea of interpellation, I am relying on the work of the philosopher Louis Althusser. Depicting a scene in which the subject is hailed by an officer of the law, Althusser writes:

> Naturally for the convenience and clarity of my little theoretical theatre I have had to present things in the form of a sequence, with a before and an after, and thus in the form of a temporal succession. There are individuals walking along. Somewhere (usually behind them) the hail rings out: "Hey, you there!" One individual (nine times out of ten it is the right one) turns around, believing/suspecting/knowing that it is for him, i.e., recognizing that "it really is he" who is meant by the hailing. But in reality these things happen without any succession. The existence of ideology and the hailing or interpellation of individuals as subjects are one and the same thing.

As Althusser says, this is not a temporal process that takes place in sequence. It is instead how ideology functions: individuals are "always-already subjects" of ideology.[30]

Through positing an identity dimension of citizenship as a process of interpellation, I want to emphasize how certain individuals and communities are positioned as objects of exclusion. Imagine the hail, "Hey, you noncitizen!" (or foreigner, or enemy alien, or terrorist). This process of interpellation of those who appear to be "Middle Eastern, Arab, or Muslim" is taking place through the racial profiling by both government officials and the U.S. public. As the individual is hailed in this manner and recognizes the hail, he or she is transformed into a subject of ideology—here, the subject of nationalist ideology that patrols borders through exclusions.

In the American imagination, those who appear "Middle Eastern, Arab, or Muslim" may be theoretically entitled to formal rights, but they do not stand in for or represent the nation. Instead, they are interpellated as antithetical to the citizen's sense of identity. Citizenship in the form of legal status does not guarantee that they will be constitutive of the American body politic. In fact, quite the opposite: the consolidation of American identity takes place against them.

While many scholars approach citizenship as identity as if it were derivative of citizenship's other dimensions, it seems as if the guarantees of citizenship as status, rights, and politics are insufficient to produce citizenship as identity. Thus one may formally be a U.S. citizen and formally entitled to various legal guarantees, but one will stand outside the membership of kinship/solidarity that structures the U.S. nation. And, clearly, falling outside the identity of the "citizen" can reduce the ability to exercise citizenship as a political or legal matter. This means that the general failure to identify people who appear "Middle Eastern, Arab, or Muslim" as constituting American national identity reappears to haunt their ability to enjoy citizenship as a matter of rights, in the form of being free from violent attack.

Thus the boundaries of the nation continue to be constructed through excluding certain groups. The "imagined community" of the American nation, constituted by loyal citizens, is relying on difference from the "Middle Eastern terrorist" and the "Arab world" to fuse its identity at a moment of crisis. Discourses of democracy used to support the U.S. war effort rest on an image of anti-democracy, in the form of those who seek to destroy the "American way of life." We can see this, for example, in the name given by the administration to the bombardment of Afghanistan, and to the war on terrorism more generally: "Operation Enduring Freedom." The idea that there are norms that are antithetical to "Western values" of freedom and equality helps solidify this conclusion.

We can consider whether the way in which identity disrupts citizenship is inevitable. Race has fundamentally contradicted the promise of liberal democracy, including citizenship. While liberalism claimed to promise universal liberty and equality, these were in fact only guaranteed to propertied, European male subjects. While some might believe in the promise of universality—that one can infinitely expand the ambit of who is entitled to rights and freedoms—race and other markers appear and reappear to patrol the borders of belonging to political communities. Despite the liberal universalizing discourse of citizenship, not all citizens are equal. These events make apparent how identity in the form of foreignness, or perpetual extraterritorialization—the manner in which certain immigrants are always already assumed to come from elsewhere, and to belong elsewhere when their behavior affronts—means that the circling of wagons is an uneven process, that drawing tighter together takes place through the expulsion of some.

Recent theorizing about diasporic or transnational subjects, while productive in many regards, has on occasion minimized the continued salience of the nation, both in terms of shaping identity and in the form of governmental control. In particular, discussions charting the decline of the nation-state have led to unfortunate implications when two points are stretched to extremes: first, the idea that immigrant communities have complete agency in determining their location and their national identity; and second, the idea that the borders of the nation can be traversed with the greatest of ease and are so reduced as to become almost meaningless.

Anthropologist Arjun Appadurai, in an essay titled "Patriotism and its Futures," written at what was perhaps a more optimistic moment, suggests that we "need to think ourselves beyond the nation," for we now find ourselves in a postnational era. America, he suggests, is "eminently suited to be a sort of cultural laboratory and a free trade zone" to test a "world organized around diasporic diversity." Appadurai argues that the United States should be considered "yet another diasporic switching point, to which people come to seek their fortunes but are no longer content to leave their homelands behind." [31]

If only this were indeed a postnational era. In a response, titled "Transnationalism and Its Pasts," literary theorist Kandice Chuh criticizes the evenness of power relations within and across national borders implied in Appadurai's postnation. Chuh emphasizes the link between transnationalism and state coercion and reminds us of the forced removal and internment of Japanese Americans by the U.S. government during World War II. [32] A transnational extension of Japan into the United States was relied on to justify this dispossession. This memory is instructive to us now. We should remember that the idea of transnationality is not solely one where immigrants function as agents in maintaining diasporic ties; it can also be one where a state, or its people, brands its citizens with foreign membership, extraterritorializing them into internment camps or ejecting them from membership through violence against their bodies.

We function not just as agents of our own imaginings, but also as the objects of others' exclusions. Despite frequent rhetorical claims to the contrary, this society is neither colorblind nor a happy "nation of immigrants." Certain racialized bodies are always marked and disrupt the idea of integration or assimilation.

Those who appear "Middle Eastern, Arab, or Muslim" and who are formally citizens of the United States have been thrust outside the protective ambit of citizenship as identity. Post–September 11, there is a new national imagining as to what bodies are assumed to stand in for "the citizen" and its new opposite, "the terrorist." But I want to shift our attention here to bodies that disappear: what of those members of this group who are not formally citizens? Those individuals who are noncitizens—those who were interviewed, deported, and detained—have been made even more vulnerable by their noncitizen status and the power of immigration law to control their fate. They are even farther removed from the "us" of America because of the ways in which we understand citizenship to correlate with membership.

The reaction to the Michigan chapter of the American Civil Liberties Union offering to assist the 566 men the FBI contacted for investigatory interviews in the Detroit area, as recorded on the ACLU hotline and reported in the *Detroit Free Press,* offers a sense of these sentiments:

> *Female Caller:* How can you guys tell us that people who are not American citizens have rights? Bull crap!
> *Male Caller:* What makes you think these people have rights? Those are Arabs; they have no rights. Deal with it![33]

The writer Ariel Dorfman, early after September 11, wrote that the photographs of those missing in the World Trade Center reminded him of the photographs of the *desaparecidos* of Chile.[34] What might it mean to shift who occupies the category of our disappeared, from those killed in the World Trade Center, to consider also those noncitizens in detention? Our government has taken them, and we do not know where they are. Are those in detention our disappeared? If not, why not? I raise this to provoke a rethinking of what bodies are centered in our consideration and what bodies disappear. Who is the "us" in the U.S.?

Notes

An earlier version of this essay was published in the *UCLA Law Review* 49 (2002): 1575–99. It is adapted here with permission.

1. As of February 8, 2002, 1,717 cases of "anti-Muslim incidents" had been reported to the Council on American-Islamic Relations (CAIR) since September 11, 2001; see http://www.cair-net.org.

2. For a discussion of the equation of "Muslim" with "Middle Eastern" or "Arab" and the use of "Muslim" as if it were a racial category, see Moustafa Bayoumi, "How Does It Feel to Be a Problem?" *Amerasia Journal* 27, no. 3 / 28, no. 1 (2001/2002): 69–73.

3. Tom Brune, "Taking Liberties," *Newsday,* September 16, 2002, sec. A, p. 8.

4. See Guidance for Absconder Apprehension Initiative (January 25, 2002), http://news.findlaw.com/legalnews/us/terrorism/documents (last visited February 28, 2002). This appears to be an expansion of a similar program upheld by the U.S. Court of Appeals for the D.C. Circuit during the Iran hostage crisis, when the attorney general promulgated a regulation requiring all Iranian citizens on nonimmigrant student visas to report to local INS offices to provide information as to their residence and status. Students who failed to comply were subjected to deportation. See *Narenji v. Civiletti,* 617 F.2d 745, 747 (D.C. Cir. 1979).

5. See South Asian American Leaders of Tomorrow, "American Backlash: Terrorists Bring War Home in More Ways Than One" (2001), http://www.peopleforpeace.org/docs/BiasReport.pdf; "'We Are Not the Enemy': Hate Crimes against Arabs, Muslims, and

Those Perceived to Be Arab or Muslim after September 11," *Human Rights Watch Report* 14, no. 6 (November 2002), http://www.hrw.org/reports/2002/usahate.

6. Muneer Ahmad, "Homeland Insecurities: Racial Profiling the Day after 9/11," *Social Text* 72, vol. 20, no. 3 (2002): 101–115. How many killings post–September 11 should be understood as motivated by anti-Arab or anti-Muslim bias is a subject of dispute—numbers range from five to seventeen. See, e.g., Alan Cooperman, "Sept. 11 Backlash Murders and the State of 'Hate': Between Families and Police, a Gulf on Victim Count," *Washington Post,* January 20, 2002, sec. A, p. 3.

7. Michel Foucault, "Governmentality," in *The Foucault Effect: Studies in Governmentality,* ed. Graham Burchell, Colin Gordon, and Peter Miller (Chicago: University of Chicago Press, 1991), 102.

8. Michel Foucault, *The History of Sexuality* (1978; reprint, New York: Vintage Books, 1990), 94.

9. I recognize here that I may be said to read Foucault against the grain, through taking his arguments regarding how power is not solely concentrated in the state to suggest that such dispersed power has links to the state. For an analogous argument, see Kendall Thomas, "Beyond the Privacy Principle," *Columbia Law Review* 92 (1992): 1477–90.

10. Inderpal Grewal, *Transnational America: Gender, Class and Ethnicity in the South Asian Diaspora* (Durham, N.C.: Duke University Press, forthcoming 2003).

11. Paola Bacchetta, Tina Campt, Inderpal Grewal, Caren Kaplan, Minoo Moallem, and Jennifer Terry, "Transnational Feminist Practices Against War," October 2001, http://home. earthlink.net/~jenniferterry/transnationalstatement.html.

12. Leti Volpp, "Blaming Culture for Bad Behavior," *Yale Journal of Law and the Humanities* 12 (2000): 89–99.

13. Linda Greenhouse, "Exposed: Again, Bombs in the Land of the Free," *New York Times,* April 23, 1995, sec. 4, p. 1.

14. See Donald G. McNeil Jr., "The Foreign Soldier: Body Confirms Suspicions about Frenchmen in Al Qaeda," *New York Times,* December 28, 2001, sec. B, p. 5.

15. See Arundhati Roy, "War Is Peace," *Outlook India,* October 29, 2001, http://www. outlookindia.com/archivecontents.asp?fnt=20011029.

16. I borrow this metaphor from Lisa Lowe, who writes of the phantasmic role played by the figure of the Asian immigrant on which the U.S. nation projects a series of complicated anxieties. See Lisa Lowe, *Immigrant Acts: On Asian American Cultural Politics* (Durham, N.C.: Duke University Press, 1996), 18.

17. Edward Said, *Orientalism* (New York: Vintage Books, 1978). For a discussion of the heterogeneity of Orientalism, see Lisa Lowe, *Critical Terrains: French and British Orientalisms* (Ithaca, N.Y.: Cornell University Press, 1991).

18. Gayatri Spivak, "Can the Subaltern Speak?" in *Marxism and the Interpretation of Culture,* ed. Cary Nelson and Lawrence Grossberg (Urbana: University of Illinois Press, 1988): 271, 297.

19. Bacchetta et al., "Transnational Feminist Practices Against War." For more information on the history of U.S. funding in Afghanistan, see Eqbal Ahmad and David Barsamian, *Terrorism: Theirs and Ours* (New York: Seven Stories Press, 2001).

20. See Charles Hirschkind and Saba Mahmood, "Feminism, the Taliban, and the Politics of Counter-Insurgency," *Anthropological Quarterly* 75 (2002): 339–354.

21. M. Ahmad, "Homeland Insecurities," 110.

22. Eliza Byard, "Queerly Un-American," *Feminist News: The Newsletter of the Institute for Research on Women and Gender* (Columbia University), January 2002, 6.

23. Bacchetta et al, "Transnational Feminist Practices Against War."

24. Lauren Berlant, *The Queen of America Goes to Washington City: Essays on Sex and Citizenship* (Durham N.C.: Duke University Press, 1997).

25. M. Ahmad, "Homeland Insecurities"; "Death for 11 Sept. Revenge Killer," *BBC News,* April 5, 2002, http://news.bbc.co.uk/hi/english/world/americas/newsid_1912000/1912221.stm.

26. Timothy Egan, "In Sacramento, a Publisher's Questions Draw the Wrath of the Crowd," *New York Times,* December 21, 2001, sec. B, p. 1.

27. "Gallup Poll Analysis: The Impact of the Attacks on America," http:// www.gallup.com/poll/releases/pr010914c.asp.

28. Linda Bosniak, "Citizenship Denationalized," *Indiana Journal of Global Legal Studies* 7 (2000): 447–88.

29. Judith Butler, *The Psychic Life of Power: Theories in Subjection* (Stanford: Stanford University Press, 1997).

30. Louis Althusser, "Ideology and Ideological State Apparatuses," in *Lenin and Philosophy and Other Essays,* trans. Ben Brewster (New York: Monthly Review Press, 1971), 170–77.

31. Arjun Appadurai, "Patriotism and Its Futures," *Public Culture* 5 (1993): 411–25.

32. Kandice Chuh, "Transnationalism and Its Pasts," *Public Culture* 9 (1996): 90–104.

33. Brian Dickerson, "ACLU Finds Intervention Not Welcome," *Detroit Free Press,* December 7, 2001, http://www.freep.com/news/metro/dicker7_20011207.htm.

34. Ariel Dorfman, "America Looks at Itself through Humanity's Mirror," *Los Angeles Times,* September 21, 2001, sec. B, p. 15.

Civil Liberties in the Dragons' Domain: Negotiating the Blurred Boundary between Domestic Law and Foreign Affairs after 9/11

CHRISTOPHER L. EISGRUBER AND

LAWRENCE G. SAGER

Cartographers once drew mythical, menacing beasts to mark the edges of the known world. The mapmakers diagrammed what information they had and then warned prudent travelers about the unfathomable perils of unknowable places—"Here, There be Dragons!" In some ways, American jurisprudence is like those old maps. It, too, divides the world into comfortable spaces and forbidden regions. It, too, has dangerous borders and, one might say, dragons. The known world coincides with the realm of domestic policy. In that domain, courts and legislatures have partnered to articulate a rich lattice of constitutional and statutory rights. Courts have mapped out procedures and rights that restrict police behavior and protect persons accused of heinous crimes. Here, reason rules. But this known, comfortable world ends at the nation's border. Doubtful of their competence and fearful that their errors might jeopardize national interests, judges have traditionally granted Congress and the president almost complete discretion over questions about immigration, the military, espionage, and many other aspects of foreign affairs. To American judges, foreign policy is an unordered wilderness, the domain of realpolitik rather than reason. Here, there are unfathomable perils; here, there be dragons.

The horrible events of September 11, 2001, made hash of these boundaries. Viewed one way, the attacks were in the domestic domain, a terrible crime of unprecedented magnitude. Nineteen people living in the United States hijacked American airplanes from American airports to destroy buildings and murder thousands of people in the United States. Viewed differently, the tragedy was in the domain of foreign affairs, a gruesome and chilling military strike in a new kind of global war. Enemy agents under the direction of a hostile foreign organization infiltrated the United States by posing as ordinary immigrants and then struck American targets.

The antiterrorism measures developed in response to September 11 reflect these complexities. The new policies blend criminal law enforcement with immigration policy, foreign intelligence operations, and military force. In essence, the president and Congress have invoked their discretion over foreign affairs in order to escape restrictions that courts have imposed on domestic police activities. This strategy has enabled the government to search and detain terrorism suspects even when it lacks the kind of evidence normally required by current doctrines of criminal procedure. Three examples typify the new, mixed regime.

Domestic intelligence operations. The USA Patriot Act, the major piece of antiterrorism legislation enacted by Congress, expanded the range of activity subject to intelligence operations (bluntly put, spying) within the United States.[1] The act also allowed for more sharing of information between intelligence agents and law enforcement agents—between, roughly speaking, "spies" and "police." These changes matter because it is easier for the government to collect information about Americans if it plans to use that information for intelligence purposes (such as guiding policy makers in the State Department) rather than for law enforcement purposes (such as assembling evidence for prosecutors in the Justice Department). The government's efforts to spy on people inside the United States have been covered by the Foreign Intelligence Surveillance Act (FISA).[2] Under FISA, the FBI can obtain a search warrant for intelligence-gathering without observing all the restrictions that apply to warrants granted for ordinary law enforcement operations. Moreover, the government can submit its intelligence-gathering requests to a special court— the "FISA court"—that meets secretly inside the Justice Department. The FISA court is designed to safeguard the confidentiality of intelligence-gathering activities, but many observers have regarded it as a highly deferential court that would "rubber stamp" any request it received.[3] These observers were accordingly stunned when the FISA court not only disapproved of the new information-sharing regulations proposed by the Justice Department after passage of the USA Patriot Act, but also issued an opinion that rebuked the FBI for having lied in several of its submissions to the FISA court.[4] The government appealed to another secret court, which eventually reversed the FISA court's decision and approved the Justice Department's proposed procedures.[5]

Military detention. President Bush has claimed that suspected terrorists are "enemy combatants" whom the government may jail, or even execute, without first convicting them in ordinary courts. On November 13, 2001, he issued a presidential order authorizing the creation of military tribunals to try noncitizens suspected of terrorism.[6] The order gave the secretary of defense complete discretion to stipulate procedures to govern the tribunals—it was up to the secretary to determine, for example, whether defendants would have legal counsel, whether they would be tried under the "reasonable doubt" standard, and what evidentiary rules would be used. The order also specified that military tribunals had the power to impose the death penalty and that defendants had no right to appeal to any American, foreign, or international court.[7] The order provoked intense public controversy, and, at the time this book went to press, it lay dormant: no military tribunal had yet been convened, although the order had not been revoked, either. The administration apparently decided to shift course: rather than using military tribunals to convict accused terrorists of crimes, it would simply hold them indefinitely as prisoners of war.[8] That was the strategy adopted in the case of Jose Padilla, an American citizen arrested at O'Hare Airport and then detained at a military facility. The government said that Padilla was trying to gather materials to make a "dirty bomb" (a bomb that would spread radioactive material over a large area), but it never filed any charges against him in any tribunal, military or civilian—instead, it simply held him, without access to legal counsel, as a prisoner of war.[9]

Immigration proceedings. The government has used immigration proceedings to detain or deport noncitizens whom it suspects of participating in, or having knowledge about, terrorist activities. If the government were to prosecute these suspects for crimes, they would have all the rights of ordinary citizens: in general, the Constitution guarantees rights to persons rather than citizens, and noncitizens accused of crimes have the same rights that citizens have.[10] There is one respect, however, in which noncitizens are dramatically more vulnerable than citizens: they are subject to deportation proceedings. Courts have traditionally held, with very few exceptions, that the national government's power to regulate immigration is "plenary," which is to say, virtually unfettered by any constitutional restrictions.[11] As a result, the government can diminish the rights of noncitizen suspects if it proceeds on the immigration track, seeking deportation, rather than on the criminal law track, seeking conviction. The USA Patriot Act expanded the government's power to detain immigrants for long periods in connection with deportation proceedings, and the government has increased its use of immigration violations as a pretext to detain people from whom it wants information.[12] Because the immigration laws are technical and complex, the pretext is often available. For example, Ali Maqtari, a Yemeni citizen married to a soldier in the U.S. Army, accompanied his wife when she reported to an army base in Kentucky. He was arrested and held for two months on suspicion of terrorism; the government did not charge him with terrorism; it instead justified his detention on the ground that he had been in the United States illegally during a ten-day period while he was converting his visa from tourist status to permanent resident status.[13]

We do not intend this list of developments as a "parade of horribles." Since the attacks of September 11 spanned the border between domestic policy and foreign affairs, it is hardly surprising that the policy response to those attacks has also done so. For our purposes, the crucial question is whether that response is (or can be made, through modest and realistic revisions) consistent with basic principles of constitutional justice. For the moment, at least, the answer remains unclear. The USA Patriot Act is complex and lengthy—indeed, the official text of this legislation runs to more than 340 pages. Some of its provisions may prove benign; in any event, the act's impact will depend in part on how it is interpreted by the courts and implemented by the president. The president's order authorizing secret trials in front of military tribunals is disturbing, but, as this book went to press, the tribunals had yet to hear their first case.[14] Most of the terrorism suspects arrested in the United States have been charged in ordinary courts and afforded the full protection of the criminal law; the most salient exception is Padilla, who is being held as a military prisoner. The administration's aggressive use of its immigration powers is worrisome, but some institutions are pushing back. For example, some local law enforcement officials have resisted federal efforts to use immigration violations to pressure immigrant communities; local police chiefs worry that such tactics will erode community support for their police officers.[15] And certainly none of the federal government's current policies approach the injustice of, for example, the massive internment of innocent Japanese Americans during World War II. Far from treating every Muslim as an enemy, President Bush has gone out of his way to urge tolerance— even visiting the Islamic Center of Washington in September 2001, when hate crimes against Islamic Americans (and others, such as Sikhs, who were mistaken for Islamic Americans) peaked.[16]

In many respects, then, September 11's legacy in the domain of civil liberties is mixed, uncertain, and inchoate. It may take years for the full shape and impact of that legacy to emerge, and its character may depend on whether September 11 turns out to be the first of many equally bloody attacks on Americans, or whether it proves to be the worst of a relatively small set. This much, however, seems clear. September 11 has changed the conceptual context for civil liberties in the United States by blurring the boundary between domestic policy and foreign policy. If courts are to play any role in sculpting antiterrorism policy so that it respects civil liberties, they can no longer treat foreign affairs as terra incognita. Unless judges are willing to scrutinize the government's behavior in the domain of foreign policy, their supervision of the criminal law process will be subject to evasion, as the government reclassifies law enforcement within the categories of foreign affairs.

The task will not be easy. There may not be literal dragons lurking in the uncharted precincts of foreign policy, but there are daunting problems: military threats that pose catastrophic risks to national security, human well-being, and world peace; remote places and unfamiliar practices that judges have little capacity to understand or analyze; jurisdictions in which the mandates of American courts carry no authority and where local laws operate on premises utterly inconsistent with the U.S. Constitution; and vast numbers of persons (including enemy soldiers and potential immigrants) whose claims against the United States could not possibly be entertained on a case-by-case basis by American courts. It would be ridiculously naive to suppose that American courts should solve the problems now facing them through brute extension of domestic constitutional rights into immigration law and other transnational domains.

We expect that the judicial response will depend on active partnership between the courts and Congress and that it will have to employ at least three different doctrinal devices. The most obvious device is *increased procedural regulation* of domains, such as immigration law, where the courts have traditionally left the legislature and the executive with a free hand. In *Zadvydas v. Davis,* decided in June 2001, the Supreme Court began to move slowly in that direction, holding that the Constitution prohibited the government from detaining deportable aliens indefinitely.[17] Yet, for the reasons suggested in the last paragraph, we doubt that it is likely or, indeed, desirable for the courts to venture far in this direction on purely constitutional grounds; they will require statutory support from Congress. That may also be true with regard to a second doctrinal device, *sunshine provisions* designed to ensure that the government is publicly accountable for its use of the discretionary authority it enjoys within the field of foreign affairs. Courts have already issued important decisions of this form, although it is not clear whether they will be upheld on appellate review. Thus, for example, Judge Gladys Kessler of the U.S. District Court for the District of Columbia ruled that the government must respond to Freedom of Information Act requests seeking the names of persons being detained on immigration-related charges.[18] The U.S. Court of Appeals for the Sixth Circuit required that deportation proceedings be open to the press unless the government could demonstrate case-specific reasons for making hearings secret (the U.S. Court of Appeals for the Third Circuit, however, reached the opposite conclusion, upholding the government's across-the-board policy of secret hearings in cases involving immigrants suspected of involvement with terrorism).[19] The FISA court's surprising public rebuke to the justice department, though not itself requiring openness, supplied additional information about intelligence processes and thereby helped citizens and legislators to monitor the executive's behavior. Notably, both Judge Kessler's decision and the FISA court's ruling relied on statutory rather than constitutional grounds.

The third device consists of *gatekeeping doctrines* that would regulate the executive's discretion to reroute cases from the criminal law track to the foreign affairs track. Many of these may have, or even require, a statutory foundation. For example, the FISA court's decision (later reversed on appeal) was predicated on statutory restrictions on the government's ability to shift law enforcement functions to an espionage track. Immigration laws currently provide that when defendants in a deportation proceeding claim to be American citizens, they are entitled to have the relevant factual issues resolved by a federal district court (rather than by the Immigration and Naturalization Service).[20]

Of course, in recognizing the importance of statutory law, we do not mean to suggest that courts should be passive executors of legislative instructions. We doubt that such a model of judicial behavior is conceptually coherent: statutes are inevitably ambiguous, and when they are ambiguous, a direction to follow "actual intent" begs the crucial question. In any event, we believe that it is preferable for courts to regard themselves as partners rather than agents of legislatures, with a responsibility to participate actively in shaping the meaning of statutes to serve the interests of justice.[21] Courts may, for example, implement "clear statement rules," pursuant to which statutes will be construed to preserve the rights of defendants in deportation proceedings unless Congress has clearly stated its intention to do otherwise.[22]

Nor do we mean to suggest that statutory law, even supplemented with clear statement rules, should be the whole story. We think it both normatively desirable and practically feasible for courts to enforce some constitutional constraints on the government's use of its foreign affairs powers, and we believe that such constitutional rulings have an important role to play in the preservation of American civil liberties. We shall turn to some examples in a moment. We think it important to stress, however, that courts will be able to negotiate the blurred boundaries between domestic policy and foreign affairs only if they are able to draw on a supportive body of statutory law—a body of law that will include statutes enacted before the events of September 11 (such as the Freedom of Information Act and the Foreign Intelligence Surveillance Act) and statutes enacted afterward (such as the USA Patriot Act and its successors).

To illustrate the range of possibilities, we now consider in more detail the civil liberties questions associated with military detention of suspected terrorists captured in the United States. We focus on these cases for several reasons. First, they present especially stark issues about the relationship of domestic criminal law to the government's foreign affairs powers. The Bush administration's position about these detentions has been extreme. The administration claims not simply that those whom it deems "enemy combatants" are entitled to fewer rights than ordinary criminal defendants, but also that they are entitled to only such rights as the government chooses to give them—which may mean, in cases such as Jose Padilla's, no procedural protections whatsoever. Second, the questions presented are relatively novel. In the immigration field, the government has a great deal of discretion, but that discretion has been implemented and codified through a complex web of statutes and case law. By contrast, the government's new policy of military detentions has sent experts scrambling to recover peculiar, forgotten precedents from World War II and before. Third, the number of terrorism suspects seized within the United States is likely to be small, which means that the federal courts could reasonably demand jurisdiction over them (it would, by contrast, be unimaginable for the federal courts to take over basic fact-finding functions with regard to all immigration cases or to examine the treatment of all prisoners of war on a case-by-case basis).

As this book went to press, lawyers acting on behalf of Padilla were seeking a writ of habeas corpus, arguing that the government should either file criminal charges against the prisoner or release him. The government had answered by insisting that Padilla's case falls in the domain of foreign affairs and military policy in which (it says) courts have no business intervening.[23] To resolve the argument, the courts will have to develop a gatekeeping doctrine. They will have to specify when government can move prisoners from the ordinary criminal law track to the prisoner-of-war track. In an ordinary war, each of these tracks supplies detainees with a distinctive set of rights. If the government proceeds on the criminal law track, it may imprison persons for long periods of time, or even execute them, but it is bound by procedural constraints: defendants are entitled to a trial in which they have a lawyer and in which the government must abide by strict evidentiary rules and convince a jury that the defendants are guilty beyond a reasonable doubt of well-defined crimes. The government has no comparable obligations on the prisoner-of-war track. It can hold prisoners without giving them trials. Prisoners of war, however, are generally supposed to enjoy a privilege unavailable to criminal defendants: when the war ends, they are entitled to be released and allowed to return home.

Because the prisoner-of-war track permits the government to hold persons without making an individualized determination of guilt, the track presents obvious risks. The government may detain innocent persons whom it wrongly suspects of being enemy agents. That is, in effect, what happened during World War II, when the United States forced Japanese Americans into internment camps. As that episode illustrates, it is no comfort to innocent persons, whose homes are destroyed and lives disrupted for months or years, that they may be free to go home when the war ends. If that is so in an ordinary war, it is all the more true in today's "war on terrorism." The entire notion of an "end" to the war seems doubtful, if only because there is no obvious party capable of surrendering. Moreover, it seems implausible that the United States has any intention of letting Jose Padilla or other suspected terrorists "return home," whatever happens. The policy of releasing prisoners at the end of the war presumes that they will peacefully return to their families and businesses, happy to put hostilities behind them. That premise fails in the case of terrorists with a personal hatred of the United States. In the new "war on terrorism," prisoner-of-war status may be equivalent to a lifetime prison sentence.

If the government had unfettered discretion to seize persons within the United States and hold them indefinitely as "prisoners of war," that power would enable it to circumvent several of the Constitution's most basic principles. It would, for example, authorize the shameful internment of Japanese Americans during World War II. It would also effectively nullify the Constitution's guarantee that the writ of habeas corpus will not be suspended except "in Cases of Rebellion or Invasion."[24] The writ is a procedural device by which prisoners can compel the government to show that it has legally sound authority to hold them. That device is pointless if the government can meet its obligation merely by declaring, without presenting any evidence, that it suspects the prisoner of being an enemy. More generally, the right not to be imprisoned absent proof of guilt is basic to due process of law and is embodied in the Fourth Amendment's prohibition of unreasonable seizures of persons.[25]

Principles so fundamental to the American constitutional order should yield, if at all, only to the most compelling claims of necessity. Necessity helps to explain, for example, why we do not oblige the government to make individualized determinations of guilt with respect to prisoners captured in the theater of war. If the government must fight wars, it must take prisoners. In light of the numbers of persons involved and the chaos of battle, it would be unreasonable to ask the military to conduct individualized trial proceedings with respect to every person it captured. These considerations would continue to apply if the theater of war were within the United States—which is why the Constitution provides for the suspension of the writ of habeas corpus "in Cases of Rebellion or Invasion." But these considerations do not seem at all compelling with regard to persons captured in the United States in present circumstances, when the number of persons seized is small and when the civilian courts are open and functioning.

To prevent the sacrifice of basic constitutional rights, courts will have to establish an evidentiary "gate" that the government must pass through before using the prisoner-of-war track to detain persons arrested inside the United States. The crucial, and difficult, question is what sort of showing the government must make. If judges are fearful of constraining the government's capacity to pursue terrorists, they might impose only a minimal burden. They might, for example, ask the government to provide evidence on the basis of which a reasonable person could conclude that the detainee was affiliated with Al Qaeda or some other organization hostile to the United States. It is hard to see, however, why national security interests should require judges to be so timid. Judges should instead demand that the government prove combatant status by a preponderance of the evidence. This test would not hold the government to the demanding standards of the criminal law: the government would not need to prove membership in Al Qaeda "beyond a reasonable doubt," nor would it need to show that the detainee was guilty of any specific crime. It would not have to identify all of its witnesses or make them available for cross-examination. If the government has solid grounds for holding a detainee, this "preponderance of the evidence" standard should be relatively easy to meet. Certainly that would seem to be the case with regard to Padilla himself, if the government is to be taken at its word: the Bush administration has said that it has plentiful and specific evidence, from multiple sources, linking Padilla to plots against the United States.[26]

Indeed, the problem with the "preponderance of the evidence" standard is not that it is too demanding, but that it may be too weak. In an ordinary war, the standard might well suffice: it would prevent the government from using the prisoner-of-war track without having any individualized evidence that the detainee was an enemy agent, and the harm from remaining errors would at least be limited by the "catch-and-release" character of prisoner-of-war status. Persons erroneously detained would go home at the war's end. But, as we have already noted, prisoners in the "war on terrorism" may anticipate lifetime detention. Put differently, their liability seems personal, rather than derivative of some state's or foreign power's. In that sense, they are being treated more like convicted criminals than captured soldiers.

In effect, the Bush administration has created a third track for detention of suspected terrorists and enemy agents, one that features neither the protections of the ordinary criminal process nor the protections of ordinary prisoner-of-war status. It is not clear that courts should permit this innovation, even if combatant status is proven by a preponderance of the evidence. Courts might, in other words, not only play a gatekeeping function with regard to prisoner-of-war status, but also insist that the government choose between the criminal law track and the prisoner-of-war track. Such a doctrine would demand that in order for the government to hold people as prisoners of war, it must specify conditions that, if satisfied, would constitute an end to the "war" and hence entitle the prisoners to release. If the government were unwilling to do that, and wanted the power to incarcerate people indefinitely on the basis of the dangerous plots in which they have been engaged, then it would have to try them for crimes.

Laying down such a rule would entail that if the government wanted to hold Jose Padilla (and others like him) indefinitely, it would not only have to prove by a preponderance of the evidence that he was an enemy agent, but also prove that he had committed crimes. Another set of questions would then arise. Courts would have to decide what procedures the government could use to establish that an enemy combatant was guilty of a crime. Must the government give enemy agents all the rights afforded to ordinary criminal defendants? Or may it proceed under less demanding standards, perhaps in specially constituted courts? The Bush administration's answer to these questions is clear, at least in cases involving noncitizens. The administration's presidential order, issued on November 13, 2001, declares that noncitizens suspected of terrorism may be tried in front of military tribunals pursuant to whatever procedures the secretary of defense considers appropriate. The administration has not said whether it believes citizens have more rights—but its treatment of Padilla suggests it does not.

In defense of this position, the Bush administration has relied heavily on a legal precedent from World War II, *Ex parte Quirin*.[27] The case dealt with German saboteurs on a covert mission in the United States. After receiving extensive training in Germany, the saboteurs waded ashore from U-boats and landed on Long Island. On coming ashore, they quickly shed their military badges and buried them in the sand. They went to New York City, where they posed as ordinary civilians. One of the saboteurs, however, got cold feet and turned himself in to the FBI. Acting on his tip, the FBI easily captured his coconspirators.

The story is already exotic, but now it becomes wilder and a bit tawdry.[28] J. Edgar Hoover wanted to claim the capture as an intelligence coup for the bureau. It would have embarrassed Hoover and the FBI if the public learned that the spies were captured through brute luck rather than keen detective work. Hoover knew that the true story would emerge if the Germans were given an ordinary trial, so he persuaded Franklin Roosevelt that they should be tried by freshly constituted military tribunals. Roosevelt issued an order creating the tribunals, and the agents were tried, convicted, and sentenced to death. They sought Supreme Court review, arguing that they were entitled to a trial before ordinary civilian courts. The case was briefed and argued in less than a week. The day after oral argument, the Court upheld the authority of the tribunals, and the agents were rapidly put to death; only months later did the Court issue an opinion. The opinion upheld the military tribunals on the ground that there was a long historical tradition of using such tribunals to try "illegal combatants."

The Bush administration claims that suspected terrorists captured in the United States are no different than the Nazi saboteurs in *Quirin:* if it was constitutional to try the German spies in front of military tribunals, then so too it must be lawful to try accused Al Qaeda operatives in front of similar bodies.[29] In one crucial respect, the administration's interpretation of *Quirin* overreaches. In *Quirin,* the defendants stipulated that they were German military agents operating secretly within the United States; they defended themselves only by arguing that they did not intend to carry out their orders. There was accordingly no factual dispute about whether the defendants were combatants. Because the *Quirin* defendants admitted "illegal combatant" status, *Quirin* tells us nothing about the constitutional rules that govern when defendants deny that they are combatants. The Bush administration's effort to try all *suspected* terrorists in military tribunals therefore depends on extending *Quirin's* rule beyond the facts of that case. We are back, once again, to the gatekeeping issue: insofar as the government may proceed on separate tracks with regard to enemy combatants and criminal defendants, courts have a role to play in making sure that those on the "combatant" track actually belong there.[30]

Let's suppose, however, that this hurdle has been cleared. Suppose, for example, that the government has proven by a preponderance of the evidence that Jose Padilla was, at the time of his capture, affiliated with Al Qaeda. With that determination in place, does *Quirin* authorize the government to try Padilla in front of a military tribunal rather than continuing in ordinary, civilian courts? We believe so: once the gatekeeping issue is out of the way, the Bush administration's interpretation of *Quirin* stands on much firmer ground.

To readers concerned about civil liberties, that may at first seem dismal news. Trials designed to hide truth from the public; executions first and reasons later; an opinion that relied almost entirely on contestable history without exploring issues of principle—*Quirin* was not a bright day for the American justice system. It is understandable that both Felix Frankfurter and William O. Douglas later expressed regret about the way the case was handled.[31] *Quirin* may be a precedent for the Bush administration's order concerning military tribunals, but the fact that it is a precedent does not mean it is worth following. Perhaps it should be regarded, along with other World War II decisions such as *Korematsu v. United States*,[32] as a classic example of what courts ought *not* to do.[33]

Quirin is indeed odious if it means that enemy combatants have no procedural rights at all, or that the government may try prisoners in front of biased tribunals in order to maximize the chance of conviction. The case lends itself to that reading, and the Bush administration seems inclined to favor such a broad construction: the presidential order of November 13, 2001, provides suspected terrorists no procedural rights of any kind. Yet, were *Quirin* read more narrowly, for the limited proposition that enemy combatants can be tried in front of properly constituted military tribunals rather than civilian courts, more might be said in its favor.

Military tribunals are not inherently unfair. Indeed, the United States uses military courts ("courts-martial") to judge its own soldiers. It is tempting to suppose that military courts are justified in substantial part by the military's occasional need to produce fair adjudications rapidly near the field of battle during the chaos of wartime. Under such circumstances, civilian courts may be unreachable and their procedures unwieldy. But this justification is far too narrow to support the ordinary operations of military courts today, which try soldiers even in peacetime for offenses committed within American borders, when a civilian courthouse is nearby and easily accessible.

We suggest that the justification for military courts relates to speed and specialized knowledge. The military world is different from the one known to ordinary citizens. Authority relationships are strict; privacy is minimal; discipline is essential; and the use of deadly weapons is a feature of everyday life. Long, drawn-out litigation about chains of authority would compromise the order and discipline that enable the military to act decisively in crises. Civilian judges and juries might have little ability to determine what courses of behavior were reasonable, what statements were credible, and so on.

These considerations are *epistemic* in character—that is, they deal with the comparative competence of civilian and military courts to get at the truth in disputes about the conduct of soldiers. Such considerations speak to the need for military courts. They do not, of course, entail that the military should be allowed to create whatever adjudicative procedures it deems expedient. Basic norms of fairness may apply differently to military and civilian circumstances, but they remain applicable nonetheless. The Supreme Court has given the military great latitude to design procedures for military courts; here, as elsewhere, the judiciary has probably deferred too much to claims of military necessity.[34] Still, the military has incentives to create fair procedures, since, after all, they will be used to judge its own soldiers. The Uniform Code of Military Justice, enacted in 1950, provides a comprehensive procedural framework for American military courts.[35] Through a combination of these internal pressures, external criticism, congressional oversight, and occasional judicial prodding, the military justice system has evolved into a settled and well-defined system that respects basic principles of fairness and contains detailed, interconnecting elements that work reasonably well together.[36]

If we recognize the constitutional propriety of military courts, it seems prima facie reasonable to allow such courts to try enemy combatants along with our own soldiers. The epistemic arguments that justify a separate system of military justice for our own soldiers are also applicable with regard to enemy soldiers. Enemy soldiers, too, operate in a realm of martial discipline and lethal force far removed from the norms that govern ordinary civil society. Moreover, it would be jarring (as supporters of the Bush administration plan have frequently observed) to offer enemy soldiers a different and on the whole more exacting standard than the one we apply to our own troops. Finally, if the same procedural protections that apply to our own soldiers are extended to enemy combatants, then there is no reason to suspect that the procedures have been designed ad hoc with the whole or partial purpose of making conviction more likely.

This last requisite is, of course, not satisfied by the Bush administration's executive order, which allows for the creation of rules entirely different from those applied in ordinary military courts. Yet, while our argument does not support the use of ad hoc tribunals of the kind created by the Bush administration, it would justify the use of military tribunals, rather than civilian courts, to try suspected terrorists, provided that (1) the government first proves (in a civilian court) that the suspects are indeed enemy combatants and (2) the tribunals operate pursuant to the same rules as ordinary military courts. The first of these requirements is an example of what we have called *gatekeeping;* the second is an example of *increased procedural regulation* of a matter—the trial of enemy combatants—over which the courts have heretofore granted the government wide discretion.

Through the combination of these two techniques, courts can extend basic constitutional principles to govern the treatment of military prisoners, a topic heretofore regarded as within the domain of foreign affairs and hence (almost) beyond judicial regulation. Courts would thereby ensure that government could not circumvent basic principles of due process simply by invoking the specter of "foreign terrorism." In that limited sense, doctrines of the kind we describe would enable courts to negotiate the blurred boundary between domestic policy and foreign affairs, preventing the government's traditional discretion with regard to the latter domain from destroying rights carefully cultivated in the former one.

It is a separate question whether the resulting solution is fully satisfactory from the standpoint of civil liberties. On the one hand, international lawyers may be pleased by our narrow construction of *Quirin,* since it conforms that ruling to the requirements imposed by the Geneva Conventions of 1949. The conventions permit captured soldiers to be tried in front of military tribunals, so long as the prosecuting nation affords them the same rights it gives to its own soldiers.[37] On the other hand, stalwart defenders of constitutional principle may plausibly suggest that the United States should hold itself to a higher standard when it tries suspected terrorists. After all, even if we think that military courts treat our own soldiers fairly, there is no guarantee that they will treat the enemy fairly.

Yet, courts would have to act boldly in order to impose even the relatively spare constitutional restrictions we have suggested, and it is unlikely that they would go further without statutory support. Here as elsewhere, full enforcement of constitutional principles will require supportive collaboration between Congress and the courts.[38] And if that is true with regard to the treatment of detainees arrested within the United States, it is doubly so with regard to noncitizen prisoners captured abroad. Though our focus in this essay has been on the intrusion of foreign affairs into the sphere of domestic civil liberties, we should not forget that some of the most urgent questions of constitutional justice arise in settings that remain (at least according to the conceptual apparatus of American jurisprudence) unambiguously foreign. The treatment of prisoners of war being held at Guantánamo Bay, Cuba, is a disturbing example. For them, as for persons arrested inside the United States, prisoner-of-war status may entail a life sentence, since it is hard to imagine what it would mean for the war to end. Moreover, the Bush administration has repeatedly declared itself unbound by the international law rules normally applicable to prisoners of war. Yet, under longstanding precedents, American courts have no jurisdiction to hear complaints from the Guantánamo prisoners.[39] It is unlikely that courts will revisit those precedents, and, indeed, one leading appellate court has already reaffirmed them.[40] Though the events of September 11, 2001, may compel judges to trespass into the dragons' domain, they will not go very far without a statutory warrant. The dangers, both real and imagined, will seem too great to allow for constitutionally based judicial review.

Notes

1. *Uniting and Strengthening America by Providing Appropriate Tools Required to Intercept and Obstruct Terrorism Act of 2001 (USA Patriot Act), U.S. Statutes at Large* 115 (2001): 272, sec. 218.
2. *U.S. Code,* vol. 50, secs. 1801–63 (2001).
3. Daniel Malooly, "Physical Searches under FISA," *American Criminal Law Review* 35 (1998): 415.
4. *In re All Matters Submitted to the Foreign Intelligence Surveillance Court,* Unpublished Memorandum Opinion, May 17, 2002. The opinion was issued in May 2002 and made public by Congress in August 2002. Philip Shenon, "Secret Court Says F.B.I. Aides Misled Judges in 75 Cases," *New York Times,* August 23, 2002, sec. A, p. 1.
5. *In re Sealed Case No. 02-001,* Unpublished Memorandum Opinion, November 18, 2002. Somewhat remarkably, the appellate court asserted that both the FISA court and the Justice Department had misread the Foreign Intelligence Surveillance Act for more than twenty years. For example, in the appellate court's view, FISA had never mandated that intelligence and law enforcement operations be carefully separated. Neil A. Lewis, "Court Overturns Limits on Wiretaps to Combat Terror," *New York Times,* November 19, 2002, sec. A, p. 1.
6. Elisabeth Bumiller and David Johnston, "Bush Sets Option of Military Trials in Terrorist Cases," *New York Times,* November 14, 2001, sec. A, p. 1; "President Bush's Order on Trial of Terrorists by Military Commission," *New York Times,* November 14, 2001, sec. 8, p. 8.
7. One thorough discussion of the order, with attention to some of the constitutional issues raised by it, is Neal K. Katyal and Laurence H. Tribe, "Waging War, Deciding Guilt: Trying the Military Tribunals," *Yale Law Journal* 111 (2002): 1259–1310.
8. Neil A. Lewis, "Administration's Position Shifts on Plans for Tribunals," *New York Times,* November 2, 2002, sec. A, p. 8.
9. See, e.g., Adam Liptak, Neil Lewis, and Benjamin Weiser, "After September 11, a Legal

Battle on the Limits of Civil Liberty," *New York Times*, August 4, 2002, sec. 1, p. 1; Adam Liptak, "Accord Suggests U.S. Prefers to Avoid Courts," *New York Times*, July 16, 2002, sec. A, p. 14.

10. *Wong Wing v. United States*, 163 U.S. 228 (1896); David Cole, "Enemy Aliens," *Stanford Law Review* 54 (2002): 978–85.

11. Cole, "Enemy Aliens," 981.

12. Ibid., 961–65, 970–72.

13. Ibid., 963.

14. Some administration officials were, however, suggesting that the government should transfer the trial of Zacarias Moussaoui to a military tribunal. Moussaoui had been charged in civilian court with participating in the attack on the World Trade Center towers, but his case was presenting the government with an increasingly difficult set of challenges. Philip Shenon and Eric Schmitt, "White House Weighs Letting Military Tribunal Try Moussaoui," *New York Times*, November 9, 2002, sec. 1, p. 17.

15. Eric Schmitt, "Administration Split on Local Role in Terror Fight," *New York Times*, April 29, 2002, sec. A, p. 1.

16. David E. Sanger, "Bin Laden Is Wanted in Attacks, 'Dead or Alive,' President Says," *New York Times*, September 18, 2001, sec. A, p. 1.

17. 533 U.S. 678 (2001); Peter J. Spiro, "Explaining the End of Plenary Power," *Georgetown Immigration Law Journal* 16 (2002): 339–63.

18. *Center for National Security Studies v. United States Department of Justice*, 215 F. Supp. 2d 94 (Dist. D.C. 2002). Just as this book went to press, an appellate court reversed Judge Kessler's ruling. *Center for National Security Studies v. United States Department of Justice*, 2003 U.S. App. LEXIS 11910 (June 17, 2003). The plaintiffs vowed to pursue further appeals.

19. *Detroit Free Press v. Ashcroft*, 303 F.3d 681 (6th Cir. 2002); *New Jersey Media Group, Inc. v. Ashcroft*, 308 F.3d 198 (3d Cir. 2002).

20. *U.S. Code*, vol. 8, sec. 1252(b)(5)(B).

21. Christopher L. Eisgruber and Lawrence G. Sager, "Why the Religious Freedom Restoration Act Is Unconstitutional," *New York University Law Review* 69 (1994): 462–63.

22. A leading discussion of the use of "clear statement rules" is William N. Eskridge and Philip P. Frickey, "Quasi-Constitutional Law: Clear Statement Rules as Constitutional Lawmaking," *Vanderbilt Law Review* 45 (1992): 593–646.

23. Benjamin Weiser, "Bomb Suspect's Lawyers Decry Detention," *New York Times*, September 27, 2002, sec. A, p. A20; Benjamin Weiser, "Judge Affirms Terror Suspect Must Meet with Lawyers," *New York Times*, March 12, 2003, sec. A, p. A17. Similar arguments occurred in connection with the case of Yasser Esam Hamdi, an American citizen seized on the field of battle in Afghanistan and later transported to a military detention facility in the United States. Katharine Q. Seelye, "Court to Hear Arguments in Groundbreaking Case of U.S. Citizen Seized with Taliban," *New York Times*, October 28, 2002, sec. A, p. 13. The United States Court of Appeals for the Fourth Circuit largely rejected these arguments; *Hamdi v. Rumsfeld*, 316 F.3d 450 (4th Cir. 2003).

24. U.S. Constitution, art. 1, sec. 9, para. 2.

25. See, e.g., *Davis v. Mississippi*, 394 U.S. 721, 726–27 (1969): "Investigatory seizures would subject unlimited numbers of innocent persons to the harassment and ignominy incident to involuntary detention. Nothing is more clear than that the Fourth Amendment was meant to prevent wholesale intrusions upon the personal security of our citizenry, whether these intrusions be termed 'arrests' or 'investigatory detentions.' "

26. James Risen and Philip Shenon, "U.S. Says It Halted Qaeda Plot to Use Radioactive Bomb," *New York Times,* June 11, 2002, sec. A, p. 1.

27. 317 U.S. 1 (1942).

28. For discussion of this matter, see, e.g., David J. Danelski, "The Saboteurs' Case," *Journal of Supreme Court History* 1 (1996): 61–80; Tony Mauro, "A Mixed Precedent for Military Tribunals," *Legal Times,* November 19, 2001, 15.

29. Alberto R. Gonzales, "Martial Justice: Full and Fair," *New York Times,* November 30, 2001, sec. A, p. 27.

30. The Supreme Court has in the past suggested that civilian courts have jurisdiction to determine whether alleged "enemy aliens" held during wartime within the United States are in fact "enemy aliens." *Ludecke v. Watkins,* 335 U.S. 160, 171 n. 17 (1948) ("The additional question as to whether the person restrained is in fact an alien enemy fourteen years of age or older may also be reviewed by the courts").

31. Danelski, "The Saboteurs' Case," 80.

32. 323 U.S. 214 (1944).

33. "If there is any lesson to be learned from the case, it is that the Court should be wary of departing from its established rules and practices, even in times of national crisis, for at such times the Court is especially susceptible to co-optation by the executive." Danelski, "The Saboteurs' Case," 80.

34. The Supreme Court briefly surveyed some basic features of American courts-martial in *Weiss v. United States,* 510 U.S. 163 (1994). Pursuant to congressionally conferred jurisdiction, the Supreme Court now reviews some constitutional challenges to the procedures used in military courts, though its review has generally been highly deferential.

35. *U.S. Code,* vol. 10, secs. 801 et seq.

36. Of course, we do not mean to suggest that the Uniform Code of Military Justice is ideal, or even close to ideal. Commentators have suggested that although the UCMJ once set a worldwide standard for procedural fairness in military trials, the United States now lags behind many other countries in this area of law. Beth Hillman, "Chains of Command," *Legal Affairs* 1, no. 1 (2002): 50–52.

37. According to Article 102 of the Geneva Conventions of 1949, "A prisoner of war can be validly sentenced only if the sentence has been pronounced by the same courts according to the same procedure as in the case of members of the armed forces of the Detaining Power, and if, furthermore, the provisions of the present Chapter have been observed."

38. Lawrence G. Sager, "Fair Measure: The Legal Status of Underenforced Constitutional Norms," *Harvard Law Review* 91 (1978): 1212–64.

39. *Johnson v. Eisentrager,* 339 U.S. 763 (1950).

40. *Al Odah v. United States,* 2003 U.S. App. LEXIS 4250 (D.C. Cir. 2003). As this book neared publication, the Justice Department's Inspector General, Glen Fine, issued a 239-page report that documented the wrongful detention and mistreatment of noncitizens charged with immigration violations in the wake of the September 11 attacks. Eric Lichtblau, "U.S. Report Faults the Roundup of Illegal Immigrants after 9/11," *New York Times,* June 2, 2003, sec. A, p. 1. The report demonstrates how the pressure to fight terrorism may lead officials to abuse their powers. It thus provides important evidence of the need to design new procedures that will protect rights effectively while also enabling the executive branch to prevent terrorist acts. The Justice Department responded defensively to the report but promised to make some of the changes recommended in it. Eric Lichtblau, "U.S. Will Tighten Rules on Holding Terror Suspects," *New York Times,* June 13, 2003, sec. A, p. 1.

Transforming International Law after the September 11 Attacks? Three Evolving Paradigms for Regulating International Terrorism

LAURENCE R. HELFER

The allure of transformative moments transcends academic disciplines. Their inherent appeal to scholars lies in their ability to serve as an interpretive lens through which to view transitions between old eras and emerging ones. The search for points of transformation is especially strong when a single event creates uncertainty or stress, destabilizing seemingly settled principles of order. The labeling of that event as transformative alleviates these tensions. It brings coherence to a world that existing paradigms no longer adequately explain, and it enables scholars to suggest new paradigms as guideposts for the future. But identifying such critical junctures is a dangerous business. History is littered with erroneous labelings of watershed events that, in hindsight, seem little more than one in a series of points on a Cartesian line mapped out decades earlier.[1]

International law is no stranger to this allure of the transformative. The political and often fluid nature of international legal rules makes adapting to and predicting change a central concern of the scholars who study it and the lawyers who practice it. As international order evolves, so too do international law's actors and observers seek to identify the salient characteristics of that evolution. But whether such processes of adaptation and prediction should be labeled as genuinely transformative events is often highly contested.

One of the founders of modern international law, the seventeenth-century Dutch scholar Hugo Grotius, is widely credited with identifying the discipline's first and only undisputed transformative moment—the change from a medieval world in which ecclesiastical authority dominated secular power to a world controlled by independent and sovereign nation-states. Grotius accurately identified his age as a time of transition and comprehensively categorized the features of the incipient legal order.[2] His predictive powers were validated two decades later when the 1648 Peace of Westphalia ended the Thirty Years' War and codified the core principles of a new "law of nations" to govern relations among sovereign states, principles that endured for the next three centuries.

Grotius's legacy for international affairs was twofold. On the one hand, modern scholars have continued to scrutinize his writings for insights into current problems, in the process identifying a distinctive "Grotian tradition" of international law.[3] On the other, a different group of scholars and policy makers has been attracted to Grotius's efforts to predict change as valuable in itself.[4] As international relations in the twentieth century became increasingly complex and populated by a diverse set of state and nonstate actors with divergent interests, these individuals associated Grotius with their own efforts to identify transformative change. By the waning years of the last millennium, questioning whether international society was on the cusp of a new "Grotian moment" had become a leitmotif in international discourse. Eminent legal scholars such as Richard Falk devoted considerable energy to identifying the content and contours of the new international society,[5] and their clarion calls for change were taken up by world leaders such as former UN secretary general Boutros Boutros-Ghali[6] and by international judges and commentators.[7]

Falk's writings deserve particular attention, for they help to situate the September 11 terrorist attacks against the backdrop of broader quests to remap the legal landscape of world affairs. Falk argues that the state-centric legal order that has prevailed since Westphalia is rapidly eroding. Taking its place is a world in which individuals and nonterritorial actors no longer maintain allegiances to the state but instead to centralized structures above the state and to local communities and subnational movements operating within it. The task Falk sets for himself is to "give judicial shape to [this] new paradigm of global relations, one that corresponds more closely than statist thinking to the needs, trends, and values of the present state of global politics."[8] After canvassing alternative ways in which this new Grotian moment could evolve, Falk argues in favor of a world order based on global populism, human solidarity, and a new "law of humanity,"[9] in which the needs and interests of individuals and nonstate actors take precedence over the geopolitics of a handful of great powers or the economics of global capitalism.[10]

The events of September 11 suggest a far less sanguine view of the place of individuals and other private actors in international society. Terrorist groups such as Al Qaeda are perhaps the ultimate "nonterritorial actors"—autonomous entities operating largely outside the state system.[11] To quote two prescient commentators, these "revolutionary forces of the future" consist of "widespread multi-organizational networks that have no particular national identity, claim to arise from civil society, and include . . . aggressive groups and individuals who are keenly adept at using advanced technology, for communications as well as munitions."[12] If, therefore, as Falk argues, an emerging law of humanity is to supplant or even to supplement the existing law of nations, mechanisms for confronting threats by these private terrorist groups must necessarily be included within it.

Seen from this perspective, it may be superficially tempting to view the September 11 attacks and their aftermath as a Grotian moment in international law—a time for creating fresh paradigms of responsibility for acts of international terror. But I believe those events can more accurately be understood by using three existing frameworks that international law already offers to respond to terrorism: first, "terrorism as international crime"; second, "terrorism as armed conflict"; and finally, "terrorism as atrocity." None of these three framings is new. Each of them existed well before September 11, and each contains its own distinct set of norms, institutions, and restrictions on states seeking to punish perpetrators and deter future harm.

What has changed since September 11, however, is the readiness of the United States to pick and choose among these three categories and to claim for itself the right to respond to terrorism unilaterally. Whether this "naked, crusading" U.S. unilateralism (as Marilyn Young describes it in her essay in this book) can engender normative legal change is uncertain and contested. Modern international law is principally created multilaterally, through treaty negotiations and customary rules formed by the consistent practice of many states. Nonconforming unilateral action by a single state—even the world's only superpower—is formally labeled as a breach of multilateral rules, not as an act that transforms them. But the critical role of power in maintaining international order often undermines that formalism and subtly shifts prevailing legal constructs.

In the sections that follow, I identify the three extant frameworks that international law uses to categorize terrorism. I then explain how the United States invoked these frameworks in response to past terrorist acts against it, and how it has altered its approach and blurred distinctions among the categories after September 11. I conclude with a discussion of the possible pathways along which international law might evolve in a post–September 11 world.

Consider first terrorism as "international crime." When transborder acts of violence for political ends became a pressing subject of international concern in the 1960s and 1970s,[13] national governments actively sought ways to suppress it. The international community first turned its attention to defining terrorism. But north-south and east-west geopolitical fault lines—including developing nations' desire to allow revolutionary movements to use force against colonial repression—ruptured any possibility of agreement over definitional first principles.[14]

As a second-best strategy, states sought to outlaw a more limited number of violent acts when a solid international consensus could be forged to do so.[15] Over the next quarter century, governments negotiated a dozen or so international conventions on subjects such as aircraft hijacking and sabotage, hostage taking, harm to diplomats,[16] and, most recently, treaties on the suppression of terrorist bombings and the financing of terrorism.[17] These conventions adopt a criminalization approach to international terrorism. States parties are required to make the acts proscribed in the treaties offenses under their domestic criminal laws and to exercise jurisdiction over alleged offenders, even those who are merely found within their territory. Once a state asserts jurisdiction, it is required either to investigate with a view to prosecuting the offender or to extradite the individual to another treaty party with a nexus to the conduct. States are also required to assist each other in investigations and prosecutions.[18] Finally, constitutional or human rights guarantees provide a full panoply of due process protections to defendants prosecuted under these treaty-inspired domestic criminal laws.[19]

Over the last fifteen years, the United States has repeatedly although by no means exclusively invoked this criminal law model as its dominant strategy in response to international terrorism. After the December 1988 bombing of Pan Am flight 103 over Lockerbie, Scotland, the United States sought the extradition of two Libyan intelligence agents believed to have masterminded the bombing. Similarly, the February 1993 bombing of the World Trade Center led to the criminal investigation and prosecution of the Islamic terrorists alleged to be responsible. Most recently, U.S. prosecutors filed indictments against Osama bin Laden and fourteen other individuals who orchestrated the August 1998 bombings of two American embassies in East Africa. In each of these instances, the United States consciously adopted a multilateral strategy, seeking the assistance of foreign governments in identifying, apprehending, and extraditing suspects to stand trial for their crimes under U.S. law.[20]

Applying this strategy to the September 11 attacks exposes significant limitations of the criminalization approach. Outlawing terrorist acts through international treaties makes two critical assumptions: first, that terrorists are private parties or rogue officials acting without the support of their governments; and, second, that states are both willing and able to fulfill their obligations under the treaties. Where either of these assumptions does not hold, the international criminalization model breaks down.

Consider the 1988 bombing of Pan Am flight 103. The United States ultimately determined that Libya was responsible for the destruction. Not surprisingly, the United States was rebuffed by Muammar el-Qaddafi when it asked him to turn over the accused Libyan intelligence officers for trial in the United States or the United Kingdom. Libya then filed suit before the International Court of Justice, asking the court to confirm that Libya's investigation into the bombings would be conclusive of its international obligations. Ultimately, a compromise was reached whereby the defendants were extradited to the Netherlands to be tried by a special Scottish court established solely for purposes of their prosecution.[21] After a trial and an appeal, one suspect was convicted and sentenced to life in prison, and the other was acquitted and freed.[22] These events exposed critical weaknesses in the international extradite-or-prosecute regime.[23]

Although the facts of the September 11 attacks differ, they are equally incapable of being addressed solely through a criminalization approach. True, Al Qaeda is a private terrorist network and thus its members are the type of individuals contemplated for prosecution under the treaties. But Al Qaeda's base of operations was located in a state that, although nominally a party to three terrorism conventions,[24] was ruled by a government that endorsed Al Qaeda's activities and provided safe haven for its worldwide operations.[25] Thus little could be gained for the United States by seeking the extradition of senior Al Qaeda members from a state that openly flouted its treaty commitments.[26]

Perhaps more importantly, a criminalization approach to terrorism is inconsistent with the more assertively unilateralist objectives that the United States has for a post-9/11 world. These objectives include, first, the immediate and effective deterrence of Al Qaeda's activities and, second, a desire for justice that eschews standard judicial prosecutions and their associated rights protections[27] in favor of indefinite detentions[28] and procedures tailor-made to favor conviction and punishment.[29]

If a criminal law approach to punishing the September 11 attackers was problematic, the United States had at the ready an alternative framing of terrorism, one more attuned to its invigorated preference for unilateral responses. This framing views terrorism not as a crime but as a form of armed conflict. In the days following September 11, President Bush expressly invoked the rhetoric of a "war" against terrorism and began a military campaign in Afghanistan less than a month later.[30] Over the last fifteen years, there has also been ample precedent for this use of force in response to terrorist attacks against U.S. citizens and property.

Following the April 1986 bombing of a nightclub in West Berlin frequented by American troops, the United States bombed military and paramilitary targets in Libya.[31] Following the 1998 East Africa embassy bombings, the United States took similar military action against terrorist training camps in Afghanistan and against a pharmaceutical plant in Sudan believed to be producing chemical weapons. In both instances, the United States defended its response by invoking its inherent right of self-defense under Article 51 of the UN Charter.[32]

These uses of force by the United States were, however, in tension with an international system designed to regulate armed conflict between states and to confine unilateral responses within multilateral limits. Only states may ratify the UN Charter, and thus only states are obligated to refrain from "the threat or use of force against the territorial integrity or political independence" of any other state.[33] Similarly, the four 1949 Geneva Conventions that codify the core principles of international humanitarian law principally concern conflicts among states parties.[34] By invoking its inherent right of self-defense in response to September 11, the United States has claimed that nonstate actors can carry out an "armed attack" against a state within the meaning of the UN Charter.[35] It thus seeks to justify unilateral use of force against private terrorist networks by invoking responses traditionally reserved for interstate conflicts, including the view that attackers are "enemies"—not "criminals"—who can be killed in battle rather than prosecuted.

Precisely how international law will respond to this framing of private terrorism as armed conflict is still uncertain.[36] On the one hand, a detailed set of rules exists for attributing the conduct of private parties to states. These rules of state responsibility make it possible to transform a conflict that is nominally between a state and private actors into a classic interstate dispute.[37] The U.S. bombings in Afghanistan are consistent with these rules, given that state's support and harboring of Al Qaeda.[38] But any attempt by the United States to expand its military campaign to private terrorist operations in other states without the consent of those states or the authorization of the Security Council would seriously undermine existing international law restrictions on the unilateral use of force.

Finally, international terrorism can be viewed as a type of atrocity, a term that Steven Ratner has defined as encompassing criminal acts "characterized by the directness and gravity of their assault upon the human person, both corporeal and spiritual."[39] The most significant among these acts are genocide, war crimes, and crimes against humanity. International law imposes criminal responsibility directly on individuals who perpetrate these horrific acts. State action is not required, nor is criminality conditioned on the voluntary ratification of a treaty.[40]

States have increasingly claimed universal jurisdiction to try individuals who commit these atrocities in their domestic courts regardless of the offenders' nationality or the place where the crimes occurred.[41] Since the Nuremberg and Tokyo tribunals following World War II, however, states have also empowered international jurists and prosecutors to assess criminal responsibility and mete out punishments. The most recent and most far-reaching of these institutions is the International Criminal Court, which commenced operations in July 2002.[42]

Although the contours of international atrocity law are slowly expanding, it may at first appear that terrorist acts do not rise to the level of true atrocities.[43] But the magnitude of the attacks in New York fit comfortably within the International Criminal Court's definition of crimes against humanity, which include murder and other inhumane acts intentionally causing great suffering that are "committed as part of a widespread or systematic attack directed against any civilian population, with knowledge of the attack."[44]

Why then is the United States not seeking to prosecute Al Qaeda agents before an international tribunal,[45] as Anne-Marie Slaughter has suggested?[46] In part, the answer lies in its preference for framing terrorism as armed conflict, an approach that makes the United States profoundly suspicious of multilateral institutions that it perceives as limiting its options for a unilateral response. The likelihood of a prolonged war on terrorism and the global scope of its targets would require granting any international tribunal a broad jurisdictional mandate, a mandate inconsistent with the steadfast, if overblown, opposition of the United States to the International Criminal Court.[47]

I conclude with a few brief observations about the ways in which each of the three paradigms for controlling international terrorism might evolve in the wake of the September 11 attacks. First, with regard to criminalization, we are already seeing the beginnings of a more robust condemnation of terrorism in international law extending beyond the suppression of specific wrongful acts. This condemnation is endorsed by states of all political stripes, including Muslim and Arab states and states once suspicious of criminalization's impact on postcolonial independence movements.[48] The more extensive state support is reflected in Security Council Resolution 1373,[49] adopted less than three weeks after the September 11 attacks. This broadly worded and unanimous resolution requires member states to target terrorists and those who harbor or support them, to suppress the financing of terrorism, and to exchange information on possible terrorist acts.[50] The resolution also creates a special committee to review whether states are complying with these new obligations.[51]

The evidence that the committee gathers will also be useful in assessing refinements to the second paradigm—terrorism as armed conflict. The response to September 11 indicates acceptance of the U.S. claim that private terrorist networks can carry out an armed attack under the UN Charter, at least where that attack emanates from a rogue state widely condemned by the international community. A far more difficult question is whether the use of force can be justified against other states unable to control or exclude terrorists[52] or that do not otherwise meet U.S. antiterrorism demands. Interactions between this category of states and those aggressively seeking to deter terrorism is likely to determine international law's evolution. One plausible pathway would preserve the primacy of state-to-state conflict but dilute the rules of state responsibility to allow for greater attribution of nonstate conduct based on more attenuated forms of state acquiescence.[53] Another pathway would retain existing attribution rules but accept as lawful some types of unilateral, nonterritorially circumscribed uses of military force against autonomous terrorist networks who operate across borders.

With respect to the atrocities paradigm, international law may evolve to include terrorism as a genuine atrocity at which the world levels its most dire condemnation and most extensive punishment mechanisms. U.S. commentators, for example, have long argued that certain terrorist acts should be subject to universal jurisdiction in national courts, even in states that are not parties to specific terrorism conventions.[54] Terrorists might also be prosecuted before the International Criminal Court. But such prosecutions will be possible only for acts committed by the nationals of a state party or in the territory of a state party, and only for those acts that clearly meet the definitions of genocide, war crimes, or crimes against humanity. Other forms of terrorism will be beyond the new court's power, a fact confirmed by the express exclusion of terrorism as such from the court's statute.[55]

In sum, therefore, I do not see the September 11 attacks as a "Grotian moment" that changed the world order. Instead, their enduring legacy for international law is likely to be as a catalyst for both multilateral and unilateral efforts—sometimes consistent efforts, sometimes conflictual

ones—to recalibrate existing legal paradigms in light of the changed geo-
strategic climate that transborder private terrorist networks have engendered.

Notes

My thanks to Jeff Atik and Greg Fox for comments on earlier versions of this essay.

1. One recent identification of a transformative event in law (both international and national) is the creation of the Internet. An initial wave of legal scholarship framed the Internet as destabilizing existing legal categories and compelling a reconceptualization of legal
relationships in both virtual and real space. David R. Johnson and David Post, "Law and
Borders—The Rise of Law in Cyberspace," *Stanford Law Review* 48 (1996): 1367, 1387–
91 (discussing the rise of a separate law of cyberspace). A second generation of scholars
quickly challenged this characterization, arguing that legal rules and paradigms developed offline are sufficient in their present form to address the legal dimensions of online
conduct. See e.g., Jack L. Goldsmith, "The Internet and the Abiding Significance of Territorial Sovereignty," *Indiana Journal of Global Legal Studies* 5 (1998): 475–491. The truth
is likely to lie somewhere between these two polar extremes. While academic debates
continue, national and international lawmaking institutions regulating the Internet are
applying both existing norms and developing new ones, in the process generating experience and insights that will eventually affect legal regulation in the offline world. See
Laurence R. Helfer and Graeme B. Dinwoodie, "Designing Non-national Systems: The
Case of the Uniform Domain Name Dispute Resolution Policy," *William and Mary Law
Review* 43 (2001): 141, 253–68.

2. Grotius's most renowned work is *De jure belli ac pacis,* first published in 1635. See Hugo
Grotius, *De jure belli ac pacis,* trans. A. C. Campbell Eng (Washington, D.C.: M. Walter
Dunne, 1901). For a discussion of the significance of Grotius's writings, see Hedley Bull,
Benedict Kingsbury, and Adam Roberts, eds., *Hugo Grotius and International Relations*
(Oxford: Clarendon Press, 1990); H. Lauterpacht, "The Grotian Tradition in International
Law," *British Year Book of International Law* 23 (1946): 1–53.

3. See, e.g., Hedley Bull, "The Importance of Grotius in the Study of International Relations" in Bull et al., *Grotius and International Relations,* 65, 78–91 (identifying five enduring features of Grotius's view of international society: the centrality of natural law,
universality, the place of individuals and nonstate groups, solidarism in the enforcement
of rules, and the absence of international institutions).

4. As Benedict Kingsbury has written, these "internationalist references to Grotius scarcely
claim to be more than purely emblematic, conveying little beyond a spirit or sense long
received into the culture and lexicon of legal internationalism." Benedict Kingsbury, "A
Grotian Tradition of Theory and Practice? Grotius, Law, and Moral Skepticism in the
Thought of Hedley Bull," *Quinnipiac Law Review* 17 (1997): 3, 10. The association of Grotius with the idea of transformation fails to convey an accurate conception of his endeav-
ors or accomplishments, but it is nevertheless an important feature of how international
legal scholars have sought to conceptualize change.

5. See, e.g., Richard Falk, *Law in an Emerging Global Village: A Post-Westphalian Perspective* (Ardsley, N.Y.: Transnational Publishers, 1998); Richard Falk, "A New Paradigm
for International Legal Studies: Prospects and Proposals," in *International Law: A Contemporary Perspective,* ed. Richard Falk, Friedrich Kratochwil, and Saul H. Mendlovitz

(Boulder, Colo.: Westview Press, 1985), 651–702. Falk's efforts to identify and articulate a "Grotian moment" stretch back nearly twenty years. See Richard Falk, introduction to *Hugo Grotius: The Miracle of Holland,* by Charles S. Edwards (Chicago: Nelson-Hall, 1981), xiii–xxi.

6. Boutros Boutros-Ghali, "The Role of International Law in the Twenty-First Century: A Grotian Moment," *Fordham International Law Journal* 18 (1995): 1609–1616.

7. Christopher Weeramantry and Nathaniel Berman, "The Grotius Lecture Series," *American University International Law Review* 14 (1999): 1515–59. See also Robert Jackson, "The Grotian Moment in World Jurisprudence," *International Insights* 13 (special issue, fall 1997): 35–55; Samuel K. Murumba, "Grappling with a Grotian Moment: Sovereignty and the Quest for Normative World Order," *Brooklyn Journal of International Law* 19 (1993): 829–69.

8. Falk, "A New Paradigm," 666.

9. Falk, *Law in an Emerging Global Village,* 33.

10. Falk, "A New Paradigm," 673.

11. See W. Michael Reisman, "International Legal Responses to Terrorism," *Houston Journal of International Law* 22 (1999): 3, 55–56 (distinguishing terrorist organizations that act as private contractors for governments from terrorist groups acting as "autonomous private operators" and stating that "the international decision process has been remarkably ambivalent about the appropriate responses to be taken with respect to private terrorists").

12. John Arquilla and David Rondfeldt, *Cyberwar Is Coming!* Rand Occasional Paper P-7791 1992, reprinted in *In Athena's Camp: Preparing for Conflict in the Information Age,* ed. John Arquilla and David Rondfeldt (Santa Monica, Calif.: Rand Corp., 1997), 23, 49.

13. See U.S. Department of State, *Significant Terrorist Incidents, 1961–2001,* http://www.state.gov/r/pa/ho/pubs/fs/5902.htm.

14. See, e.g., UN General Assembly Resolution 3034 (1972), which expressed concern over acts of international terrorism but also reaffirmed "the inalienable right to self-determination and independence of all peoples under colonial and racist regimes and other forms of alien domination and upholds the legitimacy of their struggle." General Assembly Resolution 3034, 27 UN GAOR [General Assembly Official Records] Supp. (no. 30) at 119, UN Doc. A/8730 (1972), reprinted in *United Nations Year Book* 26 (1972): 649–50.

15. M. Cherif Bassiouni, "Legal Control of International Terrorism: A Policy-Oriented Assessment," *Harvard Journal of International Law* 43 (2002): 83, 91 (noting the absence of a comprehensive convention governing the international dimensions of the fight against terrorism).

16. The major international conventions on the subject include the 1963 Tokyo Convention on Offenses and Certain Other Acts Committed on Board Aircraft, entered into force December 4, 1969, 20 U.S.T. [U.S. Treaties] 2941, T.I.A.S. [Treaties and Other International Acts Series] no. 6768, 704 U.N.T.S. [UN Treaty Series] 219, 2 I.L.M. [International Legal Materials] 1042; the 1970 Hague Convention for the Unlawful Seizure of Aircraft, entered into force October 14, 1981, 22 U.S.T. 1641, T.I.A.S. no. 7192, 10 I.L.M. 133; the 1971 Montreal Convention for the Suppression of Unlawful Acts against the Safety of Civil Aviation, entered into force January 26, 1973, 24 U.S.T. 565, T.I.A.S. no. 7570, 10 I.L.M. 1151; the 1973 Convention on the Prevention and Punishment of Crimes against Internationally Protected Persons, Including Diplomatic Agents, entered into force February 20, 1977, 28 U.S.T. 1975, T.I.A.S. no. 8532, 13 I.L.M. 41; the 1979 Convention against the Taking of Hostages, entered into force June 3, 1983, T.I.A.S. no. 11081, 18 I.L.M. 1456; the 1988 Rome Convention for the Suppression of Unlawful Acts against the Safety of Maritime Navigation, entered into

force March 1, 1992, S. Treaty Doc. no. 101-1, 27 I.L.M. 668; and the 1991 Convention on the Marking of Plastic Explosives for the Purpose of Detection, March 1, 1991, 30 I.L.M. 726.

17. See Convention for the Suppression of Terrorist Bombings, adopted by the General Assembly on January 9, 1998, G.A. Res. 52/164, 37 I.L.M. 249; Convention for the Suppression of the Financing of Terrorism, adopted by the General Assembly on December 9, 1999, G.A. Res. 54/109 (December 9, 1999), 39 I.L.M. 270 (2000). The Terrorist Bombings Convention entered into force in May 2001. The Financing of Terrorism Convention will enter into force after twenty-two states have ratified it. See Sean D. Murphy, "Contemporary Practice of the United States Relating to International Law—Conventions on the Suppression of Terrorist Bombings and on Financing," *American Journal of International Law* 98 (2002): 255.

18. See Murphy, "Contemporary Practice," 256 (identifying these obligations of conventions relating to international terrorism).

19. The most widely ratified human rights treaty protecting the rights of defendants during the trial and appellate process is the International Covenant on Civil and Political Rights, adopted December 19, 1966, 999 U.N.T.S. 171 (entered into force March 23, 1976).

20. See Harvard Law Review, "Responding to Terrorism: Crime, Punishment, and War," *Harvard Law Review* 115 (2002): 1217, 1281–21 (discussing United States responses to these three acts of international terrorism).

21. Marlise Simons, "2 Libyans Formally Charged in 1988 Pan Am Bombing," *New York Times,* April 7, 1999, sec. A, p. 8.

22. Anthony Deutsch, "Lockerbie Appeal Is Rejected," *Chicago Tribune,* March 15, 2002, p. 6; Harvard Law Review, "Responding to Terrorism," 1219.

23. See Reisman, "International Legal Responses," 22–23 (referring to these events as the "Lockerbie problem" and stating that terrorism treaties are "by themselves of little use if the terrorism in question is state-sponsored and the terrorist state is expected to cooperate in its own investigation and conviction").

24. Afghanistan is a party to the Tokyo, Hague, and Montreal Conventions protecting civil aircraft and civil aviation. See United Nations Treaty Collection, *Conventions on Terrorism,* http://untreaty.un.org/English/Terrorism.asp. In general, the obligations a state assumes in the international agreements it ratifies persist even after a change in its internal governance structure. See Lucinda Love, "International Agreement Obligations after the Soviet Union's Break-Up: Current United States Practice and Its Consistency with International Law," *Vanderbilt Journal of Transnational Law* 26 (1993): 373, 375 n. 1 (citing authorities).

25. See UN Security Council Resolution 1378, s/Res/1378 (November 14, 2001) (condemning "the Taliban for allowing Afghanistan to be used as a base for the export of terrorism by the Al-Qaida network and other terrorist groups and for providing safe haven to Usama Bin Laden, Al-Qaida and others associated with them").

26. See Charles Hoskinson, "Bush Warns Taliban 'Time Is Running Out,'" Agence France-Presse, 2001 WL [Westlaw] 25030468 (October 6, 2001) (stating that Taliban refused to hand over bin Laden and called for a holy war against the United States). See also Bassiouni, "Legal Control of International Terrorism," 87 (noting that United States never formally sought Osama bin Laden's extradition from Afghanistan).

27. Cf. Elizabeth Olson, "U.N. Fears 'Bloc' Voters Are Abetting Rights Abuses," *New York Times,* April 28, 2002, p. 17 (noting that divisions within the UN Human Rights Commission required tabling of a resolution that antiterrorist measures must conform with international human rights and humanitarian law).

28. See Bryan Bender, "U.S. Affirms Indefinite Detentions; Sets Trial Rules for Afghanistan

Combatants," *Boston Globe,* March 22, 2002, sec. A, p. 1; Katherine W. Seelye, "Pentagon Says Acquittals May Not Free Detainees," *New York Times,* March 22, 2002, sec. A, p. 13.

29. See Military Order, *Detention, Treatment, and Trial of Certain Non-citizens in the War against Terrorism,* 66 Fed. Reg. 57,833 (November 16, 2001). See also Harvard Law Review, "Responding to Terrorism," 1235–37 (arguing that the "primary American interest created by the September 11 attacks is the successful punishment of those responsible" and that military tribunals serve that interest by "reduc[ing] the probability that a suspected terrorist will escape conviction"). For debates about the propriety of prosecuting terrorists before military tribunals, see Jordan J. Paust, "Antiterrorism Military Commissions: Courting Illegality," *Michigan Journal of International Law* 23 (2002): 1–29; Kenneth Anderson, "What to Do with bin Laden and Al Qaeda Terrorists? A Qualified Defense of Military Commissions and United States Policy on Detainees at Guantánamo Bay Naval Base," *Harvard Journal of Law and Public Policy* 25 (2002): 591–633.

30. See George W. Bush, "Address before a Joint Session of the Congress on the United States Response to the Terrorist Attacks of September 11," *Weekly Compilation of Presidential Documents* 37 (September 20, 2001): 1347 ("On September 11th, enemies of freedom committed an act of war against our country.").

31. See Reisman, "International Legal Responses," 31–34 and n. 109.

32. See Michael J. Glennon, "The Fog of Law: Self-Defense, Inherence, and Incoherence in Article 51 of the United Nations Charter," *Harvard Journal of Law and Public Policy* 25 (2002): 539, 543 n. 15 (bombing of Libya); Jules Lobel, "The Use of Force to Respond to Terrorist Attacks: The Bombing of Sudan and Afghanistan," *Yale Journal of International Law* 24 (1999): 537, 537 (bombing of Sudan and Afghanistan).

33. UN Charter, art. 2(4).

34. See, e.g., Third Geneva Convention Relative to the Treatment of Prisoners of War, 75 U.N.T.S. 287, art. 2, entered into force October 21, 1950 ("In addition to the provisions which shall be implemented in peace time, the present Convention shall apply to all cases of declared war or of any other armed conflict *which may arise between two or more of the High Contracting Parties,* even if the state of war is not recognized by one of them.") (emphasis added).

35. See Curtis A. Bradley and Jack L. Goldsmith, "The Constitutional Validity of Military Commissions," *Green Bag* 5 (2002): 249, 256.

36. See Anne-Marie Slaughter and William Burke-White, "An International Constitutional Moment," *Harvard Journal of International Law* 43 (2002): 1, 7–8 (stating that one important and unsettled issue raised by September 11 is the extent to which "armed conflict," in particular as defined in the Geneva Conventions, also applies to terrorist attacks).

37. See Responsibility of States for Internationally Wrongful Acts, UN GAOR, International Law Commission 53d sess., pt. 1, UN Doc. A/CN.4/L.602/Rev.1 (2001).

38. See UN Security Council Resolution 1378 (condemning the Taliban for harboring and supporting the Al Qaeda network). But see Gregory H. Fox, "Addendum to *ASIL Insight* on Terrorist Attacks," *ASIL Insight,* September 2001, http://www.asil.org/insights/insigh77.htm#addendum (noting that in 1985 the UN Security Council condemned Israel for bombing the headquarters of the Palestine Liberation Organization located in Tunisia and rejected the claim that the bombing of Tunisia was justifiable in light of that state's harboring of terrorists who had targeted Israel).

39. Steven R. Ratner and Jason S. Abrams, *Accountability for Human Rights Atrocities in International Law: Beyond the Nuremberg Legacy,* 2d ed. (Oxford: Oxford University Press, 2001), 13.

40. See Bruno Simma and Andreas L. Paulus, "The Responsibility of Individuals for Human Rights Abuses in Internal Conflicts: A Positivist View," *American Journal of International Law* 93 (1999): 302, 308. See also Bradley and Goldsmith, "The Constitutional Validity of Military Commissions," 257 ("even if the September 11 attacks cannot be attributed to the Taliban, there is good reason to believe that the laws of war apply to nonstate actors like al Qaeda").

41. For a recent discussion of how universal jurisdiction interacts with the immunity of high-ranking government officials, see Arrest Warrant of April 11, 2000 (*Democratic Republic of the Congo v. Belgium*), 2002 I.C.J. [International Court of Justice] (February 14), http://www.icj-cij.org/icjwww/idecisions.htm (Joint Separate Opinion of Judges Higgins, Kooijmans, and Buergenthal).

42. William Orme, "An International Criminal Court Comes into Being," *Los Angeles Times,* April 12, 2002, sec. A, p. 3.

43. See Bradley and Goldsmith, "The Constitutional Validity of Military Commissions," 256 ("The laws of war apply in the context of an 'armed conflict' regardless of whether war has been formally declared. These laws, however, do not apply to isolated or sporadic acts of violence and thus may not apply to some acts of terrorism.").

44. Rome Statute of the International Criminal Court, July 17, 1998, art. 7, UN DOC. A/CONF. 183.9. See Frederic L. Kirgis, "Terrorist Attacks on the World Center and the Pentagon," *ASIL Insights,* September 2001, http://www.asil.org./insights/insigh77.htm (suggesting that the September 11 attacks "may be a crime against humanity under international law").

In addition, Protocol 1 to the Geneva Conventions treats nonstate actors in national liberation wars on a par with state armed forces and thus subject to those conventions' atrocities ban. Protocol Additional to the Geneva Conventions of August 12, 1949 and Relating to the Protection of Victims of International Armed Conflicts, opened for signature December 12, 1977, 1125 U.N.T.S. 3, 6 I.L.M. 1391. Many of these same nonstate actors have been labeled "terrorists" by their opponents. See Theodor Meron, "The Time Has Come for the United States to Ratify Geneva Protocol I," in *War Crimes Law Comes of Age* (New York: Oxford University Press, 1999), 175, 181 (noting U.S. perception that Protocol 1 was "proterrorist" and created "the specter of the PLO, the African National Congress and countless others both terrorizing civilian populations and successfully claiming combatant and POW privileges").

45. A special international criminal tribunal would need to be convened to try the perpetrators of the September 11 attacks, inasmuch as the International Criminal Court has no jurisdiction over offenses committed before the Rome Statute entered into force in July 2002. Rome Statute, art. 11(1).

46. Anne-Marie Slaughter, "Terrorism and Justice," *Financial Times,* October 12, 2001, 15.

47. Letter of May 6, 2002 to UN Secretary General Kofi Annan from Under Secretary of State for Arms Control and International Security John R. Bolton, http://www.state.gov/r/pa/prs/ps/2002/9968.htm (expressing the intention of the United States not to become a party to the treaty establishing the International Criminal Court).

48. See Kuala Lumpur Declaration on International Terrorism, adopted at the Extraordinary Session of the Islamic Conference of Foreign Ministers on Terrorism par. 7 (April 1–3, 2002), http://www.oic-oci.org/english/fm/11_extraordinary/declaration.htm ("We unequivocally condemn acts of international terrorism in all its forms and manifestations, including state terrorism, irrespective of motives, perpetrators and victims as terrorism poses a serious threat to international peace and security and is a grave violation of human

rights."). The League of Arab States stated that the attacks against the World Trade Center and the Pentagon were "deserving of all condemnation." See http://www.avot.org/stories/storyreader$63.

49. UN Security Council Resolution 1373, S/Res/1373 (September 28, 2001).

50. Ibid., pars. 1–2 (providing that "all States shall," *inter alia,* "prevent and suppress the financing of terrorist acts" and "refrain from any form of support, active, or passive, to entities or persons involved in terrorist acts").

51. Ibid., par. 6.

52. See Reisman, "International Legal Responses," 50–54 (discussing terrorist attacks emanating from states in this category).

53. The two most significant international court decisions addressing state responsibility are Case Concerning Military and Paramilitary Activities in and against Nicaragua (*Nicaragua v. USA*), [1986] I.C.J. Rep. 14, 64–5 (holding a state responsible for the actions of private paramilitary actors where such actors are "agents" of the state or under the "effective control" of the state), and *Prosecutor v. Dusko Tadic,* case no. IT-94-1-A, Judgment, Appeals Chamber, July 15, 1999, 115–45, available at http://www.un.org/icty (adopting a standard for state responsibility based on state's "overall control" of private actors or "the assimilation of individuals to state organs on account of their actual behaviour within the structure of a state"). For a discussion of the conflicting standards these two cases adopt, see Shane Spelliscy, "The Proliferation of International Tribunals: A Chink in the Armor," *Columbia Journal of Transnational Law* 40 (2001): 143, 159–68.

54. See Restatement (Third) of the Foreign Relations Law of the United States, sec. 404, comment a (1986) ("Universal jurisdiction is increasingly accepted for certain acts of terrorism, such as assaults on the life or physical integrity of diplomatic personnel, kidnapping, and indiscriminate violent assaults on people at large.").

55. Reisman, "International Legal Responses," 58 (noting that the United States successfully resisted including terrorism within the jurisdiction of the International Criminal Court).

Empire's Law: Foreign Relations by Presidential Fiat

RUTI G. TEITEL

This essay considers the question of whether September 11 had an impact on the relationship of law and politics. It begins with the question of methodology. While recognition of historical continuities is important, my essay primarily focuses, instead, on new developments in the particular relationship of law and politics. The essay contends, first, that an analysis of the law post–September 11 can illuminate the politics involved and, moreover, that such an analysis suggests that we are indeed in a constructed transformative moment—that analysis of the legal responses to 9/11 reveals the concerted attempt to shift the site of political sovereignty at present and, in particular, to the U.S. executive.

The Problem of Method

Consider to begin with the methodological question regarding the extent to which September 11 is a transformative moment in the relationship of law and politics.[1] What this essay explores here is the relationship between the legal responses of the Bush administration and the events themselves in order to better understand how the sense of the transformative significance of these political events is constructed by the law.

The prevailing approach to the relationship of law and politics tends to miss the particular significance of the role of law because, in regard to the current administration, there is a tendency to adopt a highly "realist" approach to law and politics, one that is almost nihilistic as to the expectations of the law.[2] The realists tend to conflate the question of the rule of law with the political. In the realist approach, the legal response to September 11 is largely a product of the politics of September 11, which in turn is thought to relate to the prevailing power balance of the various relevant political actors, such as the administration, the Congress, and the people, as well as the international community.

While it explains a lot, a problem with the realist approach is that it does not provide an adequate account for the role of law. An alternative approach to understanding September 11 emerges in the vivid debate between the realists and the idealists. From the idealist perspective on the post–September 11 political situation, there are a number of principles of law and normative values that should have been adhered to during this period, in particular relating to civil liberties and to the tradeoffs posed between the interests of the state and the rights of individuals and groups.[3] The antinomy posed here relates to varying conceptions of the relation of law and politics: idealists tend to consider law to be largely independent of political factors, while realist (and critical) legal theorizing tends to emphasize law's close relationship to politics.

This essay attempts to navigate the shoals of Scylla and Charybdis, to negotiate the constraints of the realist and idealist approaches, and to discuss the relationship of law and politics during this period via an alternative interpretive approach, which I contend offers a better account of what happened. One might characterize this interpretation as reflecting a pragmatic approach to the relationship of law and politics. That approach is aimed at trying to clarify to what extent we are in a transformative moment and precisely how one might understand the constructive impact of the Bush administration's responses.

The historical perspective that Marilyn Young adopts in her essay in this volume helpfully illuminates for us the continuities in the administration's approach. Young contends that the current responses in the war against terrorism involve a geopolitical balance of power historically reminiscent of the high Cold War period, namely, the period immediately following the Second World War, when the United States clearly emerged as the world's sole global power for a time. Young then goes on to suggest a way in which the current behavior of the United States is continuous with its historical political role and to point to other ways in which current U.S. unilateralism appears to go even farther than that of the high Cold War period. Beyond the Cold War analogy in Young's essay lies another analogy to a broader war model. One question this raises is whether the right analogy here is to the Cold War, to a hotter war, or to something other than war.

In my own view, understanding the current administration's actions may necessitate thinking in terms of other paradigms. The argument here is that we should turn away from the exceptional character of a war and turn instead to the juridical-political regime associated with absolute sovereignty and security, tentatively termed here "empire's law."[4]

Narrating September 11: Transitional Narratives of War and Justice

Shortly after September 11, a debate began about the political and social construction of the events being played out in the media and in the Bush administration. The first narrative after the events begins with the story of the World Trade Center towers' collapse, and thousands killed, as a deplorable tragedy. This tragic narrative lasts a very short time, for such a narrative elicits no necessary response, but fatalism. This is un-American; there has to be something to do. Almost immediately thereafter, the tragic narrative gives way to a "justice" narrative. When the World Trade towers' collapse is characterized as an "attack,"[5] it reframes the administration's response. In "Operation Infinite Justice," the administration begins to characterize the events as a failure of criminal law; and the call is issued to bring Osama bin Laden to "justice." Almost from the start, the term "Operation Infinite Justice" was criticized for its absolutist, jihad-sounding language, yet it was perhaps an honest reflection of the administration's position and policy direction. To respond to extremist fundamentalism, there must be universals. And there would later be a similar rhetoric of morality aligned with the administration's political response.

Thereafter, there commenced an evident debate within the administration regarding what the proper response to the September 11 events should be. While there was an appeal to launching the "war against terrorism," there was also language alluding to alternative, competing juridical-political models. The reference to "campaigns" suggests that what is at stake is not a conventional war but, rather, an ongoing police operation: "Operation Infinite Justice."

What then took center stage was a growing debate over which model—war or justice—was most apropos for explaining September 11 and its aftermath. In this regard, there were various camps, with the defense establishment supporting the military model, while the legal establishment, some members of Congress, and civil libertarians, in particular, were insisting that the events of September 11 posed a problem of justice and that its perpetrators ought to be treated like those implicated in the 1993 attempts on the World Trade Center, namely, along the lines of ordinary federal judicial processes.[6] No coherent explanation was offered for why the events of 2002 should not be handled like those in 1993.

While there has been discussion of diverse war-versus-justice responses to September 11, at the start these responses were not always so easily distinguishable in the realm of international affairs, as there has historically been a close nexus in the discourses of war and justice. Indeed, historically, there has been an established role for international criminal trials in the justification of war, meant to rationalize and support the aims of military intervention in the name of humanity.[7]

Yet it hardly mattered which side of the debate one followed: whether it was the war model that would treat the Taliban regime and its allies as the enemy, guided by the relevant law of war, or the justice model that would treat members of Al Qaeda and those who harbored them as criminals subject to domestic law. The more profound problem here was that the administration saw no reason to commit to either of these conditions, seeking to follow neither the law of war, including the agreements binding on the United States in periods of conflict,[8] nor, ordinarily, applicable domestic criminal or constitutional law.[9] Instead, it seemed to be deliberately seeking out gray areas of nonlaw, or "no-law."

The position that emerged is that the military appeared not to be accountable to the ordinary domestic legal regime, but neither was it subject to a general application of an international humanitarian regime. Whereas in ordinary times the military would have been fully subject to a juridical regime, what became apparent was the attempt to use September 11 as an occasion for an extended "emergency" and a state of exception regarding the law. More and more, the administration called for law that was "exceptional." The claim was that because the United States was in an exceptional position, whatever related law was exceptional, and determining instances of departure, or exception, from law would be fully up to the administration.[10]

To what extent is this administration's position new, and to what extent is it related to September 11? Just how much continuity is there in the administration's approach? Even before September 11, there had already been a substantial collapse of the law of war and the law of peace and a move toward significant overlap of these in the discourse of human rights and other foreign affairs. The political conditions of the heightened political transitions at the close of the twentieth century, along with spiraling political fragmentation, have led to failed or weak states, steady-state small wars, and the apparent toleration of ongoing conflict. I have characterized this as the "normalization" of transitional political conditions, which are associated with the apparent entrenchment of an ongoing law of conflicts. A central concern of the international rule of law at present has become how to manage ongoing situations of conflict in global politics.[11]

What has become more and more acceptable in the international realm is the possibility of the violation of national sovereignty, particularly intervention in states that are already in recognized situations of diminished sovereignty.[12] This scenario has become increasingly common as a result of the end-of-century transitions, which have given rise to weak states and pervasive political violence. A leading example is Kosovo, where political conditions were such that it was considered largely in keeping with international legitimacy to engage in a campaign of humanitarian intervention.[13] This was the political backdrop to the September 11 events and the subsequent U.S. intervention in Afghanistan, which, although more controversial than the intervention in the former Yugoslavia, garnered a good measure of European support and was not opposed by the United Nations.

What becomes apparent is that, in the context of present political realities, there is a greater acceptance of an evidently politicized jurisprudence, that is, the "normalization" of transitional justice.[14] This is the hyperpoliticized law associated with periods of political flux. What would ordinarily have been considered to be exceptional uses of the law, associated with extraordinary periods of conflict, have now became entrenched and generalized. Where the humanitarian law regime is used to justify intervention it reflects an instrumentalized relationship of international law to politics as well as the uses of the connection between the ethical aspects of the humanitarian law regime and the administration's explicit political aims.

I turn next to what I consider to be a plausible paradigm by which to understand the juridical-political regime post–September 11. The evidently politicized jurisprudence suggests that the apt analogy here is neither to a simple justice model nor to a model of war but rather to the world-sovereign security state. I shall also attempt to show the flaws in this model.

Law as Enforcement

The confluence of law and politics after September 11 suggests that the current administration's paradigm regarding law is really a form of "law of the exception" and that this is associated with the regime's conception of itself as the "sovereign police." It sees the role of the United States in the world as that of the one and only "superpower."[15] In this world vision, the United States has sovereign power over the "law of the exception."[16]

Moreover, the appeal to a state of permanent exception of lawlessness is being justified on a somewhat paradoxical moral basis. The exercise of power is being rationalized by an appeal to "universal" values. Consider to what extent the move out of law in the current regime is rationalized in terms of moral justifications invoked for the departure from the regular application of the law.[17] Both the response and its justification appear to be a move away from the rhetoric of politics and toward the realm of political theology.

It is the security model, rather than that of war or of justice, that best explains the United States in its present operative role and the U.S. approach to the reigning legal regime. The suspension of the law, which operates in the state of exception, is justified in terms of a police operation. Under this view, other countries are thought to have limited sovereignty, while the United States argues that it has a "right" to intervene in order to enforce the "violations" of the "law." Accordingly, the violation of the law constitutes the police justification enabling the U.S. "right" to intervene. Indeed, the law enforcement justification helps to explain the existing U.S. unilateralism seen in international affairs: the "sovereign police" paradigm is a model implying "limited" sovereignty for other countries, but nearly absolute sovereignty for the United States.[18]

In the security model, law's relationship to enforcement is utterly pragmatic. Moreover, police generally have full legal authority, and by analogy, in its foreign affairs, the United States generally observes international law and even deploys courts. For example, the United States supported the ad hoc tribunal for the former Yugoslavia, which inter alia served to legitimize NATO intervention in Kosovo.[19]

Still, the paradigm of the sovereign security state clarifies the limited potential for international law: namely, that its role must be fully reconcilable with a sovereign police power. This paradigm of the sovereign police model in current political realities helps to explain the logic of the U.S. approach to the International Criminal Court (ICC) and, more generally, to multilateral responses to violence. The logic is that the United States constitutes the world sovereign; it follows, therefore, that the United States can never be the subject of police action. For the United States to be the object of police power would pose a serious contradiction to the reigning logic. Accordingly, in this view, unilateralism is not hypocrisy but rather a position fully consistent with the United States's self-perception of its role in the world for some time now, particularly since September 11. Of course, the problem with the sovereign security argument here is that, while this administration view may be shared by others and offer some surface legal plausibility, it is ultimately lacking in coherence.

As a matter of political reality, the United States is currently not a world sovereign. Instead, today "security sovereignty" is shared, and it depends on bodies of principles that are widely applicable and enforceable, rendering the U.S. position favoring "nonlaw," or law of the exception, as out of step with the emerging consensus. This is elaborated below.

The Law of the Exception

Consider some illustrations of the use of law in the sovereign security state model. Relatedly, consider the relationship of the expansion of the security state to the growth in the executive, and the resulting risks, of an imperial presidency. I shall discuss three issues: first, the expansion of executive discretion that is characteristic of the police power and, in particular, the executive discretion in the administration's "military order" authorizing detentions in the war against terrorism; next, the proposed military tribunals and how and to what extent these illustrate the "police power" model; and, last, the U.S. position in the international community and, in particular, regarding the new International Criminal Court, the institution established to prosecute the most heinous offenses under international humanitarian law. The creation of the ICC has coincided with the post–September 11 responses and, therefore, offers a further illustration of the sovereign security state model.

Framing the lawless emergency: the November 13th order. Here, I address the "military" order authorizing the detention, treatment, and trial of certain noncitizens in the war against terrorism. Two months after September 11, on November 13, 2001, the Bush administration tried to impose regulations concerning the security situation at the time, and its characterization of the events reflects the invocation of the security state model.[20] It eventually became clear that the administration was not exactly looking for a legal analogy; just the reverse—it appeared to be looking for a way out of any applicable law. What became evident during this period, through the order's definition of the applicable administrative regime, was the creation of a state of exception: leading the order's findings are that the post–September 11 situation is a "national emergency." Moreover, the November 13 order asserts that it is "not practicable to apply in the proposed military commissions under order" "the principles of law and the rules of evidence generally recognized in the trials of criminal cases in the U.S. District Courts."[21] Indeed, this frames the state of exception regarding the applicable law. Present political realities are characterized as posing an "extraordinary emergency," and the related exceptions are justified by "an urgent and compelling government interest."²² "Compelling" interests are those of a constitutional order.

The political conditions being considered are exceptional and are defined in terms of security. This language already constitutes a move away from law, for the rationale of security is being used to justify the suspension of law, that is, law's operation in a state of exception. The definition in "security" terms is a regime definition of conditions that relate to the police role. The next point goes to the problem of defining just who is subject to the order. What is remarkable in light of the above statement of the "emergency" is the absence of a definition of the relevant subject of the order, whether of the substantive offenses or of the status of the individual subjects. According to the order, a person can be tried for violations of the "laws of war and other applicable laws"²³ with respect to "acts of international terrorism."²⁴ Yet the November 13 order lacks a definition of terrorism. Because of that, in addition to various definitions, including membership in Al Qaeda, the individuals subject to the military order and eligible for detention include "non-U.S. citizens," with respect to whom the presidency "determine[s] from time to time"²⁵ that, if they do not fit one of the other definitions, "it is in the interest of the U.S. that such individual[s] be subject to this order."²⁶ What this essentially means is that the definition of individuals subject to the detention order will be left entirely to the president.

The problem with the lack of definition in the November 13 order is that it shows the extent to which, despite the use of the term "military order" and the reference to "military commissions," this promulgation is hardly an exercise necessarily within the law of war. It is not clear whether mere membership in Al Qaeda, harboring terrorists, and other offenses left undefined in the order violate the law of war, which is, after all, the necessary predicate for the jurisdiction of the military commission, under both the common law and Article 21 of the Uniform Code of Military Justice.²⁷ Not all acts of international terrorism are necessarily violations of the law of war. Therefore, for the order to be applicable to the intended categories of acts and persons, added specific authority from Congress would be necessary. What is plain about the administration's November 13 order is the extent to which it is an illustration of apparently unbridled executive discretion.

Another problem of expanded executive prerogatives that threatens the separation of powers is the order's attempt to extend the jurisdiction of the proposed military commissions to acts not associated with September 11. This uncouples the authority of the proposed military commissions from Congress's September 18 joint resolution, which sanctioned force against those who planned, authorized, committed, or aided the terrorist attacks on September 11.[28] There is a remarkable gap between the predicate bases of the Bush order and the definition of the substantive offenses in the authority granted by the congressional resolution. For the congressional authority granted was rather limited, and it was defined in terms of September 11. Congress's resolution was most certainly not a declaration of war, whereas the administration's order is far more ambiguous—and a somewhat tautological statement of executive fiat. The November 13 order, which proposes military commissions to address offenses unrelated to the September 11 attacks, particularly against persons in the United States, in the absence of further congressional action, raises serious questions of both constitutional and statutory authority. What is patently clear is that the order constitutes an act of pure executive discretion.

Many months after September 11, this state of affairs has continued. Indeed, to this day, the administration has failed to publicly identify the suspects in its sweep.[29] Moreover, because of the secrecy and nontransparency of these detentions, even if there were definitions of the subjects or offenses in the order, it would be nearly impossible to verify the definition by the application of the order. Such secret detentions are the hallmark of the police state.[30]

There are other aspects of the military order, particularly in reference to the military tribunals, that raise serious problems of abuse of executive discretion. Even though the terms of the Bush order could apply to prisoners of war, it is not limited to them because it also includes "unlawful combatants" and others.[31] At least two categories of persons are protected under the law of war: "prisoners of war" and "unlawful combatants." However, the November 13 order also potentially applies to other categories of persons. Moreover, there is no attempt to reconcile the order with international law. That the order gives the president exclusive authority to make the determination of whether a person fits the categories of the order renders the order standardless and sweeping, a perfect illustration of pure executive discretion. It is remarkable to have a standardless order of this kind, without an independent appeal. This is in clear conflict with prevailing international law. Article 106 of the Third Geneva Convention requires a right of appeal for prisoners of war and provides that prisoners of war should be treated in the same manner as "the members of the armed forces of the detaining power."[32] The extraordinary unilateral nature of the president's decision pursuant to the order, together with the absence of standards, conflicts with the Third Geneva Convention, which specifically provides for a hearing by a competent tribunal to determine whether a person might fall into the category of either "unlawful combatant" or "prisoner of war." Indeed, in the absence of such hearings, persons in custody are supposed to be given the benefit of the presumption that they are prisoners of war.[33]

Moreover, under domestic law, the military order denies the basic remedy of habeas corpus provided by the U.S. Constitution. Denial of this supreme constitutional right, which is guaranteed except in the extraordinary emergency of "cases of rebellion or invasion,"[34] raises serious constitutional questions because the existence of such limiting political conditions would ordinarily be determined by Congress.[35] Indeed, the choice of Guantánamo Bay itself points to a deliberate selection of a site intended to be outside the parameters of the Constitution.[36]

Subsequent rules promulgated by the administration for guiding the proposed military tribunals may mitigate some of the problems with the original order.[37] Under the March 21, 2002, rules, a military tribunal's decisions will be reviewed by a three-member panel; however, without an independent appeals process,[38] many of the original concerns remain. Once again, what is underscored in the post–September 11 expanded prosecutorial powers is the nearly unfettered executive discretion over who will be prosecuted and under what rules, as well as what standards will guide the review of convictions and sentences.

The military tribunals. Next, I shall discuss aspects of the military tribunals that further illustrate the deployment of what I have characterized as the "law of exception." The November 13 order concerning the military tribunals proposed that suspected Al Qaeda members or supporters would be tried before them but also lumped together all sorts of disparate defendants and related laws. Again, what is suggested is that the United States is operating largely outside established legal regimes in the area of "exception." This is indeed a law of exception because the military tribunals follow neither U.S. law nor international law; nor are they commensurate with either the war model or the justice model. Instead, they are consistent with a security regime that functions at the limits of the law.

That the exceptional character of the military tribunals for terrorism suspects puts them in an "in between" or "no-law" legal zone can be seen in the mixed character of the offenses to be tried. "Terrorism" and "assisting terrorism" do not necessarily fall under the law of war. The hybridity of the proposed military tribunals is similarly seen in the judging powers of both civilian and military judges; and it is also evident in the potential subjects, which include both alien civilians and prisoners of war.

The extraordinary power arrogated by the executive epitomizes the sovereign police state. The president asserts the power to punish any noncitizen who violates a broadly defined understanding of the laws of war, but it is nevertheless a power that is not consistent with the laws of war. What is remarkable is the extent to which the president is going it alone here. There has not been a classic declaration of war regarding the events of September 11; the limited authority that Congress gave to the president was to engage in the "necessary and appropriate" use of force. Therefore, the so-called military tribunals actually have very little connection to September 11, but rather appear to be an illustration of the exploitation of contemporary political conditions to expand executive power in a remarkable way. Where the standard is "necessary and appropriate," then the review standard in the relevant inquiry would go to whether the actions taken are disproportionate, that is, whether secret detentions, military tribunals, and the absence of appeals are disproportionate to the limited state of emergency associated with September 11. To what extent will there be any judicial constraints on or any meaningful judicial review of the current policies?

The other characteristic aspect of the security regime seen here is that the notion of the "terrorist" has no fixed meaning and is left always open to definition (and expansion) by the executive; moreover, it is increasingly defined in terms of the classic "friend/enemy" distinction of politics.[39] This is clearly evident in the November 13 order when it refers to "non-citizens," who, by definition, are not full members of the decision-making community and are being treated in ways that ought to imply close judicial scrutiny.

In the present security regime, law is all about what allows enforcement, what enables the police operation. There is little other independent meaning. While this use of police operations in the world did not begin with September 11 (for example, the "Gulf War" represents a historical precedent), we can nevertheless expect to see more of this in the campaign against terrorism.

The United States and the international community. So far, I have been discussing the administration's overt response to terrorism, a problem that transcends the conventional discrete lines of domestic and international politics and law. Indeed, it is definitional of terrorism, given its aims and objects, that it destabilizes established categories in the law along those lines. Now, I turn to the realm that is explicitly international. The international context makes clear the administration's conception of sovereignty, particularly, its view of the U.S. position in the world.

As discussed above, in its response to September 11, the United States has largely sought to eschew the parameters of international law. Moreover, it has elided the other political constraints of allies, making it plain that it will pursue a unilateral action, whether with respect to detained terrorists, the attack on Afghanistan, or, more currently, in its plan to extend the war on terrorism to Iraq, despite the fact that other multilateral options would have been possible, as the terrorist attacks on the U.S. civilians clearly constituted a crime against humanity.[40] Nevertheless, this unilateral stance has become the norm.

The final illustration of "empire's law" discussed here is the U.S. position regarding a permanent International Criminal Court.[41] The debate over whether the United States would become a party to the ICC had long been under way during the post–September 11 responses, yet, prior to September 11, the final U.S. position had not been fully reached. Had history gone differently, one could speculate that the U.S. position on the ICC's fateful development might also have been different.

Despite some impetus toward the creation of a permanent international criminal tribunal after Nuremberg, the geopolitical U.S.-Soviet balance delayed its development until half a century later. During the spring of 2002, more than sixty countries ratified the "Rome Treaty," enough to establish a permanent ICC. The jurisdiction of this court over the most heinous violations began during the summer of 2002.[42]

The United States has now officially "unsigned" the treaty and has indicated that it will resist the court's jurisdiction.[43] Moreover, the United States now appears to be on the road to full-fledged opposition to the ICC, as evidenced in its diplomacy with other countries as well as in the remarkable conditions of exception that the administration has demanded regarding its role in so-called peace operations around the world.[44]

Consider the U.S. position during the debate about the ICC and the extent to which it follows the structure of the sovereign police argument discussed above. In the ICC debate, the administration once again is operating at the limits of the law, as it follows neither the regime of ordinary peacetime law nor the regime of military justice.[45] Moreover, in the ICC debate, the military is invoked as the basis of the administration's opposition.[46] This is particularly problematic as the administration justifies its opposition in terms of security concerns, where it finds itself regularly juxtaposing military authority to that of the law.

This notion of a military authority above the law is characteristic of non-rule-of-law states. However, the position defended by the United States, adopting that of the Department of Defense, is premised on a more complex, even paradoxical, police argument: namely, that the claim to exception from the law is grounded from within the law and its enforcement. According to this argument, as the sole military superpower and functioning as a worldwide cop, the United States has a greater potential exposure to the ICC's jurisdiction, and, the administration contends, there is a strong possibility of politicized prosecutions. Therefore, so the argument goes, the United States needs privileged protection from the ICC's jurisdiction.[47]

While at first the United States pushed for the strategy of "exception at will"—with the United States having the power to lobby referral of all cases by the UN Security Council and block any it opposed with a veto—it became clear that exclusive Security Council referral jurisdiction in the ICC would not be accepted. In the final treaty, the Security Council retains referral power, as well as the power to temporarily defer prosecutions that arrive in the court via alternative routes. For some time, the United States continued to try to find a legal formula for exemption, but, by the end of the Rome conference, it dropped even the pretense of a formula, peremptorily demanding, instead, a full and total exemption from the court's prosecutions. This stance rendered impossible further engagement by the United States in the ICC. The final decision to "unsign" the preceding administration's signature to the Rome Treaty, executed in the Clinton presidency's last days, was merely the formal extension of the Bush administration's stated position that it did not intend to cooperate with the court.[48]

In Europe, as well as in U.S. human rights circles, there has been a substantial outcry over the American position. The claim is that the Bush administration is being hypocritical because it insists that other countries adhere to international law while always seeking a full exemption for the United States. Much is made of the occasional U.S. support for international institutions, such as the ad hoc criminal tribunal presently trying former Yugoslav president Slobodan Milosevic[49] and adjudicating atrocities relating to the Rwandan genocide.[50] Of course, there are others who argue just the opposite, noting that the international institutions may be less politicized than any individual state's judiciary.[51]

Nevertheless, to some extent, the U.S. position regarding the Hague war crimes tribunal prosecuting Milosevic and the U.S. position on the ICC are not irreconcilable, but, rather, follow the present administration's logic. Since the United States conceives of itself as the world sovereign, one might argue that it would be contradictory for U.S. police operations to be subject to the ICC. Indeed, the ICC stands for the possibility that any head of state anywhere in the world could potentially be subject to the court's jurisdiction and thus to a sovereign police action.[52] Therefore, to yield to the ICC's jurisdiction would, to some extent, contravene the U.S. sovereign police logic, that is, where the United States is deemed the preeminent enforcer yet somehow liable to being the object of a police action. Indeed, the point of the United States as the sovereign police power is now being made in the ad hoc international tribunal prosecution of Milosevic to justify the enforcement of humanitarian intervention by the NATO powers. So the very question posed by the new international juridical regime is whether there ought to be review of sovereign police power. To what extent might accommodating expanded juridical sovereignty be interpreted as a challenge to the exceptional status of the U.S. police power worldwide?

Conclusion

The very definition of sovereignty today means the power to define the limits of the law, that is, the power to suspend the validity of existing international and constitutional law. The United States claims with respect to the current international humanitarian law regime that, as the self-appointed world police, it must operate in a state of exception. Yet while this argument may have surface plausibility, it is clear that the United States is not an effective world sovereign, as it has no monopoly over legitimate violence, which is in any event defined more by numerous conventions enforced in a decentralized way—in and by the law, not in its lurch.

A similar logic is being deployed at the domestic level. As with terrorism, there is substantial fluidity in the ramifications of the domestic for foreign affairs and vice versa. Here, the contradictions are only more evident, clearly revealing a politicized executive, attempting to maneuver on the basis of terrorism, free of congressional oversight or constitutional checks. At the domestic level, one can see that the administration's rhetoric reflects a freewheeling, nontransparent executive. There is only a veneer of the sovereignty of law.[53] For the most part, to date, the administration's various operations have proceeded without congressional or judicial check, and the challenge to the rule of law is even greater in the domestic context.

We need to better understand the contemporary expansion in the presidential police power in the name of emergency. These developments should be interpreted in the context of other broader political changes, for the most part related to globalization politics that have threatened many of the established institutions and processes that have hitherto provided accountability and legitimacy. In thinking about political institutions in hard times, we should not allow the extension of what ought to be limited emergencies as a pretext for the permanent expansion of the security state. States of exception should be treated as such—at best, as provisional accommodations, subject to constitutional limitations. While the problem of terrorism may defy facile analogies, whether to war, to the police state, to ordinary times, it ought not become an occasion for lawlessness. Indeed, the last century saw a history of such abuses in the war against communism.

Analysis of the law after September 11 illuminates the U.S. attempt to construct a sovereign role in international affairs. Yet, in many ways, this construction is paradoxical, and even beside the point, for September 11 makes clear the obsolescence of the prevailing understanding of national security premised on territory and force. Rather than lying outside law, the emerging notion of security will depend on greater international cooperation within the law.

Notes

1. For a useful discussion of method, see Steven R. Ratner and Anne-Marie Slaughter, eds., "Symposium on Method in International Law," *American Journal of International Law* 93 (1999): 291.

2. On realism generally, see Stephen Krasner, "Abiding Sovereignty," *International Political Science Review* (forthcoming 2003); John Mearshimer, *The Tragedy of Great Power Politics* (New York: Norton, 2001). See also Ruth Wedgwood, "The Rules of War Can't Protect Al Qaeda," *New York Times,* December 31, 2001, sec. A, p. 17.

3. See Aryeh Neier, "The Military Tribunals on Trial," *New York Review of Books,* February 14, 2002, 11–15; Ronald Dworkin, "The Trouble with the Tribunals," *New York Review of Books,* April 25, 2002, 10–12; Lawrence H. Tribe, "Trial by Fury: Why Congress Must Curb Bush's Military Courts," *New Republic,* December 10, 2001, 18.

4. On "empire" in political theory, see Michael Hardt and Antonio Negri, *Empire* (Cambridge: Harvard University Press, 2001). See also Robert Cooper, "The Post-Modern State," in *Re-Ordering the World: The Long-Term Implications of 11 September,* ed. Mark Leonard (London: Foreign Policy Centre, 2002), 11–20, calling for a new imperialism of "cooperative empire." On American unilateralism, see Nicholas Lemann, "The Next World Order," *New Yorker,* April 1, 2002, 42–48.

5. See Elizabeth Becker, "A Nation Challenged; Renaming an Operation to Fit the Mood," *New York Times,* September 26, 2001, sec. B, p. 3; CNN, "Army Gets Orders: 'We're Ready to Go,'" September 20, 2001, http://fyi.cnn.com/2001/US/09/20/ret.deploy.

6. See Harold Koh, "We Have the Right Courts for bin Laden," *New York Times,* November 23, 2002, sec. A, p. 39; George Fletcher, "War and the Constitution," *American Pros-*

pect, January 14, 2002, 26; Bruce Ackerman, "On the Home Front, a Winnable War," *New York Times,* November 6, 2001, sec. A, p. 21.

7. See Michael Walzer, *Just and Unjust Wars: A Moral Argument with Historical Illustrations,* 3d ed. (New York: Basic Books, 2000).

8. Namely, the Geneva Conventions that regulate the treatment of prisoners of war. See Geneva Convention (3) Relative to the Treatment of Prisoners of War, 75 U.N.T.S. [UN Treaty Series] 135, adopted August 12, 1949, entered into force October 21, 1950.

9. See Alberto R. Gonzalez, "Martial Justice, Full and Fair," *New York Times,* November 30, 2001, sec. A, p. 27.

10. See CNN, "Bush Advisers Debate Detainees' Status," January 26, 2002, http://www.cnn.com/2002/US/01/26/ret.powell.detainees/?related.

11. See Ruti Teitel, "Humanity's Law: Rule of Law for a Global Politics," *Cornell International Law Journal* 35, no. 2 (2002): 356–87.

12. See Stephen D. Krasner, *Sovereignty: Organized Hypocrisy* (Princeton: Princeton University Press, 1999); see also Michael Ross Fowler and Julie Marie Bunck, *Law, Power, and the Sovereign State: The Evolution and the Concept of Sovereignty* (University Park: Pennsylvania State University Press, 1995).

13. For discussion of the legitimacy of this intervention, see Louis Henkin, "Kosovo and the Law of 'Humanitarian Intervention,'" *American Journal of International Law* 93, no. 4 (October 1999): 824–27.

14. See Ruti Teitel, "Transitional Justice Genealogy," *Harvard Human Rights Journal* 16 (spring 2003): 69–94; Ruti Teitel, *Transitional Justice* (Oxford: Oxford University Press, 2000), epilogue.

15. See Thomas Donnelly, "The Past as Prologue: An Imperial Manual," *Foreign Affairs,* July/August 2002, 165–70; Lemann, "The Next World Order," 42; Thomas L. Friedman, "Foreign Affairs: Was Kosovo World War III?" *New York Times,* July 2, 1999, sec. A, p. 17.

16. On the philosophical implications of contemporary sovereignty, see Giorgio Agamben, *Means without End: Notes on Politics* (Minneapolis: University of Minnesota Press, 2000), 103–6.

17. Indeed, this approach appears to be a move away from the increasing shift to positive law from natural law, which seems to be a throwback in the history of international law and international relations. See Peter Malanczuk, *Akehurst's Modern Introduction to International Law,* 7th ed. (London: Routledge, 1997).

18. See statement of Richard Haass, State Department director of policy and planning, in Lemann, "The Next World Order," 44. Referring to the current policy of "limited sovereignty" as representing the emergence of a new principle, Haass says, "sovereignty entails obligations," principally "not to massacre your own people" and "not to support terrorism in any way." Failure to meet these obligations means the forfeiture of "the normal advantages of sovereignty, including the right to be left alone inside your own territory." Ibid., 45.

19. See Alessandra Stanley, "Conference Opens on Creating Court to Try War Crimes," *New York Times,* June 15, 1998, sec. A, p. 1; Roger Cohen, "The World: Europe's New Policeman," *New York Times,* October 18, 1998, Week in Review, 3.

20. See President, Military Order of November 13, 2001, "Detention, Treatment, and Trial of Certain Non-Citizens in the War against Terrorism," *Federal Register* 66, no. 222 (November 16, 2001): 57,833.

21. Ibid., sec. 1(f).

22. Ibid., sec. 1(g).
23. Ibid., sec. 1(e).
24. Ibid., sec. 2(a)(1)(ii).
25. Ibid., sec 2(a).
26. Ibid., sec. 2(a)(2).
27. Art. 21 of the Uniform Code of Military Justice, 10 U.S.C. 821 (2001).
28. See *Authorization for Use of Military Force,* Public Law 107-40, 107th Cong., 1st sess., September 18, 2001 (authorizing "necessary and appropriate" force against the terrorist network involved in the terrorist attacks of September 11).
29. *Center for National Security Studies v. U.S. Department of Justice,* Docket no. 01-2500 (GK), 215 F. Supp. 2d 94 (D.C. Cir. Aug. 2, 2002) (following litigation, a judge ordered the disclosure of the list of U.S.-based detainees), stay granted pending appeal in *Center for National Security Studies v. U.S. Department of Justice,* no. 01-2500 (GK), 215 F. Supp. 2d 58 (D.C. Cir. Aug. 15, 2002). Contrast *North Jersey Media Group, Inc. v. Ashcroft,* 308 F.3d 198 (3d Cir. 2002) (finding that the attorney general may conduct deportation hearings in secret when the individual involved might have connections to or knowledge of the 9/11 attacks) and *Detroit Free Press v. Ashcroft,* 303 F.3d 681 (6th Cir. 2002) (finding that there is a First Amendment right of access to deportation proceedings).
30. See Ruti Teitel, "Persecution and Inquisition," in *The Transition to Democracy in Latin America: The Role of the Judiciary,* ed. Irwin Stotsky (Boulder, Colo.: Westview Press, 1994): 141–153.
31. See Military Order of November 13, 2001, section 2(a)(1).
32. See Geneva Convention (3) Relative to the Treatment of Prisoners of War, art. 106, 75 U.N.T.S. [UN Treaty Series] 135, entered into force October 21, 1950 (requiring for every law "the right of appeal or petition from any sentence").
33. Geneva Convention (3) Relative to the Treatment of Prisoners of War. There are other rights that the relevant Geneva Convention article refers to that are not guaranteed, even in the subsequent draft regulation.
34. See U.S. Constitution, Art. I, sec. 9.
35. Indeed, there are precedents during the American Civil War. See *Ex Parte Milligan,* 71 U.S. 2 (1866).
36. Compare *United States v. Verdugo-Urguidez,* 494 U.S. 259 (1990), with *Reid v. Covert,* 354 U.S. 1 (1957) (regarding the extraterritorial reach of the U.S. Constitution).
37. See Department of Defense, Military Commission Order no. 1, March 21, 2002.
38. Ibid., sec. 6 (4).
39. See Carl Schmitt, *The Concept of the Political* (Chicago: University of Chicago Press, 1996).
40. See Rome Statute of the International Criminal Court, UN Doc. A/CONF. 183/9, July 17, 1998, art. 7, reprinted in 37 I.L.M. [International Legal Materials] 999 (1998). See also Frederic L. Kirgis, "Terrorist Attacks on the World Trade Center and the Pentagon," *ASIL Insights,* September 2001, http://www.asil.org./insights/insigh77.htm.
41. See Rome Statute of the International Criminal Court, 37 I.L.M. 999 (1998); Undersecretary of State for Political Affairs Marc Grossman, Address at the Center for Strategic and International Studies, Washington, D.C., May 6, 2002 (United States will not join the International Criminal Court).
42. Neil A. Lewis, "U.S. Is Set to Renounce Its Role in Pact for World Tribunal," *New York Times,* May 5, 2002, sec. A, p. 18.
43. See U.S. Defense Secretary Donald Rumsfeld, Statement on the ICC Treaty, May 6, 2002,

http://www.defenselink.mil/news/May2002/b05062002_bt233-02.html. See also Department of State, Under Secretary of State for Arms Control and International Security John R. Bolton, Letter to UN Secretary General Kofi Annan, indicating the United States's intention is not to become a party to the ICC treaty, May 6, 2002, USDOS Press Release, http://www.state.gov/r/pa/prs/ps/2002/9968.htm.

44. See Colum Lynch, "United States Seeks Court Immunity for East Timor Peacekeepers," *Washington Post,* May 16, 2002, sec. A, p. 22; Christopher Marquis, "United States Is Seeking Pledges to Shield Its Peacekeepers from Tribunal," *New York Times,* August 7, 2002, sec. A, p. 1.

45. See Somini Sengupta, "U.S. Fails in U.N. to Exempt Peacekeepers from New Court," *New York Times,* May 18, 2002, sec. A, p. 4; Serge Schmemann, "U.S. Peacekeepers Given Year's Immunity from New Court," *New York Times,* July 12, 2002, sec. A, p. 3. There was a recent resolution of the matter on a case-by-case basis with involvement of the Security Council, as contemplated under Article 16 of the ICC Treaty.

46. See the American Servicemembers' Protection Act, which is an attempt to challenge any future U.S. participation in the ICC. *The American Servicemembers' Protection Act of 2002,* U.S. Public Law 107–206, 107th Cong., 2nd sess., August 2, 2002.

47. See Rumsfeld, Statement on the ICC Treaty, May 6, 2002.

48. Such cooperation would have been required by the Rome Statute, art. 86. The Bush administration's decision to resort to "unsigning" appears to take seriously the possibility of legal obligations arising from its signature. See Vienna Convention, art. 18, which asks nations to refrain from taking steps to undermine treaties that they sign. For discussion of the contradiction in this interpretive approach, see Ruti Teitel, "Global Rule of Law: Universal and Particular" (paper presented at Central European University Conference, Universalism in Law: Human Rights and the Rule of Law, Budapest, June 14–16, 2002).

49. See Statute of the International Tribunal for the Prosecution of Persons Responsible for Serious Violations of International Humanitarian Law Committed in the Territory of the Former Yugoslavia since 1991, Security Council Resolution 827, UN SCOR [Security Council Official Records], adopting UN Doc. s/25704 at 36, annex, and UN Doc. s/25704/Add.1 (1993), available at http://www1.umn.edu/humanrts/icty/statute.html; Statute of the International Criminal Tribunal for the Former Yugoslavia, Security Council Resolution 827, UN SCOR, 48th sess., 3,217th mtg., UN Doc. s/RES/827 (1993), as amended by Security Council Resolution 1166, UN SCOR, 3,878th mtg., annex, UN Doc. s/RES/1166 (1998), available at http://www1.umn.edu/humanrts/resolutions/SC98/1166SC98.html.

50. See Statute of the International Tribunal for Rwanda, Security Council Resolution 955, UN SCOR, 49th sess., 3,453rd mtg., UN Doc. s/RES/955 (1994), available at http://www1.umn.edu/humanrts/peace/docs/scres955.html.

51. See Henry Kissinger, "The Pitfalls of Universal Jurisdiction," *Foreign Affairs,* July/August 2001, 86.

52. This is not to say that such an indictment requires an international court. See *Regina v. Bow St. Metro.,* Stipendiary Magistrate, *Ex parte Pinochet Ugarte,* [2000] 1 A.C. [Advisory Circular] 61 (H.L. [House of Lords] 1998), reprinted in 37 I.L.M. 1302 (1998), vacated by *Regina v. Bow St. Metro.,* Stipendiary Magistrate, *Ex parte Pinochet Ugarte* (no. 2), [2000] 1 A.C. 119 (H.L. 1999), reprinted in 38 I.L.M. 430 (1999); *Regina v. Bow St. Metro.* Stipendiary Magistrate, *Ex parte Pinochet Ugarte* (no. 3), [2000] 1 A.C. 147 (1999).

53. See, e.g., American Servicemembers' Protection Act.

MARY L. DUDZIAK

Twelve months after the terrorist attacks, the nation remembered September 11, 2001. One year exactly after the first plane exploded into the World Trade Center, a moment of silence was observed in New York City. Across the nation, at the very same time, vigils were held, some in the dark of the early morning. Around the world, many stopped to remember. At St. Paul's Cathedral in London, Prime Minister Tony Blair joined cabinet ministers, Prince Charles, and others in a moment of silence. In Bangkok, Thailand, the Bangkok Orchestra singers joined 180 choirs around the world in singing Mozart's Requiem, "to replace the cries of shock and fear that rang out one year ago" with song. In New York, the name of each victim was read aloud at a memorial event at Ground Zero. The names were broadcast without commercial interruption. Advertisers had been concerned that it would be unseemly to sell products during commercial breaks, although in the days before, some did market 9/11-related merchandise, while others broadcast memorial messages to customers.[1]

Reflecting a theme that permeated anniversary news coverage, Neil Conan of National Public Radio began his program that morning by reflecting on the moment when "we were all about to change, together." The banner headline on America Online was simply "The Day We Changed." The assumption that September 11 had been a moment of change was again ubiquitous. Yet, in an unscientific poll taken by the Web site for historians History News Network, 67 percent of respondents answered "no" to the question, "On balance, would you say that 9-11 changed America in a decisive way?" Only 28 percent thought that it had.[2]

Perhaps the idea of change was comforting. After the horror, how could life simply go on as usual? For those who had lost loved ones, their lives had, of course, been forever altered. For those who lived and worked in lower Manhattan, their daily experience of the city would never look and feel the same again. But for others, untouched by the fire and destruction, daily routines continued. Yet how could so many murders have happened at once on American soil, without the nation itself shifting under the burden of sorrow?

Beneath the polling data, the days after September 11 brought changes of their own. At New York's Ground Zero, the site was stripped bare of rubble, and the city debated how to rebuild and how to create a physical space dedicated to remembering. In Washington, D.C., repairs to the Pentagon were completed, with one seared stone from the rubble placed at the foundation, bearing simply the date: September 11, 2001. Outside Shanksville, Pennsylvania, a "temporary" memorial with messages to flight 93 continued to stand against the wind.[3]

Individuals had their own stories of change. Keiko Masubuchi is not a sentimental person, yet she described a change in her life as resulting from September 11. She was at work in midtown Manhattan when the towers fell and was not aware of the extent of devastation until she saw the television coverage later that day. She received frantic calls from friends and family in Japan. Come back here where it is safe, they urged her. It was at that moment that Masubuchi decided that first and foremost she was a New Yorker. To seal her fate to her injured city, she would become a U.S. citizen. Out of this crisis, for Masubuchi, came a reconfigured relationship with the nation.[4]

Within the United States and across the world, memories of September 11 have become ways of negotiating our relationship with America. American flag lapel pins, flags draped from buildings, flags on car windows, now tattered. The American flag itself has become an icon for remembering.

Constructing a memory involves forgetting. Creating the narrative structure of a memory requires us to choose what to place in the story, and what to leave out. As Marita Sturken has written, "The desire for narrative closure . . . forces upon historical events the limits of narrative form and enables forgetting."[5] This process of forgetting in order to remember was a part of the September 11 anniversary events themselves. As family members and political celebrities read the names of the dead at Ground Zero, one reader followed each name with the word "American." People from many nations had perished, but at the anniversary they were remembered as Americans.[6]

September 11 is remembered as an American event, yet it is a contested memory. "We Are all Americans" was a headline in *Le Monde* on September 13, 2001; "We are all still Americans—but not every day now," wrote a *Le Monde* columnist a year later. By calling the dead "Americans," the reader at Ground Zero can be seen as resonating with this capacious identification with America, with the sea of American flags after September 11 across the world. Yet the Americanness of the event is called forth in a different way in some political rhetoric that sees the terrorist attacks as one moment in a struggle between the United States and the forces of evil in the world. Deprived of the neat categories that characterized the Cold War, President Bush constructed a new dichotomy when he saw terrorism as emanating from an "axis of evil."[7] Seeing the evil residing in particular nation-states, he lay the basis for the justification of a new American war effort to redeem America as a world power dedicated to the eradication of evil. This narrative move remembers September 11 as a passage in a longer story about American power and destiny. And so, although memories of September 11 converge on constructions of and engagements with America, in that very site of narrative convergence lies the basis for division.

Having settled into our imaginations, the series of events that transpired on September 11, 2001, continue to play out, although the moniker itself, September 11, seems frozen in time. Was this a day when we all changed together? Was this a transformative moment in the history of the United States and of the world? Did the terrorist attacks usher in a new age of terror? The presence of change, the nature of change, of a historical moment so near may be, for this generation, impossible to measure. And yet one thing, at least, is new and is enduring. The one change most certain is the perpetual creation—that is, the construction and reconstruction—of memories of September 11.

Notes

1. Dan Barry, "Day of Tributes, Tears, and the Litany of the Lost," *New York Times*, September 12, 2002, sec. A, p. 12; Sebastian Rotella and Michael Slackman, "A Year After: The World," *Los Angeles Times*, September 12, 2002, pt. 1, p. 25; "Sept 11 Remembrance Rites Held across the World," *Straits Times*, http://straitstimes.asia1.com.sg/sept11/story/ 0,1870,142774,00.html; Stuart Elliot, "To Avoid Looking Exploitive, a Great Many Big Marketers Will Not Run Advertising Tomorrow," *New York Times*, September 10, 2002, sec. C, p. 5.

   During the week before September 11, 2002, the Web site bloomingdales.com sent out e-mail advertisements regarding September 11 memorial Christmas tree ornaments and coldwatercreek.com sent messages to customers with the subject line "We Remember."
2. Neil Conan, *Talk of the Nation*, National Public Radio, September 11, 2002; America Online, September 11, 2002, http://www.aol.com; "HNN Poll: Did It Change Us?" *History News Network*, http://hnn.us/articles/961.html.

3. Herbert Muschamp, "Don't Rebuild: Reimagine." *New York Times Magazine,* September 8, 2002, 41; Edward Wyatt, "At Trade Center Site, a Wealth of Ideas: Competing Interests are Fighting to Have a Say in Reviving Downtown," *New York Times,* July 28, 2002, sec. 1, p. 25; Steve Vogel, "Final Stone Placed in Exterior of Pentagon: Nine Months after Attacks Crews Shift Focus to Interior," *Washington Post,* June 12, 2002, sec. B, p. 1; Francis X. Clines, "At Rural Campsite, a Museum in the Making," *New York Times,* December 3, 2001, sec. B, p. 8; Francis X. Clines, "Pilgrims Flock to Site of Crash near Rural Hill," *New York Times,* September 9, 2002, sec. A, p. 1.

4. Keiko Masubuchi, conversation with author, New York, N.Y., June 29, 2002.

5. Marita Sturken, *Tangled Memories: The Vietnam War, the AIDS Epidemic, and the Politics of Remembering* (Berkeley: University of California Press, 1997), 8.

6. Cable News Network, September 11, 2002 (coverage of memorial events). See also "An Irish Tribute," http://www.irishtribute.com (memorial tribute honoring persons of Irish descent who perished on September 11).

7. Jean-Marie Colombani, "Nous sommes tous Americains," *Le Monde* (Paris), September 13, 2001; Thomas Friedman, "Tone it Down a Notch," *New York Times,* October 2, 2002, p. A27; President George W. Bush, "Address before a Joint Session of Congress on the State of the Union," *Weekly Compilation of Presidential Documents* 38, no. 5 (February 4, 2002): 133, 135.

For Further Reading

Books

Abou El Fadl, Khaled. *The Place of Tolerance in Islam.* Boston: Beacon Press, 2002.

Alexander, Dean C., and Yonah Alexander. *Terrorism and Business: The Impact of September 11, 2001.* Ardsley, N.Y.: Transnational Publishers, 2002.

Baer, Ulrich, ed. *110 Stories: New York Writes after September 11.* New York: New York University Press, 2002.

Benjamin, Daniel, and Steven Simon. *The Age of Sacred Terror.* New York: Random House, 2002.

Bernstein, Richard, and the Staff of the *New York Times. Out of the Blue: The Story of September 11, 2001, from Jihad to Ground Zero.* New York: Times Books, 2002.

Booth, Ken, and Tim Dunne, eds. *Worlds in Collision: Terror and the Future of Global Order.* New York: Palgrave Macmillan, 2002.

Brill, Stephen. *After: How America Confronted the September 12 Era.* New York: Simon and Schuster, 2003.

Calhoun, Craig, Paul Price, and Ashley Timmer, eds. *Understanding September 11: Perspectives from the Social Sciences.* New York: New Press, 2002.

Carr, Caleb. *The Lessons of Terror: A History of Warfare against Civilians: Why It Has Always Failed and Why It Will Fail Again.* New York: Random House, 2002.

Catherwood, Christopher. *Why the Nations Rage: Killing in the Name of God,* rev. ed. Lanham, Md.: Rowman & Littlefield, 2002.

Chang, Nancy. *Silencing Political Dissent: How Post–September 11 Anti-Terrorism Measures Threaten Our Civil Liberties.* New York: Seven Stories Press, 2002.

Chomsky, Noam. *9-11.* New York: Seven Stories Press, 2001.

Crockatt, Richard. *America Embattled: September 11, Anti-Americanism, and the Global Order.* London: Routledge, 2003.

Dershowitz, Alan M. *Why Terrorism Works: Understanding the Threat, Responding to the Challenge.* New Haven: Yale University Press, 2002.

Der Spiegel. Inside 9-11: What Really Happened. Translated by Elisabeth Kaestner. New York: St. Martin's Press, 2002.

Dresang, Dennis L., ed. *American Government in a Changed World: The Effects of September 11, 2001.* New York: Longman, 2003.

Emerson, Steven. *American Jihad: The Terrorists Living among Us.* New York: Free Press, 2002.

Esposito, John L. *Unholy War: Terror in the Name of Islam.* Oxford: Oxford University Press, 2002.

Falk, Richard. *Law in an Emerging Global Village: A Post-Westphalian Perspective.* Ardsley, N.Y.: Transnational Publishers, 1998.

Friedman, Thomas L. *Longitudes and Attitudes: Exploring the World after September 11.* New York: Farrar, Straus and Giroux, 2002.

Gertz, Bill. *Breakdown: How America's Intelligence Failures Led to September 11.* Washington, D.C.: Regnery, 2002.

Halliday, Fred. *Two Hours That Shook the World: September 11, 2001: Causes and Consequences.* London: Saqi, 2002.

Hanson, Victor Davis. *An Autumn of War: What America Learned from September 11 and the War on Terrorism.* New York: Anchor Books, 2002.

Hershberg, Eric, and Kevin W. Moore, eds. *Critical Views of September 11: Analyses from around the World.* New York: New Press, 2002.

Hoge, James F., and Gideon Rose, eds. *How Did This Happen? Terrorism and the New War.* New York: PublicAffairs, 2001.

Kepel, Gilles. *Jihad: The Trail of Political Islam.* Translated by Anthony F. Roberts. Cambridge: Harvard University Press, 2002.

Kolko, Gabriel. *Another Century of War?* New York: New Press, 2002.

Markham, Ian S., and Ibrahim Abu-Rami', eds. *September 11: Historical, Theological, and Social Perspectives.* Oxford: Oneworld, 2002.

Miller, John, and Aaron Kenedi, eds. *Inside Islam: The Faith, the People, and the Conflicts of the World's Fastest Growing Religion.* New York: Marlowe, 2002.

Nasr, Seyyed Hossein, and Oliver Leaman. *History of Islamic Philosophy.* London: Routledge, 1996.

Olshansky, Barbara. *Secret Trials and Executions: Military Tribunals and the Threat to Democracy.* New York: Seven Stories Press, 2002.

Pipes, Daniel. *Militant Islam Reaches America.* New York: W. W. Norton, 2002.

Pleszcynski, Wladyslaw, ed. *Our Brave New World: Essays on the Impact of September 11.* Stanford, Calif.: Hoover Institution Press, 2002.

Pyszczynski, Thomas A., Jeff Greenberg, and Sheldon Solomon. *In the Wake of 9/11: The Psychology of Terror.* Washington, D.C.: American Psychological Association, 2002.

Ratner, Stephen R., and Jason S. Abrams. *Accountability for Human Rights Atrocities in International Law: Beyond the Nuremberg Legacy.* 2d ed. Oxford: Oxford University Press, 2001.

Reuters. *After September 11: New York and the World.* Upper Saddle River, N.J.: Prentice Hall PTR, 2002.

Sammon, Bill. *Fighting Back: The War on Terrorism—From inside the Bush White House.* Washington, D.C.: Regnery, 2002.

Silberstein, Sandra. *War of Words: Language, Politics, and 9/11.* London: Routledge, 2002.

Silvers, Robert B., and Barbara Epstein, eds. *Striking Terror: America's New War.* New York: New York Review Books, 2002.

Sorkin, Michael, and Sharon Zukin, eds. *After the World Trade Center: Rethinking New York City.* London: Routledge, 2002.

Snow, Donald M. *September 11, 2001: The New Face of War?* New York: Longman, 2002.

Talbott, Strobe, and Nayan Chanda, eds. *The Age of Terror: America and the World after September 11.* New York: Basic Books, 2002.

Vanden Heuvel, Katrina, ed. *A Just Response:* The Nation *on Terrorism, Democracy, and September 11, 2001.* New York: Thunder's Mouth Press/Nation Books, 2002.

Vidal, Gore. *Perpetual War for Perpetual Peace: How We Got to Be So Hated.* New York: Thunder's Mouth Press/Nation Books, 2002.

Periodicals with Relevant Symposium Issues

"After Words: Who Speaks on War, Justice, and Peace?" *Amerasia Journal* 27, no. 3 / 28, no. 1 (2001–2002).

"Confronting Terrorism." *Current History* 101, no. 659 (December 2002).

"Dissent from the Homeland: Essays after September 11." *South Atlantic Quarterly* 101, no. 2 (spring 2002).

"Focus: September 11, 2002—Legal Response to Terror." *Harvard International Law Journal* 43, no. 1 (2002).

"History and September 11—A Special Issue." *Journal of American History* 89, no. 2 (September 2002).

"International Justice, War Crimes, and Terrorism: The U.S. Record." *Social Research* 69, no. 1 (January 2003).

"Law and the War on Terrorism." *Harvard Journal of Law and Public Policy* 25, no. 2 (2002).

"A New Foreign Policy for a Fragmented World." *PS: Political Science and Politics* 36, no. 1 (January 2003).

"9/11: One Year Later." *Internationale Politik* 3,Transatlantic ed. (fall 2002).

"9/11 and Its Aftermath: Perspectives from Political Psychology." *Political Psychology* 23, no. 3 (September 2002).

"Political Islam." *Current History* 101, no. 658 (November 2002).

"The Road to and from September 11th: A Roundtable." *Diplomatic History* 26, no. 4 (fall 2002).

"September 11: A Public Emergency?" *Social Text* 72, vol. 20, no. 3 (2002).

"State of Emergency." *Theory, Culture, and Society* 19, no. 4 (August 2002).

"Symposium: Free Speech Rationales after September 11th: The First Amendment in Post–World Trade Center America." *Stanford Law and Policy Review* 13 (2002).

"Symposium: Memoranda on September 11, 2001 (Reflections)." *Boundary Two* 29, no. 1 (spring 2002).

"Symposium: 9/11 and After." *Foreign Affairs* 80, no. 6 (November/December 2001).

"Symposium: Reflections on 11 September." *Theory and Event* 5, no. 4 (2002).

"Symposium on Communications on September 11." *Prometheus* 20, no. 3 (Carfax, September 2002).

"Symposium on Violence in America." *Notre Dame Journal of Law, Ethics, and Public Policy* 16, no. 1 (2002).

"Terrorism and the Law." *Loyola of Los Angeles Law Review* 35, no. 4 (June 2002).

"'We Are Not the Enemy': Hate Crimes against Arabs, Muslims, and Those Perceived to Be Arab or Muslim after September 11." *Human Rights Watch Report* 14, no. 6 (November 2002).

Articles

Abou El Fadl, Khaled. "Islam and the Theology of Power." *Middle East Report* 221 (winter 2001): 28–33.

Ahmed, Samina. "The United States and Terrorism in Southwest Asia: September 11 and Beyond." *International Security* 26, no. 3 (winter 2001): 79.

Al-Sayyid, Mustapha Kamel, et al. "Impact of 9/11 on the Middle East." *Middle East Policy* 9, no. 4 (December 2002): 75–101.

Bodney, David J. "War, Wisdom, and Freedom of the Press." *Communications Lawyer* 19 (winter 2002): 3–6.

Bourne, Richard. "The Significance of 11 September 2001 and After." *Round Table* 363, no. 1 (2002): 77–90.

Braber, Liam. "Korematsu's Ghost: A Post–September 11th Analysis of Race and National Security." *Villanova Law Review* 47 (2002): 451–90.

Cameron, Fraser. "Utilitarian Multilateralism: The Implications of 11 September 2001 for U.S. Foreign Policy." *Politics* 22, no. 2 (2002): 68–75.

Casey, Leo. "Teaching the Lessons of 9/11." *Dissent* 50, no 1 (winter 2003): 50–57.

Cole, David. "Enemy Aliens," *Stanford Law Review* 54 (May 2002): 953–1004.

Cox, Michael. "American Power before and after 11 September: Dizzy with Success?" *International Affairs* 78, no. 2 (2002): 261–76.

Dickinson, Laura A. "Using the Legal Process to Fight Terrorism: Detentions, Military Commissions, International Tribunals, and the Rule of Law." *Southern California Law Review* 75, no. 6 (September 2002): 1407–92.

Drumbl, Mark A. "Judging the 11 September Terrorist Attack." *Human Rights Quarterly* 24 (2002): 323–60.

Erhlich, Paul R., and Jianguo Liu. "Some Roots of Terrorism." *Population and Environment* 24, no. 2 (November 2002): 183–92.

Fadlallah, Husayn. "11 September, Terrorism, Islam, and the Intifada: An Interview with Shaykh Muhammed." *Journal of Palestine Studies* 31, no. 2 (winter 2002): 78–84.

Fenwick, Helen. "The Anti-Terrorism, Crime, and Security Act 2001: A Proportionate Response to 11 September?" *Modern Law Review* 65, no. 5 (2002): 724–62.

Flynn, Stephen E. "America the Vulnerable." *Foreign Affairs* 81, no. 1 (January/February 2002): 60–74.

Gardner, James P., and Sarah M. Henry. "September 11 and the Mourning After: Reflections on Collecting and Interpreting the History of Tragedy." *Public Historian* 24, no. 3 (summer 2002): 37–52.

Gellman, Susan. "The First Amendment in a Time That Tries Men's Souls." *Law and Contemporary Problems* 65, no. 1 (spring 2002): 87–101.

Giuffo, John, and Joshua Lipton. "Reverberation: How Ten Regional Newspapers Responded to September 11." *Columbia Journalism Review* 40, no. 5 (January/February 2002): 44–50.

Green, Duncan, and Matthew Griffith. "Globalization and Its Discontents." *International Affairs* 78, no. 1 (2002): 49–68.

Greenstein, Fred I. "The Contemporary Presidency: The Changing Leadership of George W. Bush: A Pre- and Post-September 11 Comparison." *Presidential Studies Quarterly* 32, no. 2 (June 2002): 387–96.

Gross, Samuel R., and Debra Livingston. "Essay: Racial Profiling under Attack." *Columbia Law Review* 102, no. 5 (2002): 1413–38.

Haddad, S., and H. Khashan. "Islam and Terrorism: Lebanese Muslim Views on September 11." *Journal of Conflict Resolution* 46, no. 6 (December 2002): 812–28.

Heng, Yee-Kuang. "Unraveling the 'War' on Terrorism: A Risk-Management Exercise in War Clothing?" *Security Dialogue* 33 (2002): 227–42.

Herf, J. "What Is Old and What Is New in the Terrorism of Islamic Fundamentalism? Reflections on the September 11 Attack on the United States." *Partisan Review* 69, no. 1 (2002): 25–31.

Heyman, Philip B. "Dealing with Terrorism." *International Security* 26 (2001/2002): 24–38.

Hoffman, Bruce. "Rethinking Terrorism and Counterterrorism since 9/11." *Studies in Conflict and Terrorism* 25 (2002): 303–16.

Hollander, P. "Anti-Americanism: Murderous and Rhetorical (After the September 2001 Terrorist Attack on the United States)." *Partisan Review* 69, no. 1 (2002): 14–18.

Holliday, Ian. "When Is a Cause Just?" *Review of International Studies* 28, no. 3 (2002): 557–75.

Jackson, Sherman A. "Jihad and the Modern World." *Journal of Islamic Law and Culture* 7, no. 1 (2002): 1–26.

Katyal, Neal K., and Lawrence H. Tribe. "Waging War, Deciding Guilt: Trying the Military Tribunals." *Yale Law Journal* 111, no. 6 (April 2002): 1259–1310.

Klare, Michael T. "Waging Postindustrial Warfare on the Global Battlefield." *Current History* 100, no. 650 (2001): 433–37.

Klinger, David A., and Dave Grossman. "Who Should Deal with Foreign Terrorists on U.S. Soil? Socio-Legal Consequences of September 11 and the Ongoing Threat of Terrorist Attacks in America." *Harvard Journal of Law and Public Policy* 24 (2002): 815–34.

LaFeber, Walter. "The Post–September 11 Debate over Empire, Globalization, and Fragmentation." *Political Science Quarterly* 117, no. 1 (spring 2002): 1–17.

Lee, Alyssa, Mohan Isaac, and Aleksandar Janca. "Post-Traumatic Stress Disorder and Terrorism." *Current Opinion in Psychiatry* 15, no. 6 (November 2002): 633–37.

Lieven, Anatol. "The Secret Policemen's Ball: The United States, Russia, and the International Order after 11 September." *International Affairs* 78, no. 2 (2002): 245–59.

Markovits, A. S. "Terror and Clandestine Anti-Semitism: Thoughts on German and American Reactions to September 11, 2001." *Partisan Review* 69, no. 1 (2002): 19–24.

Mattson, Kevin. "American Culture Since 9/11." *Dissent* 50, no. 1 (winter 2003): 58–61.

McAllister, Stephen, et al. "Life after 9/11: Issues Affecting the Courts and the Nation." *Kansas Law Review 51* (February 2003): 219–47.

Micklethwait, John, and Adrian Wooldridge. "From Sarajevo to September 11: The Future of Globalization." *Policy Review* 117 (February/March 2003): 49–63.

Murphy, Sean D. "Contemporary Practice of the United States Relating to International Law." *American Journal of International Law* 96 (January 2002): 237–55.

Panitch, Leo. "Violence as a Tool of Order and Change: The War on Terrorism and the Anti-globalization Movement." *Monthly Review* 54, no. 2 (2002): 12–32.

Price, D. "Islam and Human Rights: A Case of Deceptive First Appearances." *Journal for the Scientific Study of Religion* 41, no. 2 (2002): 213–25.

Reisman, W. Michael. "International Legal Responses to Terrorism." *Houston Journal of International Law* 22 (1999): 3–61.

Rizopoulos, N. X. "The Autumn of Our Discontent." *Partisan Review* 69, no. 2 (2002): 282–92.

Shapiro, Jay. "Terrorism, the Constitution, and the Courts." *New York Law School Journal of Human Rights* 18, no. 2 (spring 2002): 189–204.

Shuja, Sharif M. "The September 11 Tragedy and the Future World Order." *Contemporary Review* 280 (April 2002): 198–205.

Smoler, Frederic. "Fighting the Last War—and the Next." *American Heritage* 52, no. 8 (2001): 38–42.

Tehranian, Majid. "Global Terrorism: Searching for Appropriate Responses." *Pacifica Review* 14 (2002): 57–65.

Whidden, Michael J. "Unequal Justice: Arabs in America and United States Antiterrorism Legislation." *Fordham Law Review* 69 (2001): 2825–88.

Yip, K. S. "An Ounce of Forgiveness Is Better than a Ton of Revenge: A Reflection on the September 11 Terrorist Attacks." *Social Work* 47, no. 3 (2002): 331.

Web Sites

http://911digitalarchive.org
George Mason University and City University of New York Graduate Center

http://september11.archive.org
Sponsored by a collaboration between the Library of Congress, Internet Archive, and Web-Archivist.org

http://www.nato.int/terrorism
North Atlantic Treaty Organization

http://www.911history.net
Sponsored by the Museum of the City of New York and the Smithsonian National Museum of American History Behring Center

http://www.september11news.com
News archive for the period from September 11, 2001, to September 11, 2002

http://www.terrorism.com
Terrorism Research Center, Inc.

http://www.terrorismanswers.com
Council on Foreign Relations

http://www.un.org/terrorism
United Nations Action against Terrorism

Contributors

KHALED ABOU EL FADL is Acting Professor, UCLA School of Law, and the Omar and Azmeralda Alfi Distinguished Fellow in Islamic Law. An expert on Islamic law and a frequent media commentator, his books include *Rebellion and Political Violence in Islamic Law* (Cambridge University Press, 2001).

MARY L. DUDZIAK is the Judge Edward J. and Ruey L. Guirado Professor of Law and History at USC Law School. A legal historian who studies the relationship between international affairs and domestic law and politics, she is the author of *Cold War Civil Rights: Race and the Image of American Democracy* (Princeton University Press, 2000).

CHRISTOPHER L. EISGRUBER is the Laurance S. Rockefeller Professor of Public Affairs in the Woodrow Wilson School and the University Center for Human Values, Princeton University. His publications include *Constitutional Self-Government* (Harvard University Press, 2001).

LAURENCE R. HELFER is a professor of law and Lloyd Tevis Fellow at the Loyola Law School, Los Angeles. He has published widely on international law and sexual orientation discrimination in scholarly journals.

SHERMAN A. JACKSON is an associate professor of medieval Arabic law and theology at the University of Michigan. He is the author of *Islamic Law and the State: The Constitutional Jurisprudence of Shihāb al-Dīn al-Qarāfī* (E. J. Brill, 1996).

AMY KAPLAN is a professor of English and American studies at the University of Pennsylvania. Her books include *The Anarchy of Empire in the Making of U.S. Culture* (Harvard University Press, 2002) and *Cultures of United States Imperialism* (Duke University Press, 1993).

ELAINE TYLER MAY is a professor of history and American studies at the University of Minnesota. A historian whose work centers on the intersections of politics and private life, she is the author of several books, including *Homeward Bound: American Families in the Cold War Era* (Basic Books, 1988).

LAWRENCE G. SAGER is the Jane Drysdale Sheffield Regents Chair, University of Texas at Austin School of Law. He has published widely in constitutional law and constitutional theory and is the author of *Justice in Plainclothes: A Theory of American Constitutional Practice* (Yale University Press, forthcoming).

RUTI G. TEITEL is the Ernst C. Stiefel Professor of Comparative Law at New York Law School. An expert on constitutional and international law, she is the author of *Transitional Justice* (Oxford University Press, 2000).

LETI VOLPP is an associate professor of law at the Washington College of Law at American University. She has published widely on race, gender, immigration, and civil rights in scholarly journals.

MARILYN B. YOUNG is a professor of history at New York University and the director of the Project on the Cold War as Global Conflict at the International Center for Advanced Studies, New York University. A leading diplomatic historian, her books include *The Vietnam Wars, 1945–1990* (HarperCollins, 1991).

224   Contributors

Acknowledgments

This volume has its origins in the events on which it centers. It was edited and revised as the post–September 11 cultural, political, and international environment continued to unfold. In that sense, it is both a primary source and a secondary source. It offers critical perspectives on September 11 in history; yet, at the same time, these essays are necessarily a product of this moment, necessarily constructed by it.

Most of the contributors to this volume gathered at the University of Southern California Law School in May 2002 for a symposium, "September 11 as a Transformative Moment," sponsored by the USC Center on Law, History, and Culture. The purpose of the symposium was to take seriously and examine critically the common assumption that September 11 had "changed everything." Speakers focused on whether September 11 had transformed the U.S., Islam, and the world. The symposium was a starting point for the collaboration that produced this collection.

All books are products of the efforts of many people, and this is especially true of this volume. I am particularly indebted to Howard Gillman, co-organizer of the September 11 symposium. It is not an overstatement to say that without Howard's support and involvement, the symposium and this collection would not have come about. I also owe special thanks to Khaled Abou El Fadl, who made time in his extremely busy schedule to help me think through the structure for the symposium and identify speakers. His ideas had an important impact on the way this collection was constructed.

I am grateful to the Center on Law, History, and Culture, particularly its codirectors Hilary Schor and Nomi Stolzenberg, for supporting the September 11 symposium, and to Matthew Spitzer, Dean of the USC Law School, and Joseph Aoun, Dean of the USC College of Letters, Arts, and Sciences, who funded the Center. Mira Hamilton, Janine Luzano, and Maria Medrano handled many logistical challenges with grace and tact. Robert Chang, Roger Dingman, Louis Fisher, Howard Gillman, Eliz Sanasarian, and Nomi Stolzenberg participated on panels, enriching our debates. I am grateful as well to other USC colleagues and members of the Los Angeles community who attended the symposium and participated in discussions.

As this project moved from symposium to book manuscript, input from colleagues, editors, and outside readers has been essential. For their comments on the introduction and other portions of the manuscript I am grateful to Robert Chang, David Cruz, Louis Fisher, Howard

Gillman, Lanita Huey-Jacobs, Dan Klerman, and Michael Shapiro. A particularly important role was played by two anonymous readers for Duke University Press. Being a reader for a press is generally a thankless task. Readers devote hours to critical commentary on the work of strangers, with little compensation. The reviewers for this volume materially affected the final product, in both the structure and composition of the essays. Their perspectives enabled me to see the volume in new ways. Valerie Millholland at Duke University Press played a critical role as well, and I am grateful for her perceptive engagement with this project and her efforts to bring the book quickly to print. Important assistance came from Kate Lothman and other Duke University Press staff, and from Maria Medrano, Jeannine Park, and James Morse at USC Law School. Rocio Herrera, Rebecca Lefler, and Femi Oguntolu provided valuable research assistance, while Greg Barchie and Hayes Robbins helped proofread. Thanks to Rebecca Lefler, Brian Raphael, Jennifer Wimer, and other USC law library staff members for their work on the list of suggested readings, and to Carol Roberts, who prepared the index.

I found many of the photographs in this book through an extraordinary Web site, the 911 Digital Archive (http://911digitalarchive.org). The Digital Archive collects personal stories, photographs, and other sources to create an online repository on September 11. I am grateful to all the photographers for having granted permission to use their work, and for their help in providing the press with publishable copies. A number of other photographers were willing to have their photos included, but the photos did not meet specifications for printing. I am nevertheless very grateful for their efforts, and I encourage readers to visit the 911 Digital Archive, where the powerful work of additional photographers can be found.

I am grateful to Chris Eisgruber, Director of the Law and Public Affairs program at Princeton University, where the bulk of the editorial work on this manuscript was completed. Thanks as well to staff members Kathleen Applegate and Cindy Schoenek and my LAPA colleagues, who help make LAPA a wonderful community for interdisciplinary legal studies.

Most of all, I must thank each contributor to this volume. Collections are notoriously difficult to coordinate, but these authors have written and rewritten their essays on schedule, making it possible to bring this work to print in a timely way. Their creativity and insight have been inspiring.

I must, of course, thank my daughter, Alicia, who was ten and a half years old on September 11, 2001, and will be twelve when this book is in print. It is traditional in acknowledgments to thank long-suffering family members for their forbearance, but it is not for her tolerance of my work that I thank Alicia. Instead it is for her engagement. My first essay on September 11, written within a week of the attacks, came out of a conversation with her about the flags in our neighborhood. On September 11 and after, children have required that we explain things that seemed to be unexplainable. It was the need to say something meaningful to my own child that first helped me find the words that might convey my understanding of September 11 to others.

Our students will inhabit a post–September 11 world for many more years than will we. It is to them, and to the future, that we dedicate this book.

Index

Page numbers in italics refer to illustrations. Some entries for U.S. presidents are accompanied by entries for their administrations (e.g., "Bush, George W." and "Bush administration") to distinguish discussions of a president's individual actions from those of his administration as a whole. In subentries, "Bush" refers to George W. Bush, unless otherwise indicated.

Burke, Kenneth, 35–36, 52
Burke-White, William, 191 n.36
Bush, George H. W., 19
Bush, George W.: on Afghan women, 153; Christian convictions of, 75–76; on consumerism/conservation, 44; criticized for flight following September 11 attacks, 37, 48; on Cuban independence, 67; fundamentalism of, 74; on the homeland, 58; on Islam, 5, 125; on presidential records, 18–19; on racial profiling, 148, 149, 150; on September 11 as a new kind of war, 3; on September 11 vs. Pearl Harbor, 14, 29 n.17; stature/popularity of, 40–41; on tolerance toward Muslims, 43, 47, 166; on trading cards, 47; ultimatum imposed on Hussein by, 27–28; war on terrorism declared by, 26–27, 38, 40–43, 45, 184–85, 191 n.30. See also Bush (George W.) administration
Bush, Laura, 153
Bush (George W.) administration: on Al Qaeda, 28; Cold War language used by, 45; on counterinsurgency, 32 n.54; on international law, U.S. exemption from, 21, 27, 34 n.77; legal responses to September 11 (see law and politics); on military detentions, 169, 171, 172–74, 175–76; on nuclear weapons, 23–24; oil policies of, 44; on Padilla, 171, 172; on prisoners of war, 177; on sovereignty of other countries, 19; and U.S. dominance, 17–19. See also United States foreign policy
Bustani, Jose, 21
Butler, Judith, 156
Byrd, James, 154
Byrd, Robert, 22

Calabrese, Carl J., 41
Campbell, Duncan, 31 n.40
Camp X-Ray (Guantánamo Bay, Cuba), 67
Carmona Estanga, Pedro, 19–20, 31 n.40
Carter, Jimmy, 13
Carter, Stephen L., 132 nn.13–14
Carter administration, 23
Case Concerning Military and Paramilitary Activities in and against Nicaragua, 193 n.53

Castro, Fidel, 67
Catholics, 118, 133–34 n.21
CBS, 12
Center for National Security Studies v. U.S. Department of Justice, 210 n.29
Central Intelligence Agency (CIA), 21
change: conceptions of, 2–3, 56; and continuity, 25; and memories of the past, 4; new policies justified by, 8
charity, 51
Charles, Prince of Wales, 212
Chavez, Hugo, 19–20, 31 n.40
chemical weapons, 23
Cheney, Lynne, 13, 49
China, 15
Chinese Americans, 155
Christianity, 75–76, 132 n.14
Christian Science Monitor, 50
Chuh, Kandice, 159
Chwaszczewski, John, 13
CIA (Central Intelligence Agency), 21
Cisneros, Gustavo, 31 n.40
citizen sentinels, 12–14, 29 nn.14–15, 50
citizenship: and democracy, 158; and identity, 156–60; as legal status, 156, 157–58; as political activity, 156; and race, 158, 159; as rights, 156; solidarity of, 6; and suffering, 154
civilizational conflict, 5, 73, 81–84, 105 n.9, 107 n.34
civil liberties, 163–77; and domestic intelligence (spying), 164, 177 n.5; and domestic policy vs. foreign policy, 163–64, 166–69, 176–77 (see also USA Patriot Act); and immigration proceedings/law, 165–66, 167, 168; and military detention, 164–65, 166, 169–76, 178 n.23, 178 n.25, 179 n.30 (see also military tribunals for terrorists); threats to, 47–48, 49, 52 (see also USA Patriot Act). See also rights
Civil Rights Movement, 44
Clinton, William Jefferson ("Bill"): Bolivian policy of, 17, 30 n.25; Iraq bombed by, 10–11, 28 n.2; and Negroponte, 20; Plan Colombia policy of, 17; war against terrorism, 10–11; on the World Trade Center bombing of 1993, 39
Clinton administration, 23

Coetzee, J. M.: *Waiting for the Barbarians,* 27

Cold War: civil defense during, 4, 14, 45, 46; and the Civil Rights Movement, 44; Communist threat in, 3, 4, 14, 42, 50; consumerism during, 44; "Evil Empire" in, 45; as a frame of acceptance, 36, 37, 52, 195; losses during, 52; loyalty oaths during, 48; politics of, 43; and poverty, 44–45; public debate stifled during, 48; security sought in marriage/family, 50

Colombia, 17

colonialism: and Al Qaeda, 80; and imperialism, 24–25; and Islam/Islamic law, 5–6, 73, 78–79, 85, 103, 108 n.39; and the Taliban, 80; and terrorism, 183, 189 n.14

Communism, 3, 4, 14, 42, 50

community spirit, 51

Conan, Neil, 212

conflict/hate/enmity, 98

conservation, 44

Constant, Emmanuel, 19

Constitution: extraterritorial reach of, 203, 210 nn.35–36; Fourth Amendment, 170, 178 n.25; on habeas corpus, 170, 171, 203

consumerism, 44, 46–47, 52

contras, 19–20

Convention against the Taking of Hostages (1983), 189 n.16

Convention for the Suppression of Terrorist Bombings (UN, 1998), 190 n.17

Convention for the Suppression of the Financing of Terrorism (UN, 1999), 190 n.17

Convention for the Suppression of Unlawful Acts against the Safety of Civil Aviation (Montreal, 1973), 189 n.16, 190 n.24

Convention for the Suppression of Unlawful Acts against the Safety of Maritime Navigation (Rome, 1992), 189–90 n.16

Convention for the Unlawful Seizure of Aircraft (The Hague, 1981), 189 n.16, 190 n.24

Convention on Offenses and Certain Other Acts Committed on Board Aircraft (Tokyo, 1969), 189 n.16, 190 n.24

Convention on the Marking of Plastic Ex-

plosives for the Purpose of Detection (1991), 190 n.16

Convention on the Prevention and Punishment of Crimes against Internationally Protected Persons, Including Diplomatic Agents (1975), 189 n.16

counterinsurgency, 17, 30 n.25, 32 n.54

Counter-Proliferation Initiative (CPI), 17

crises, 2, 35–36, 52

Cuba, 19, 33 n.64, 66–67. *See also* Guantánamo Bay

cultural relativism, 79

Dār al-Harb (abode of war), 131–32

Dār al-Islām (abode of Islam), 101, 131–32

Darwin, Charles, 117

Daschle, Tom, 48

Declaration on International Terrorism (Kuala Lumpur, 2002), 192–93 n.48

deconstructionism, 72

defense budget, 22, 42–43, 52

Defense Department, 64, 206

Defense Planning Guidance, 16

democracy, 158

Dennis, Anthony J., 107 n.34

deportation. *See* detention/deportation

Descartes, René, 117

detention/deportation: Bush administration on, 169, 171, 172–74, 175–76; and civil liberties, 164–65, 166, 169–76, 178 n.23, 178 n.25, 179 n.30 (*see also* military tribunals for terrorists); of immigrants/noncitizens, 14, 148–49, 159–60, 165–68, 200–203, 210 n.29 (*see also* Guantánamo Bay, prisoners detained at; racial profiling; USA Patriot Act); secret, 202, 210 n.29

deterrence, 18

Detroit Free Press v. Ashcroft, 210 n.29

Dewhurst, David, 62

diaspora/exile, 62–63, 158–59. *See also* immigrants

DiManno, Rosie, 36–37

Doherty, Carroll, 40

"domestic," meanings of, 59

domestic security: in airports, 4, 45–46, 52; alerts, 14; bomb shelters, 45, 46, 51–52; and closeness/intimacy, 50–51, 52;

Friedman, Thomas, 56

fundamentalism: of bin Laden, 74, 105 n.11; of Bush, 74; and false universals, 120–29; Islamic, 5–6

fuqaha (guardians of system of private endowments), 84–85

Gallup Poll, 40

gatekeeping doctrines, 168, 169, 171, 173–74, 176

Gazette (Montreal), 50

gender, 49–50, 153–54

General Assembly Resolution 3034 (UN, 1972), 189 n.14

generosity, 51

Geneva Conventions: on armed conflict, 191 n.36; on atrocities, 192 n.44; on humanitarian law, 185, 191 n.34; on prisoners of war, 13, 65, 69 n.17, 176, 179 n.37, 202–3, 209 n.8, 210 nn.32–33

Germany, 23

germ warfare, 23

al-Ghazali, Abu Hamid, 107 n.31

global warming, 21

Goldman, Adam, 12

Goldsmith, Jack L., 192 n.40, 192 n.43

Grant, George, 107 n.34

Great Britain, 23, 105 n.10

Greek philosophy, 107 n.31

Grotius, Hugo, 180–81, 188 n.3

ground zero: cleanup/rebuilding at, *144–46*, 213; meanings/use of the term, 4, 36–37, 55–58; memorial at, *140*; uncanniness of, 57–58

Guam, 66–67

Guantánamo Bay (Cuba): and imperialism, 66–68; jurisdiction over, 65–66, 67; lawlessness/uncanniness of, 67–68; meanings of, 4, 5, 65–68; prisoners detained at, 13, 65–66, 67–68, 69 n.17, 177, 203

Guardian (London), 46–47, 63

gun ownership, 51–52

Guthrie, Dan, 48

Guttig, Tom, 48

Haass, Richard, 19, 24–25, 209 n.18

habeas corpus, 170, 171, 203

Haiti, 19

Haitian refugees, 67

Hamas, 71

Hamdi, Yasser Esam, 178 n.23

Hare, Neil, 36

Harrison, Lawrence, 81

Hart-Rudman Commission on National Security, 64

Hassan, Waquar, 154–55

Hegel, Georg Wilhelm Friedrich, 117

Heimat (homeland), 58. *See also* homeland

Helfer, Laurence, 7

Heng, Yee-Kuang

Henick, Chris, 12

Hersh, Seymour, 29–30 n.19

Hiroshima, 2–3, 56–57

historical change, 2–3

historical exceptionalism, 56–57

historical memory, 3, 8, 213–14

History News Network, 212

Hizb al-Tahrir, 86

Hizbullah, 71

Hodgson, Marshall, 117

Holy Sites, 87, 88

home, focus on, 4

home front, 58, 64

homeland: and diaspora/exile, 62–63; and ethnicity, 62; of immigrants, 60–61; and imperialism, 63–64; Jewish, 58–59; meanings of, 4–5, 58–64; of Native Americans, 61; and race, 61–62

homeland security. *See* domestic security; Homeland Security, Department of

Homeland Security, Department of: on citizen sentinels, 50; creation of, 60; goals of, 61; and the Immigration and Naturalization Service, 61, 67; security systems created by, 4, 45–46. *See also* domestic security

homophobia, 154

Honduras, 20

Hoover, J. Edgar, 173

Hoskinson, Charles, 190 n.26

Human Rights Commission (UN), 190 n.27

human rights violations, 22, 32 n.54

Huntington, Samuel, 5, 73, 81, 106 n.21, 107 nn.34–35

Hussein, Saddam, 11, 15, 17, 27–28, 105 n.8

Islam (*continued*)

form by American Muslim romantics, 115–16, 120–24, 126–27, 130–31, 133 n.12, 134 n.28; reform by black American Muslims, 113–14, 115, 133 n.11; religious institutions of, 84–85; resistance ideologies of, 85; revolutionaries in, 71; Salafabi, 91–93, 94, 103, 134 n.28; Salafi, 89–92; secularism's threat to, 104 n.7; September 11's Islamic roots, 84–86; siege mentality of, 79–81; spread of, through trade, 100; and the sublime, 96–97; Sunni, 87, 122–23; teaching about, in U.S. classrooms, 13–14, 29 n.15; on terrorism, 98–99, 110 n.63; tradition vs. nontradition in, 115–16; transformation of, 74–78, 106 n.18; values of, core, 96–97, 110 n.53; values of, moral, 98–100; Wahhabi, 86–89, 91–92, 93, 108 n.44, 134 n.28; on war, 99, 100, 102, 110 n.65; Ẓāhirite, 124, 129. *See also* Muslims; Qur'an

iṣmat al-anbiyā' (Prophetic infallibility), 122–23

Israel: homeland of, 62; Palestine Liberation Organization headquarters bombed by, 191 n.38; Palestinians brutalized by, 74, 75; U.S. foreign policy on, 74; weapons of mass destruction from, 23

Jackson, Sherman A., 6

Jacobs, Lawrence, 48

Japanese American internment, 43, 155, 159, 166, 170

Jewish homeland, 58–59

Jews, 75

jihad, 86, 101–2

Judaism, 75–76

Judt, Tony, 27, 33 n.71

justice, 96, 100–101, 109 n.51, 196–98

Justice Department, 148–49, 164, 177 n.5

Kagan, Richard, 25–26, 33 n.71

Kaplan, Amy, 4–5, 7

Kennedy, John F., 60

Kessler, Gladys, 167–68

Khalilzad, Zalmay, 15, 30 n.21

Khawarij, 93–94, 98

Kinzer, Stephen, 20, 32 n.45

Klare, Michael, 33 n.67

Koran. *See* Qur'an

Korean unification, 16

Korean War, 3, 14–15

Korematsu v. United States, 174

Kosovo, 198, 199

Krauthammer, Charles, 25

Kucinich, Dennis, 13

Kuwait, 74

Lake, Anthony, 25

language of September 11, 55–68; ground zero, meanings of, 4, 55–58; Guantánamo Bay, meanings of, 4, 5, 65–68; homeland, meanings of, 4–5, 58–64; narrative/historical exceptionalism of, 56–57, 197; 9/11, meanings of, 55–56; and protected zones of language, 59

law: civil, 85; immigration, 165–66, 167, 168; and the Internet, 188 n.1; Islamic, 84–85, 90, 108 n.39. *See also* international law; law and politics; military tribunals for terrorists

law and politics, 194–208; idealist approach to, 195; and law as enforcement, 198–200; and the law of the exception, 200–208, 210 n.28; and method, 194–96; of military detention of noncitizens, 200–203, 210 n.29 (*see also* Guantánamo Bay, prisoners detained at); of military tribunals for terrorists, 202–4, 210 nn.32–33; and narratives of September 11, 196–98; and positive vs. natural law, 209 n.17; pragmatic approach to, 195; realist approach to, 194–95; and the U.S. vs. international community, 204–7, 211 n.48 (*see also* International Criminal Court, U.S. rejection of)

League of Arab States, 192–93 n.48

legal vs. philosophical discourse, 129–31

legal realism, 150, 194–95

liberty, 158

Libya, 184, 185

Lieberman, Joseph, 12, 49

Lieven, Anatol, 17, 27

Lindh, John Walker, 152

Lockerbie (Scotland), 183, 184, 190 n.23

Los Angeles Times, 51

conflict/hate/enmity, 98; on deterrence, 110 n.63; on diversity, 99; on domination, 131; on *fasad fi al-ard,* 98; on jihad, 102; on justice, 100–101; Medinan vs. Meccan phase of, 133 n.10; on the other, 99–100; on peace, 97, 102; on *qital,* 102; Salafis on, 89; "slay them wherever you find them" injunction, 126, 135 n.39; on *ta'aruf,* 100; on *ta'awun,* 100–101; on *ta'mir,* 96, 98; on terrorism, 110 n.63; on treaties/contracts, 99, 110 n.64

race, 61–62, 158, 159
racial profiling, 43–44, 147–52, 154–56, 160 n.4
al-Rahman, Umar 'Abd, 104–5 n.8
Ramadan, Tariq, 110 n.73
Ratner, Michael, 67
Ratner, Steven, 185–86
Reagan, Ronald, 21–22, 32 n.51, 45
Reagan administration, 19–20
Reich, Otto, 19–20, 31 nn.39–40
Reid, Richard, 152
Reisman, W. Michael, 189 n.11, 190 n.23, 193 n.55
relationships, focus on, 4
religion, 76, 77–78, 102–3, 132 nn.13–14. *See also* Christianity; Islam; Judaism; secularism
Rice, Condoleezza, 15, 18
Rida, Rashid, 89
Ridge, Tom, 60–61, 62
rights: citizenship as, 156; Civil Rights Movement, 44; human rights, international law on, 190 n.19, 190 n.27; human rights violations, 22, 32 n.54; of immigrants, 61, 67, 165–66. *See also* civil liberties
Robust Nuclear Earth Penetrator (RNEP), 24
Rockefeller, John D., IV, 28 n.5
Rogers, Paul, 34 n.77
Rome Treaty, 205–6, 211 n.48. *See also* International Criminal Court
Roosevelt, Franklin D., 58, 173
Rorty, Richard, 134 n.24
Rosen, Stephen Peter, 25, 34 n.78

Roy, Arundhati, 152
Rumsfeld, Donald, 26
Rushdie, Salman, 63
Rwanda, 206

Sager, Lawrence, 7
Said, Edward, 153
Salafabism, 91–93, 94, 103, 134 n.28
Salafism, 89–92
salam (peace and tranquility), 97
al-San'ani, 89
Saudi Arabia: and Egypt, 87; oil in, 88; U.S. foreign policy on, 74; Wahhabis in, 87–89, 108 n.44; weapons from, 23; women in, 106 n.18
al-Sawi, 87
Schell, Jonathan, 11, 24
scripturalism, 135 n.34
Second Amendment Sisters, 51
secularism, 104 n.7, 105 n.14, 110 n.73
security. *See* domestic security; national security
Security Council (UN), 23
Security Council Resolution 1373 (UN, 2001), 186–87, 193 n.50
Security Council Resolution 1378 (UN, 2001), 190 n.25, 191 n.38
September 11, *137–45;* destructiveness/scale of, 35, 38, 39; early reactions to, 1–2, 11, 35, 196; hate violence following, 147, 149–51, 153, 154–55, 161 n.6; Islamic roots of, 84–86; legal responses to (*see* law and politics); "9/11," meanings of, 55–56; precedents/historical references for, 35–37, 38 (*see also* Cold War; Pearl Harbor; World War II); religion's marginal role in, 76; remembering/memorials to, *139–42,* 212–14, 214 n.1; as a symbolic moment, 72; as transformative, 2–4, 7–8, 212–13; as unprecedented, 36–37, 38; war on terrorism as response to, 40 (*see also* war on terrorism)
Shafi' b. 'Ali, 125
al-Shāfi'ī, Muhammad ibn Idris, 123, 124
Shanksville (Pa.). *See* United Airlines flight 93
Shari'ah, 71

Sharon, Ariel, 22
al-Shawkani, Muhammad ibn Ali, 89
Shepard, Matthew, 154
Sherry, Michael, 41–42
Shi'i sect, 87
al-Shinqīṭī, 124
Sikhs, 155
Sinān, 117
Slaughter, Anne-Marie, 186, 191 n.36
social change, crises as moments of, 2
Sodhi, Balbir Singh, 154
Somalia, 11
South Africa, 23, 61–62
South Asian Americans, 155
sovereignty: definition of, 207; limited, of other countries, 19–21, 24–25, 199, 209 n.18; meanings of, 65; over U.S. possessions, 66–67, 69 n.24; U.S., 21, 199–200, 206–7; violation of, 197–98
Soviet Union, 16, 18, 43
Special Registration, 149
Spivak, Gayatri, 153
spying, domestic, 164, 177 n.5
Star Wars missile shield, 43
State Department, 20
Stephanson, Anders, 26
Stroman, Mark, 154–55
students, detention/investigation of, 43–44, 148–49, 160 n.4
Sturken, Marita, 56, 213
Sudan, 10
Sufism, 90
Sunnah, 89
Sunnism, 87, 122–23
sunshine provisions, 167–68
Supreme Court: on enemy aliens, 179 n.30; on immigrants, detention of, 167; on military courts, 175; on U.S. sovereignty over possessions, 66–67, 69 n.24
surveillance, electronic, 47–48

ta'aruf (obligation to know one another), 100
ta'awun (cooperation), 100–101
Taha, Mahmoud Mohamed, 133 n.10
talfiq (blending of opinions from the past to solve problems), 90
Taliban: colonialism/modernity as giving

rise to, 80; Islamic authenticity claimed by, 76–77; normativity/influence of behavior of, 78; terrorists sheltered by, 190 n.25, 191 n.38; U.S. support of, 43, 153. See also Guantánamo Bay, prisoners detained at
ta'mir (to civilize, build, construct), 96, 98
Tanzim al-Qa'idah, 86
Ṭāwūs, 125
Tehranian, Majid
Teitel, Ruti G., 8
terrorism: Al Qaeda as source of, 14; and American innocence, loss of, 11, 28 n.5, 56; as armed conflict, 7, 182, 184–85, 186, 187, 191 n.30, 191 n.34, 191 n.36, 191 n.38, 192 nn.43–45, 193 n.53; as atrocity, 7, 182, 185–86, 187, 192 n.40, 192 nn.43–44, 193 nn.54–55; autonomy of terrorist groups, 181–82, 189 n.11; and colonialism, 183, 189 n.14; as crime, 7, 39–40, 182–84, 186–87, 189–90 nn.14–17, 190 nn.23–27, 191 n.29, 192–93 n.48, 193 n.50; definition of, 204–5; domestic, 38; embassy bombings of 1998, 38, 183, 185; immigrants as terrorists, 67; international, against the U.S., 38–39; Islam on, 98–99, 110 n.63; military tribunals for terrorists, 49, 66, 173–74 (see also civil liberties, and military detention); and national liberation, 85–86; terrorists living in the U.S., 19, 31 n.38; unilateralist response by U.S., 7–8, 182, 184, 191 n.29, 205; USS Cole bombing, 38–39. See also September 11; war on terrorism
Terrorism Information and Prevention System (TIPS), 12–13, 29 n.10, 50
Terrorist Bombings Convention (2001), 190 n.17
Thirty Years' War, 181
TIPS (Terrorism Information and Prevention System), 12–13, 29 n.10, 50
Tisdall, Simon, 24
Tokyo tribunals, 186
Topps, 47
trading cards, 47
transnationalism, 158–59. See also diaspora/exile; immigrants

Truman, Harry, 14–15, 29 n.18, 58
Tunisia, 191 n.38

UN (United Nations): Charter, 185, 187; in Korean War, 14; U.S. control of, 21
unanimous consensus, 122–23, 129, 130, 135 n.43
uncanniness, 57–58
Unabomber, 38
Uniform Code of Military Justice, 175, 179 n.36, 201
United Airlines flight 93 (Pennsylvania crash), 1, 2, *139*, 213
United Airlines flight 175 (World Trade Center crash), 1
United Nations. *See* UN
United States: anger toward/hatred of, 12, 45, 46, 53 n.20; dominance of, 15–19, 22–23, 30 n.21; vs. Europe, in military strength, 25–26; vs. Europe, in values, 33 n.71; fear/mistrust of, 27, 34 n.77; on Muslim/civilian casualties, 105 n.10; sovereignty of, 21, 199–200, 206–7; war declarations in, 40; weapons of mass destruction from, 23. *See also* United States foreign policy; United States government
United States foreign policy: on Afghanistan, 21–22, 32 n.51, 74, 184–85; on Bolivia, 17, 30 n.25; on Central America, 19–20; on Colombia, 17; on counterinsurgency, 17, 30 n.25, 32 n.54; vs. domestic policy, and civil liberties, 163–64, 166–69, 176–77; on Egypt, 74; on El Salvador, 20; exceptionalism of, 26, 56, 57–58, 60, 197, 200–207, 210 n.28; on Honduras, 20; on human rights violations, 22, 32 n.54; imperialism of, 24–25, 27; on Indonesia, 30 n.24; on Israel, 74; on Korean unification, 16; on Kuwait, 74; on the Middle East, generally, 16; on Nicaragua, 19, 20; religion in, 76, 105 n.14; on Saudi Arabia, 74; on sovereignty, 19–21, 24–25, 199, 209 n.18; unilateralism of, 3–4, 7–8, 25, 182, 184, 186, 191 n.29, 195, 205; on the Venezuelan coup, 19–20, 22, 31 n.40; war on drugs, 17, 30 n.25, 32 n.54. *See also* war on terrorism
United States government: Americans'

trust in, 40; authority expanded after September 11, 47–48 (*see also* USA Patriot Act); racial profiling by, 150–51. *See also* United States foreign policy; war on terrorism; *individual departments and offices*
Uniting and Strengthening America by Providing Appropriate Tools Required to Intercept and Obstruct Terrorism Act. *See* USA Patriot Act
universals: Islamic, 79, 80–81, 116–20, 134 n.22; universal values, 79, 80–81, 106 n.21, 107 n.35. *See also* false universals
Unocal, 24
USA Patriot Act (2001), 12, 29 n.9, 47–48, 61, 164, 165, 166
USS *Cole* bombing (2000), 38–39

values: competence to represent, 81, 83; lineage of, 81, 82, 83; meaning of, 81, 82; and the other, 81, 82, 83; universal, 79, 80–81, 106 n.21, 107 n.35; Western vs. Islamic, 81–83, 107 n.31
Vandehei, Jim, 53 n.20
Venezuelan coup, 19–20, 22, 31 n.40
Vienna Convention, 211 n.48
Vietnam War, 11
visa investigations, 43–44, 148–49, 160 n.4
voice mails, federal access to, 47
Volpp, Leti, 6–7
voluntarism, 51

Wadud, Amina, 133 n.11
Wahhabism, 86–89, 91–92, 93, 108 n.44, 134 n.28
Wain, Barry, 32 n.53
Waiting for the Barbarians (Coetzee), 27
war, 26, 196–97. *See also specific wars*
war on drugs, 17, 30 n.25, 32 n.54, 43
war on terrorism: Bush's declaration of, 38, 40, 41, 42–43; Bush's popularity boosted by, 40–41; cards commemorating, 47; Clinton bombs Iraq, 10–11; and the Cold War, 12, 14–15, 29–30 nn.18–19; goals of, 22; and local politics, 22, 32 n.53; national interest invoked in, 22; and oil policy, 24, 33 n.67; preemptive war in,

war on terrorism (*continued*)
18, 19; prisoner-of-war status in, 170, 172 (*see also* civil liberties, and military detention); racial profiling in, 43–44; and U.S. dominance, 15–19, 22–23, 30 n.21. *See also* USA Patriot Act
Washington Post, 41, 49
Waters, Maxine, 13
Watson, Robert, 21
weapons of mass destruction, 17, 23
Weekly Standard, 26–27
West: hypocrisy of, perceived, 72–73, 74, 104–5 n.8; Muslims' need to appease, 125–27; secularism of, 110 n.73; universals of, 79, 80, 106 n.21, 107 n.35
West, Cornel, 134 n.25
West Berlin nightclub bombing (1986), 185
Westoxification, 80, 106 n.28
Williams, Paul L., 105 n.9, 109 n.48
Williams, William Appleman, 24
Wilson, Woodrow, 58–59

wiretaps, 47–48
Wolfowitz, Paul, 16, 21, 125–26
women: in Afghanistan, 153–54; gun ownership by, 51–52; right to equal consideration, 114–15; socioeconomic mobility of, 77, 106 n.18
World Trade Center attack (2001), *137*, 196
World Trade Center bombing (1993), 39, 183, 196
World War I, 3, 57–58
World War II, 3, 14, 41–42, 43, 44, 52. *See also* Japanese American internment; Pearl Harbor

Young, Marilyn, 3–4, 182, 195
Yugoslavia, 199, 206

Zadvydas v. Davis, 167
Ẓāhirites, 124, 129
al-Zawahiri, Ayman, 104–5 n.8

Mary L. Dudziak is Judge Edward J. and Ruey L.
Guirado Professor of Law and History at the
University of Southern California Law School.
She is the author of *Cold War Civil Rights:
Race and the Image of American Democracy*.

Library of Congress Cataloging-in-Publication Data
September 11 in history : a watershed moment? /
edited by Mary L. Dudziak.
p. cm.—(American encounters/global interactions)
Includes bibliographical references and index.
ISBN 0-8223-3229-9 (cloth : alk. paper)
ISBN 0-8223-3242-6 (pbk. : alk. paper)
1. September 11 Terrorist Attacks, 2001.
2. War on Terrorism, 2001–   3. United States—
History—21st century.   4. History, Modern—
21st century.   I. Title: September eleven in history.
II. Dudziak, Mary L., 1956–   III. Series.
HV6432.7.S45   2003   973.931—DC21   2003010840